THE PLEASURE SEEKERS

THE PRIDDEN SAGA: BOOK FOUR

Disclaimer:

All characters in this book are fictitious, and any resemblance to actual persons, living or dead, is purely coincidental.

Cover Art by Deranged Doctor Designs

Editor: Laura LaRocca

ISBN: 978-1-7389742-8-3

Printed in United States of America

Published by JMT Publishing, Canada
www.jmtpublishing.com
Second Edition, 2023

THE PLEASURE SEEKERS

THE PRIDDEN SAGA: BOOK FOUR

J. M. TIBBOTT

DEDICATION

To the man who inspired me to take the leap so many years ago—Robert Kleiber. Gone but never forgotten.

J. M. Tibbott

ACKNOWLEDGEMENTS

A special and very appreciative thanks to my critiquing partners and my wonderful Beta readers.

A huge amount of appreciation to my friend Marilyn who helped me keep focussed through a difficult year.

A special thanks to Ed Greenwood, who acted as a mentor, and steered me back on track when my focus slipped to some bright and shiny object near my path.

Much appreciation to my wonderful readers who kept requesting the next volume.

MAP OF PRIDDEN

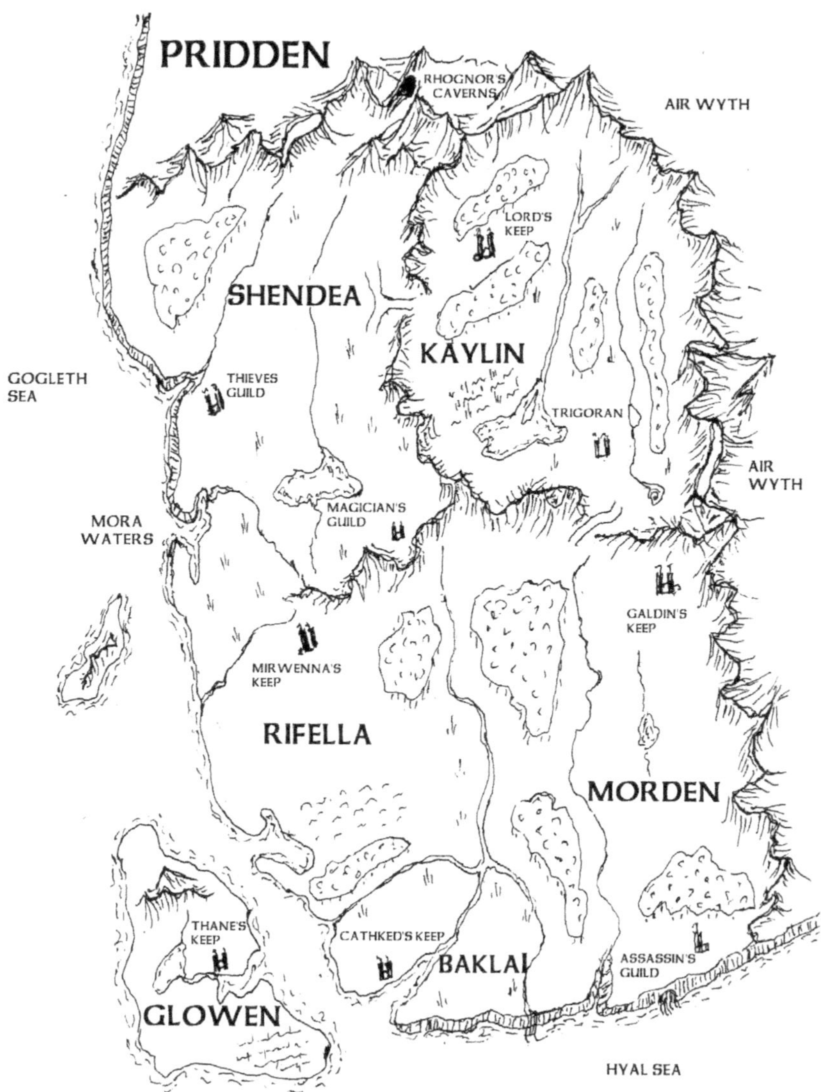

MAP OF GLOWEN

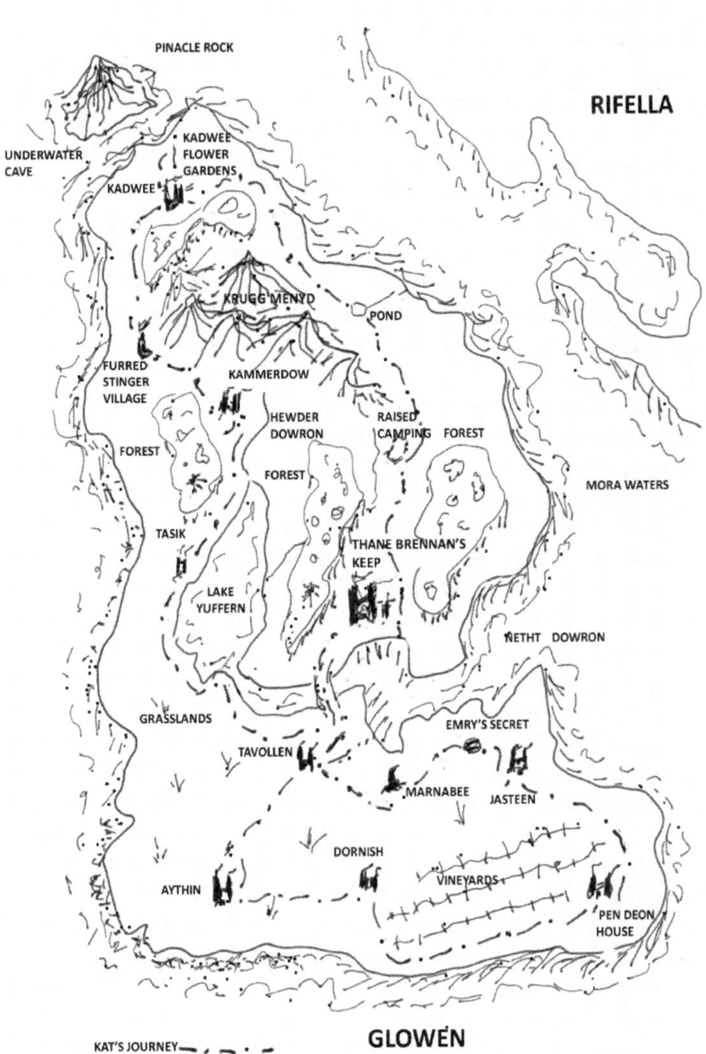

WHAT HAS HAPPENED THUS FAR.

Kat, a solitary but brilliant, video game designer is thrust into the unfamiliar world of Pridden, when while on sabbatical, her own world is turned upside down. Offered a chance by Eduardo, the ruling Lord of Kaylin, to return home if she will help save his subjects from the winds of war, Kat must decide what risks she will take and what restrictions she is willing to accept. Beset by bizarre and ferocious creatures, narrow-minded social mores, seductively erotic men, and with no idea who is friend or foe, she must wend her way through a minefield of challenges, including capture by the Assassins for transport to the foul Thane Galdin. After her rescue by Eduardo's men and other sympathetic inhabitants of Kaylin, she manages to persuade at least two people with enough power to support her in the future.

Gaining the help of an adorable pyrock, a creature who is able to convey messages instantly to any area of Pridden, the journey continues as Kat picks her way among the spiritual healers of Shendea.

In this next land, she encounters heart-stopping confrontations from a ferocious cathnog and violent strangers. Still tasked with the request by Eduardo of Kaylin to help Pridden avoid a devastating war, but without clear instructions, she is escorted by her mysterious guide, Mouse, and the glorious, but invisible big cat, Shade. How will she keep her word to Eduardo to help Lord Rhognor, the Lord of Shendea, and still return safely to her own world?

Despite her tendency to blunder through peculiar customs, she is astonished by a Thieves' Guild who do not steal, a Magicians' Guild who demonstrate no magic, and learns to sidestep the wiles of the alluring Rifellans. Despite these difficult tasks, Kat is still able to gain the trust and support of two residents of the land of Shendea.

When she enterers Rifella, Kat, with only her guide Mouse and her pyrock, Wink, is often mistaken for a red-headed, royal-born Rifellan. The inhabitants she encounters are strong, fine-looking men and women, and who are surprisingly welcoming. Rifella is a harsh land, filled with many new dangerous creatures, and often grim terrain, but she is entranced by the beauty she encounters, where she faces some delightful new animals.

Drawn to Liandock, the intensely attractive Metal-Master when he enters her life again, Kat requests his help to return her to her home.

If she can aid Rifella's ruler, Lord Murwenna and her heir, to discover the oppositions within the land of Rifella, maybe she can gain additional ways to return home. Mouse and Wink are integral in helping Kat escape from the terrifying Assassins, and further foil Thane Galdin's intent to capture this enterprising woman.

CHAPTER 1

I'm too young to die. Kat raised her head and saw Mouse standing under the shelter. *Bloody hell, he's eating.* She clutched the rail and heaved. Her stomach burned and her head pounded. She groaned and her insides spasmed again as she retched.

Another flash of lightening lit the sky. *Thankfully the rail is wood. Although if it were metal, I would be able to die sooner.*

The ship climbed a gargantuan wave and pounded down the other side, leaving her stomach somewhere in mid-air. She moaned.

"Kat?" A hand touched her arm. "Drink some of this red-leaf tea." Mouse held a cup out to her.

She attempted to shake her head, but found the pain too great, and she leaned over the rail and dry-retched again.

"This helped you before. Remember? Drink some." He thrust the cup into her hand.

"Go away. Let me die in peace."

"Drink, Kat."

To shut him up, she sipped at the tea. She blinked. The tea stayed down and she sighed in relief. She took a second sip, but when the boat gave another lurch, she hung over the rail once more, sure the small amount of liquid would reappear.

Below her in the water, a massive form, greater in length than the boat, crowded along the side of the vessel. The creature lifted its head out of the water and opened an enormous mouth ringed with three sets of huge, yellowed teeth. Water and small fish gushed from the jaws. The creature raised its body so close to the deck of the boat, Kat thought the jaws might reach out and pluck her from the ship.

She shrieked and pushed back from the rail, losing her balance, and staggered into Mouse, who caught her before she fell. The cup dropped from her hand and smashed as the tea splashed over the deck.

"Kat, what is wrong?" He ran past her to the rail and glanced over. "What startled you?"

Kat tried to reply, but hurriedly covered her mouth, as the small amount of tea she swallowed threatened to reemerge. She coughed. "Whale." Another flash of lightening lit the sky, this time accompanied by a belch of thunder and a further drenching of rain.

Mouse frowned at her. "Wale?"

She nodded, afraid to speak, and possibly gag again.

"You are soaked, and you must be cold. You should shelter below deck."

Kat put hand over her mouth, and shook her head, which caused a further bolt of pain.

Mouse led her to a chair bolted to the deck underneath a canvas shelter. "Can you sit? I will bring you more tea, which will help, I promise."

He settled Kat in the chair, with a blanket wrapped around her, and when he returned, he handed her a fresh cup of tea. Kat's stomach, while still delicate, at last stopped spasming, and, as the blanket warmed her, she relaxed in her seat.

He sat in a chair beside her. "Are you able to talk?"

She nodded, and held up two fingers and inch apart.

"What did you observe in the water?"

"Not sure, but it stretched the full length of this vessel, and had loads of teeth. A shark or a whale?"

"I am not familiar with either of those creatures. Stories exist of massive sea animals appearing in the waters around Glowen, but none have been seen in many paths. However, no tales suggested they ever attacked anyone, so we can assume they are benign."

"I don't care. The worst they can do is kill me, and I still think that would be a blessing."

"Sleep if you can, Kat. The canvas will keep the bulk of the rain off you, although I would suggest you might be better below deck"

"No. I need fresh air."

"Then sleep. I will sit beside you and gather sleep as well. Hopefully the storm will pass during the night." He patted her hand.

Kat barely noticed his gesture. She closed her eyes to avoid watching the rise and fall of the ship's rail.

All those teeth. A shark? I'm not warm enough to figure out if my stone is cold.

♋♋♋

A distant roll of thunder wakened Kat. She shivered in the cold. She yawned, turned over in the chair, and looked directly into Mouse's eyes. *He's got brown eyes, but with a bit of green. Never saw that before.*

"Ah, you are awake, so drink some more tea, Kat. We are about to enter the harbor, and the storm is almost passed. We will be landing soon, and you will be much better."

Soon, with the storm spent and the rain ceased, a sliver of sun poked a few rays through the clouds. The sea in the harbor now calm, with the jetty in sight, the vessel no longer heaved or tossed.

Land at last.

Men hurried about the deck, dousing the heavy mainsail, and tying the canvas down along the boom. Others threw a number of fat woven rope fenders over the rails to protect the sides of the vessel from the jutting edges of the wharf. Slowly, with only a small jib to provide headway, the boat glided to the dock, where others waited to catch the lines thrown by the ship's crew and lash the thick ropes to sturdy wooden bollards on the wharf.

The on-board crew cleared the way to the gate in the railing, then brought the gangplank and slid the wooden beam in place, connecting the boat and dock.

Still feeling green from the passage through the storm, Kat staggered gingerly down the gangway to the motionless wharf. She stood clinging to a post, waiting for the nausea and the swaying to subside. *Hell. The wharf's still moving.*

She stepped forward, and lurched into a solid warm body.

"I see you have already sampled our glorious wines."

She gazed up at the speaker. *Tall male. Broad shoulders. Strong legs.* She perked up. The sight of a well built man immediately brought Liandock to mind. *Wink isn't back from him. It's been days. Will he help me?* She stared up at the face of the man in front of her, and stopped. While he was handsome, he was smirking. Did he just insult her?

Mouse stepped in front of her. "You overstep yourself, sir. My Lady Kat suffered much at the hands of one of your violent storms during our voyage here."

Mouse, defending her?

"A thousand apologies, my Lady Kat." His inky black hair shone in the sun, and he flashed a brilliant smile. "Perhaps I can help escort you to your lodgings?" He stared down his hawk-like nose at her, his grey wolf's eyes disconcerted her, and he flared his nostrils at Mouse.

Kat, aware she stared at him, shook her head. *Is he flirting or being condescending? Granted he's good looking, but he's a bit too fond of himself.*

"Not necessary. Mouse arranged a carriage for us." She gestured towards her companion.

"Of course, I simply meant to be of aid. However, should you require *anything*—" he leaned toward her, "—during your visit here, please do call on me. I am Emrys pen Godron."

Kat taken aback, did not appreciate the emphasis on the word *anything*, and she particularly disliked the flared nostrils when he stared at Mouse. She glanced back at her companion and caught a flash of hatred in his darkened eyes. It appeared Mouse was infuriated.

She turned back to the man and set her face in her most insolent expression. "I doubt I will need you, Emrys, but I will keep you in mind should the occasion arise." She was aware of the ice dripping from her words.

She glanced at Mouse again. His eyes were calm, and he displayed the merest hint of a smile.

Emrys raised an eyebrow, looked down his nose at both of them, bowed, and turned to leave.

"Are these Glowens all so arrogant?" she asked Mouse as they walked to where their horses and baggage waited.

Mouse shrugged. "I have never visited Glowen before, but I am aware they are the most sensual of all the people in our lands. His name identifies him as part of the wine-making pod. They take pleasure in eating and drinking to excess, and I understand they bed any creature who stands still long enough to be persuaded. I suspect they are usually successful and thus have developed an exaggerated view of themselves."

"Any creature?"

"So I have heard. There are few aversions to possible bedmates among the Glowens. However, they rarely bond with people of the other lands. You will find your task of gaining their trust, and ultimately their help, difficult in the extreme."

"Perfect." She rolled her eyes. "Why did Eduardo send me here?"

"Think of him as Lord Eduardo, and you will understand him better." Mouse shrugged. "Eduardo is conscious that Glowens possesses challenges which also require soothing, although they are less troubled than the other lands." He scratched at his ear. "He also knows you must get cooperation from all six lands to be able to harness the power required to return you to your home world."

Kat, startled, stared at him. *How is he aware about my agreement with Eduardo?*

Mouse seemed discomforted by her expression. "Eduardo deemed my knowledge of the reason for your journey as necessary. As such, it is important you discover what will motivate all with whom you come in contact."

"So, I need to determine a way to tend to social niceties with these Glowens? This does appear to be the seemly thing to do." Kat sniffed.

Mouse's face transformed with a grin that threatened to cause him injury. "Sorry." His face resumed its normal sober expression. "You are beginning to pick up the cadence of the speech on our world. My smile was not meant to insult. I intended to indicate you are doing an excellent job. You do not wish to appear to be more alien than you truly are."

"You know, Mouse, that's the first time I've seen you smile so broadly. I like it when you smile."

He appeared embarrassed by her comment. "Ah, here's the carriage to our lodgings." Relief sounded in his voice. "We will take our horses to the stables until they are needed."

Kat watched him as he ordered the loading of their travel bags and bargained for the price of the trip. The carriage owner tied their three horses to the back of the rig.

Mouse'd make a fine leader. He's more competent than I expected. But he's hiding something from me. Her stomach still felt raw, and she shivered as a thought struck her. *Wink. Where is my pyrock? Why is Liandock taking so long to answer me?*

CHAPTER 2

The horses clopped along a wooden-laid road toward the Thane's Keep.

Mouse commented on the actions of the various inhabitants. "The harbor we arrived at is the outlet of the Netht Dowron, which is how the Glowens refer to their rivers. As you can see, the outlet has enough room to possess docks along each side." He waved at the rows of vessels. "This side of the Netht is strictly for goods being imported, while on the opposite side are located the shipyards, where they build small vessels, and are able to repair almost any water-going craft. That is also where they load goods for export."

Kat stared back at the docks along Netht Dowron, which bustled with stevedores unloading a series of goods from other lands of Pridden. She watched as bolts of cloth from Kaylin, wooden cases filled with glass bottles of various colored liquids from Shendea, and dressed planks of an unusual wood, secured in batches, appeared on the wharf. She suspected the wood came from Baklai. Bannigus, the Horse-Master in Rifella mentioned that they produced excellent and unusual woods. In another pile, huge bales of brynosh from Shendea, secured on top of sheaves of tanned leather, sat high on delivery carts bound for the Keep. Kat wondered what the fibers of brynosh would be used for in Glowen. The harbor teemed with people and goods from all over Pridden. The only exception was Kaylin, whose shipments appeared to be handled by men from Rifella.

The carriage headed toward the Keep and shortly halted at the stables. The stable master bustled outside to greet his guests. He called to an assistant to load their baggage on a cart, which the young man pulled to the gates of the Keep. Kat followed, while Mouse remained to complete some items with the stable master.

As Kat and the assistant entered the courtyard, a middle-aged woman clad in a light blue robe approached them. “Are you the Lady Kat?”

“I am, although I would request you call me Kat as I prefer to be informal.” She bobbed her head at the woman. “I assume because of the color of your robe you are the healer for Glowen?” She smiled.

The woman’s face lit up with pleasure. “I am indeed. I am Healer Marreth, and I believe you are familiar with my mentor, Healer Wynneth in Kaylin?”

“Yes. I had a pyrock message from her before I left Rifella. She appeared to be well.”

“She is. I am anticipating our next meeting in the Dark Forest with immense pleasure. The healers from all the lands meet once each path in the forest for reflection and contemplation. This is the time when we gather to heal and renew ourselves.” She paused and held up her hand. “One moment. Let me tell the stable assistant where to take your baggage.” She faced the apprentice and gave him directions. As she turned back, Mouse appeared from the direction of the stables.

“Sire Mouse. Welcome. I sent your baggage to your rooms, and if you will walk with me, I will show both of you to your respective accommodations and point out the communal dining facilities, so you may enjoy a mid-turn meal or something light in your rooms." She continued down the hall. "Later, I will come for both of you, because Thane Brennan has requested you dine with him this evening. I should advise you we are not formal here in Glowen. The first time you are introduced to him, do refer to him as Thane Brennan. He will no doubt request you drop the title, but if he does not, you may do so without concern."

"Our thanks, Healer." Mouse bowed his head to recognize her position.

"Here we are. The room on the left belongs to you, Sire Mouse, and the one further on is yours, Kat."

Kat smiled at her. "Thank you Marreth. We will wait for you to call us for the evening meal."

Marreth bid them farewell, and they watched her depart down the hall.

Mouse glanced at Kat. "I would appreciate the opportunity to change my clothing. Shall we consider a mid-turn meal?"

"Mouse, I'm weary. If you don't mind, I'll order a light snack to my room, and hopefully grab a nap. I did not rest well last night, as you're aware."

"An excellent idea, Kat. I also need more sleep, and a light snack will suit me. I shall rouse you in time to be ready for Marreth."

"Thank you." She turned back to her door, and entered the room. Kat yawned and extracted Wink's cage from her luggage, placed it on a small table, and gazed at it. She sighed, dropped her clothes on a chair, and headed for the bed, extinguishing the globes on her way.

I can't be bothered eating. Too tired.

A knock roused Kat from a deep sleep. Rubbing her eyes, she climbed out of bed and stumbled to the door. "Yes?" She addressed the closed door.

"It is Mouse. I promised I would rouse you in time to prepare to join Marreth to dine with Brennan."

Kat yawned. "Already?" She sighed. "Thanks for calling for me. I need to take a cold shower to wake myself. I will be as quick as possible."

"You do have time, Kat." He cleared his throat. "Since the Glowens are fond of pleasure, dress in something eye catching."

"OK." She heard Mouse return to his own room.

Shivering after her cold shower, she rummaged through her baggage for the emerald green dress shot with gold thread she wore for Lord Rhognor in Shendea.

She dug to the bottom of her bag to locate the gold flats that matched the dress. She sat to apply some makeup, and gasped at the dark circles below her eyes. Concealer was needed. After applying a light bronze blush and lip gloss and a vigorous brushing of her hair, she eyed herself in the mirror. *Something's missing.*

She snapped her fingers and extracted the sunrise-colored scarf from her backpack. Draping the shawl around her shoulders, she again glanced at her reflection. *Now, I'm ready.* The face smiling back at her was self-satisfied.

Another knock, and she walked over and opened her door. Marreth and Mouse stood ready for her.

Marreth's face lit up. "Kat, you seem prepared to meet royalty." She laughed. "You will find that although the Glowen people dress ornately, they are not formal people. I do believe you will enjoy meeting Brennan and his advisors."

"Is he bonded with someone?"

"He is. We should head for the Thane's dining hall, and I will tell you a little about him, his siblings, and offspring on the way."

Mouse nodded to Marreth. "I am interested as well. I am not that familiar with Glowen and the ways of their citizens."

The three sauntered down the hall, as Marreth continued with her tale. "Brennan is officially Thane Brennan pen Taddyn. His is the pod from which all our leaders spring."

Kat raised both eyebrows at Marreth. "Pod?" She remembered that Mouse mentioned the word before.

"Ah yes. Pod refers to the familial groups of people, and usually relates to their positions on Glowen. Brennan's pod hails from Lord Taddyn, the last Lord of power in Glowen, and thus all his descendants bear the extended name pen Taddyn. Should one of Brennan's offspring inherit the title of Thane, their bonded mate would become one of the pen Taddyn pod. Glowen no longer limits inheriting the title of Thane to males only."

Kat wrinkled her brow. "They are following Rifella's lead?"

"Yes. The Glowens admire the Rifellans."

Kat smiled. "I'm not surprised. Of all the people I encountered thus far, Rifellans are the strongest believers in 'live and let live'. I find the them the easiest people to relate to."

Marreth grinned. "I suspect they accepted and welcomed you because you so strongly resemble Rifellan royal born."

Kat nodded. "They did seem to." She glanced at Marreth, puzzled. "I met Glowens in the other lands, but never recalled them introducing themselves as from a pod. Why is that?"

"Glowens learned quickly that when they are in other lands, referring to their pod names can be complicating. They have sufficient challenges with the other lands, and so do not use pod names until they are home again."

Marreth paused at an enormous door, decorated with paintings of flowers, and lengths of illustrations of grape vines with ripe golden clusters of berries hanging from the vines.

Kat closed her eyes and took a deep breath. "This is so beautiful. I can almost detect the rich odor of ripe fruit, and experience warmth emanating from the painting."

Marreth turned to the guards on either side of the door. "Would you please announce Lady Kat, Sire Mouse, and me to Thane Brennan."

The guards entered the room, announced the three of them, and stood aside to allow them entrance.

Along one side of the room stood a magnificent table, set for a formal dinner with silver plates, and bowls of flowers at regular intervals along the blindingly white tablecloth. A tall man with pale, golden skin, rose from his seat at the head of the table and boomed out a welcome to Kat. He turned to Mouse and welcomed him as well. Mouse dipped his head in acknowledgement of the Thane's position, and Kat followed suit.

"Please be seated." The Thane's gravelly voice reminded Kat of rock singers from her own world, whose vocals resulted from too many cigarettes and too much alcohol. Brennan's she susptected were the result of a large man using his voice to bellow orders regularly.

Apprentices guided them to seats, Kat to the left of Brennan, beside a female sharing the head of the table with him, and Mouse on Kat's left. Next to Mouse, the apprentices seated Marreth, and across from Kat, a male who introduced himself as Gaynore, Brennan's Chief Advisor. What Kat found unnerving were the eyes of all in the hall turned toward her. Those closest to her she saw clearly had irises of light blue in color, most with darker, almost cobalt, rings around the outside. The experience felt like being in the company of a wolf pack. She had always loved the color of what she referred to as wolf eyes, although, this many, all staring at her, she found a little unsettling.

Brennan was not a handsome man, but he was oddly attractive, with a strong firm jaw, full fleshy lips, and an aquiline nose. His eyes were the most wolf-like of the entire company, piercing and strongly male. With the body of a wrestler, he was a big man and Kat, unsure how much was muscle and how much extra pounds, found herself impressed by him. He possessed the features of a leader, and his aura hinted that he could dominate both men and women. The female beside him confirmed his ability with women—she was beautiful, with fine features and lustrous black hair, streaked with strands of ash blonde.

Brennan introduced them to those seated at the table. He indicated the woman beside him. "My bonded mate, Lilliwon, also welcomes you, and across from you, Lady Kat, is my Chief Advisor, Gaynore pen Deon."

Kat lowered her head to each person as the Thane introduced them. She glanced at Mouse, who sent her a tiny nod of approval. *Interesting. They may not be as formal as some lands, but it seems the Thane speaks for all.*

Brennan snapped his fingers, and an army of serving apprentices moved through the room carrying platters of food and generous containers of Orenberry wine.

Scents and the sizzle of roasted meats wafted around the room, and Kat salivated in anticipation.

I must pin Marreth down tomorrow and ask her what the pen Deon pod represents.

CHAPTER 3

With the tables loaded with jugs of wine, Kat, curious about the platters of food filled with five or six different meat dishes and tempted by the aromas, decided to try a small amount of each. The yellowish dish, which she thought might be currie, proved to be a sweet, tender meat, served on a bed of yellow vegetables that reminded her of mangos and lichees. The extraordinary flavor tempted her to eat more, but she knew that if she did, she would not be able to sample the others. A dark brown stew contained gornog, her favorite meat, but prepared in a sauce that reminded her of Mexican chocolate, infused with the tang of chili, and was the drink she adored from home..

She turned to Mouse. "The flavors are exceptional. Have you eaten much Glowen food before?"

His mouth obviously full of food, he shook his head.

Kat had eaten nothing since she boarded the boat from Rifella and served herself a third dish—a type of fish, delicately grilled in a batter tasting of lime. By the time she tried the strips of some unknown animal, threaded on sticks of wood, and alternating with a bright orange fruit and cubes of what reminded her of Hawaiian breadfruit, her hunger seemed almost satisfied.

She wanted something sweet, so turned to the fruit dishes, which sat on huge platters, creating a rainbow of color on the table. Kat ate a purple one, a red one, and a yellow one, grimacing at the taste of the latter. It reminded her of sour cherries.

She hastily drank a mouthful of wine. *Uh oh, I feel a gornog belch coming on.* Luckily the noise level had increased as the rest of the diners imbibed large cups of Orenberry wine, and she managed to restrain herself to a discreet burp.

Kat gazed around the room at the cheerful, tipsy faces of the Glowens at Brennan's table. *So many others in Pridden find fault with them, but they appear to be a happy people.* She found the experience to be oddly discongruous to see cheerful people with the dramatic eyes of wolves. She glanced at Mouse, who appeared amused by those in the hall. "They enjoy themselves, don't they? Do you think the other lands are jealous of their abundant amount of foods?"

Mouse shrugged. "I suspect Kaylins are horrified because the Glowens enjoy life so much, while they are so restricted in their lives. The Shendeans tend to dismiss the Glowens as being wanting in spiritual matters." He chuckled. "You should not believe the Shendean attitude which belonged to the late Hesginn. He was a rigid man with little sense of humor."

Kat snorted. "He certainly disliked the Glowens. But now I think of it, he disliked quite a number of people."

Mouse grinned and continued. "Rifellans are so fond of their own way of living, I do not believe they concern themselves much with the Glowen way of life. Both they and the Baklai, whose lives are harsh, probably envy the easy existence of the Glowens. Mordens, however, are annoyed by everyone. I mean the Mordens in the north. The southerners are relatively easy-going."

Kat, about to take the conversation further, stopped when Brennan stood. "Citizens, I am aware you noticed a stranger in our midst." He motioned to Kat to stand. "Let me introduce to you the Lady Kat, whom Lord Eduardo of Kaylin sent to visit our land. Eduardo hopes she will discover any challenges we may be encumbered with." He roared with laughter and faced Kat. "I am afraid your journey will be for naught. Glowen has no challenges. However, we all encourage you to enjoy a journey through our land."

All the people laughed along with their Thane and clapped.

Brennan held up his hands. "This has been a long day for us. This feast is our welcome to Kat, and I urge you all to answer any of the questions she may request of you. I bid you all good evening." He helped his mate from her chair and left the hall.

The rest of the Glowens rose and headed to their own homes.

As Kat moved to leave the hall, she realized Marreth walked beside her. "Could we meet for the morning meal on the morrow? I have so many questions." She glanced around at Mouse who caught up with them. "Would that suit you too?"

He nodded at her. "I would appreciate joining you both. I too am seeking answers."

Marreth smiled at them. "I would be pleased to answer any questions you may pose. I shall have one of our apprentices rouse you on the morrow."

Kat grinned. "Fine. I don't want to sleep in."

The three walked down the passage to their rooms.

Kat yawned and entered her room. As she undressed, she gazed at Wink's empty cage.

A quick visit to the personal and she snuggled under the comforter on her bed.

The people of Pridden seem so contemptuous of the Glowens. Why? And why does Brennan believe there are no challenges in Glowen? Does he have another agenda?

CHAPTER 4

The night, cloying, black, and eerie, unsettled Kat's stomach. Why was she standing on the cobbled road outside the keep? She studied the dark row of trees beyond the field of thick grasses. No breeze blew, but the hairs on her arms raised, and she shivered from some nameless dread. *Something's in the forest.*

Transfixed by tendrils of terror creeping over her, she held her breath as the trees vibrated when some unknown entity moved toward the edge of the field. The same faceless tall creature she'd seen before, and whose robes absorbed all light, appeared from between the dark blanket of trees. His robes somehow extinguished the lights of the stars.

Kat stumbled backwards and lost her footing on the small slippery stones. She flailed her arms and regained her balance. He was gone, but no light returned to the scene before her.

She stared anxiously around and gasped as the inky robed form reappeared, moving soundlessly toward her along the slippery stones. The pounding of her heart and the beat of blood at her throat held her motionless. The form stopped, as if prevented by some obstacle. Once before, in Rifella, a barrier had stayed the movement of the unknown creature, imparting a sensation of safety. This time, the feeling was accompanied by a soft feather touch on her cheek and a squeak in her ear.

Kat opened her eyes and sat up in her bed, gasping for breath. "A dream? A nightmare?"

Another squeak and small leathery wings batted at her face.

"Wink." Kat smiled in relief. "How can I be frightened when you're here?"

She held up her hand and the pyrock settled in her palm, holding out a fragile foreleg with a tube attached. She slipped the tube from Wink's leg and carried the tiny creature to the desk. Kat fed her some treats and settled the ball of fur inside her cage. *I'm so glad she's back. She interrupted the dream.* Kat's heart eased its thumping in her chest. *Perhaps I should consult with Marreth about the nightmare.*

She picked up the tube Wink brought back and unrolled the lengthy note contained inside. She understood only a few words, but recognized the symbol for Liandock at the bottom of the page. *Rats, he wrote in Priddanese. Who can I ask to translate?*

Kat's stomach gurgled and she burped. She'd over indulged at Brennan's table the night before. She took a quick peak at the window, and caught the first few tendrils of light coloring the dawn sky. After a glance around the room, she strode over to the ever-present tassel and tugged it.

She had time to don a robe, when a soft knock sounded. She opened the door, and requested the young apprentice bring her red-leaf tea.

"Of course, Lady Kat. I will bring some to your room right away."

She thanked him and he scurried down the hallway. She closed the door.

She did not need to wait long. A second knock revealed he had returned with a tray containing a sizable pot of tea, a mug, and small plate of cookies. She thanked him again as he bowed his way out.

Sitting at the table, Kat experienced almost instant relief as she sipped the hot liquid. She picked up Liandock's note, and pondered how to obtain a complete translation. *I don't want to ask Mouse. He seemed to need to separate Liandock and me*.

Stomach settled, Kat headed back to her bed, anxious to grab more sleep before she talked to Marreth about her nightmare. About to pull the covers over her she sat up again and snapped her fingers. Marreth. She would ask Marreth to read her the note.

♋♋♋

A knock roused Kat from her sleep, and she called out. "Who's there?"

"I am Ferren. Healer Marreth requested I wake you. She will meet you in the dining hall when you are ready to join her."

Kat called back. "My thanks. I will go to the dining hall shortly."

She slid from her bed, removed the ball of fur from Wink's cage, and stroked her. A tiny sleepy eye opened and gazed up at her with a chirp.

"Thank you, Wink. You did well, and I missed you." Kat fed the little pyrock, and deposited her back in her cage. Wink circled three times and curled in her favorite position.

Showered and dressed, Kat touched LIandock's pendant, set with the brilliant green stone, smiled in memory, and tucked his note in her right pocket. She exited her room and headed for the dining hall.

Finding her way presented no problem. Glowens appeared to be exuberant people, and the sounds of laughter and conversation guided Kat in the right direction. Entering the room filled with the din of discussion among friends, and the delightful aroma of baked bread, Kat immediately saw Marreth waving her to a seat next to Mouse.

Marreth's face lit up as Kat approached the table. "Good morrow to you, Kat."

"And to you as well, Marreth." As she sat, she glanced at Mouse. "Did you order your meal?"

"Not as yet." His grin was lopsided. "There is no journeyklim, but the Glowens offer a variety of other foods for a morning meal. We waited for you."

Kat pursed her lips. "Marreth what do you normally consume this early?"

"My favorite is groonnan. The dish is made from grains which grow near the village of Kadwee in the northern area of this land. I naturally consumed journeyklim elsewhere, and this is similar in both flavor and texture."

"Would you order for me? Perhaps you will also order tea as well."

Mouse widened his eyes. "What, no Karri-san?"

"I only caught sight of a few Rifellans in Glowen, and I seem to be becoming more accustomed to their presence."

"Interesting. I wonder if you sailed on many more boats, would you become accustomed to them as well?"

Kat glared at him. "I've suffered from seasickness all my life. As a youngster, I often sailed with my parents. I'm only sick the first two or three da—uh turns, and then I find my sea legs."

Marreth peered at Kat. "Your sea legs? What are those?"

"When one stops being nauseated by the movement of the water."

"I understand." Marreth beckoned to a wait person, who approached their table. "Would you bring two orders of groonnan?" She paused and regarded Mouse. "Would you enjoy the same dish?"

He nodded.

Marreth completed her request, and the woman left to fill the order.

"Kat, while we wait, I received a pyrock message for you from Fenneth in Rifella." Marreth passed a piece of parchment to Kat.

Kat glanced at the message, but while she recognized many words, the bulk of the meaning eluded her. She handed the note back to Marreth. "I'm afraid I only read a few words in your writing. Would you translate for me?"

"By all means. She writes, 'Brade became restless, and I assumed she missed you. However one day when I was about to visit Murwenna, I could not detach the kamelona from my neck and was forced to visit with her on my shoulder. No sooner had I approached Murwenna, when Brade leaped from my neck and jumped to the cradle holding Troyon. Murwenna shrieked and jumped for the cradle to remove it, but the kamalona nuzzled the cheek of the heir, who giggled and reached out his hand and patted her. I grabbed Brade, but the heir wailed for her. We were all stunned. Murwenna nodded at me, so I returned Brade to the heir. He smiled and gurgled at her and patted her again. Since that day, Brade sleeps beside him and guards the young male. Troyon delights in the colors on Brade's body, and the two appear to belong to each other. Murwenna sends her thanks, because she is convinced she now has double protection for her progeny.' Fenneth also thanks you for handing Brade to her."

Kat laughed at the story. She remembered the beauty of the chameleon-like creature that many considered dangerous.

"Can you send a reply to Fenneth thanking her for the information?"

Marreth nodded. "Yes."

Mouse raised an eyebrow and shook his head at Kat. "You are most fortunate Brade proved to be an asset. I suspect you might have suffered a distinct lack of admiration from the Rifellans if the kamalona harmed Murwenna's heir in any way."

Kat frowned at him. "I don't believe Brade would harm a child. I still have not found any Rifellans who have been attacked by a kamalona."

He rose from his seat. "Nevertheless, I am convinced you are fortunate the creature turned out to be benign." He stretched. "I would appreciate time to meet with two of the Rifellan guards here in Glowen to obtain more information about the routes around the land. Their knowledge will supply us with the best places to visit. Kat, are you able to amuse yourself for the rest of this turn?"

"Yes, perfect. I wish to spend some time with Marreth." She turned to the healer. "If you are available?"

"We enjoy a well-stocked market next to the Keep, which we can visit while Mouse is occupied."

"I'd be delighted, Marreth, and I shall keep myself busy, Mouse. Shall we meet again for the evening meal?"

He nodded, left the table, and headed from the hall.

Kat faced Marreth. "Before we leave for the market, would you please translate another pyrock message for me."

Marreth eyed her with curiosity.

"I requested Liandock, my Rifellan friend, to help me return home when I have completed my travels though Pridden. He responded with this note. My challenge is I can't read enough Pridden writing, so that I can understand what he's written." Kat reached in her pocket and handed Marreth the note from Liandock.

"Why did you not ask your guide to interpret this for you?"

"While we were in Rifella, I began to suspect that Mouse wished to act as a barrier between us. I'm not sure he approves of my growing relationship with Liandock."

"And is your relationship growing?"

Kat fidgeted, felt her cheeks heating, and gazed at her hands. "I believe Mouse thinks so. But please, Marreth read me the note."

The healer unfolded the parchment, and read, "Your friend writes, 'My apologies for being so tardy in my reply to you. First, I am not sure I truly do possess the power you need. But, the real reason is, I confess, I do not desire for you to leave Pridden or me. However, as I consider your situation, I know your return is vital to both our worlds. I will await your call for my help, and anticipate seeing you again with much pleasure. My help you shall have, although I dread saying farewell.' He signed this missive with a rune, which I cannot read."

Kat peered over the healer's shoulder and smiled. "That's his name, Liandock." She gazed at Marreth and placed a hand on her arm. "Let's visit the market now."

As they rose, Kat continued to smile to herself.

He doesn't want to say goodbye either.

CHAPTER 5

Kat and Marreth exited the gates of the Keep and turned right toward the market. The pathway, covered in wooden boards, allowed the visitors and vendors to keep their feet dry and mud-free.

Kat examined the well-laid planks and the way in which the pathway was springy underfoot. "I notice Glowens make use of wood in their buildings and on their paths as well. I find this more comfortable to step on and not nearly as hard as walking on the cobblestone roads in the other lands I've visited." *Interesting. In my nightmare, I was standing on cobblestones. I wonder where it was.*

"Glowen possesses a number of forested areas which produce the wood we need for all our buildings. What we do not have, however, are places that are readily mined for stone. When you travel to the areas which contain clogs, which they call kruggs in Glowen, you will find their rocks are either exceptionally hard, and therefore difficult to shape, or are soft and crumble with ease."

"Forests? All I have seen so far were huge tracts of land, lush with fruit and various growing edible plants. I did not see forests."

"You will, Kat. When you travel to the northern area of the island, up toward Kadwee, and on the other side of Lake Ufern, you will encounter many forested areas. The Glowens manage their forests well. They only allow a certain number of trees to be culled each path. As soon as a tree is felled, they immediately plant two more in its place."

"Why two more?"

"Sometimes a tree is attacked by tree borers or fails to develop properly. If both survive to maturity, there is always a need for beautiful wood. Occasionally there are sufficient stores to export to Rifella. While Glowens are able to build their own boats, they prefer the skills demonstrated by the Rifellans."

Kat raised an eyebrow. "Yet, at the jetty where we landed, I saw batches of wood coming from Baklai."

"Yes. Baklai has some woods of different colors, which the Glowens appreciate and use in their art."

They continued to stroll among stalls displaying clothing for both men and women. Kat saw, with interest, the clothing for men was far more colorful than that for women. Marreth pointed at shirts and pants hanging from the displays, and told Kat the material came from Master Thontook's looms in Kaylin.

"I thought the Kaylins disliked dealing with the Glowens?"

"They do, Kat, but the Rifellans act as the middle men for Kaylin goods in this land."

"Ah." Kat smiled. "The more I view of the lands of Pridden, the more I understand how important the symbiosis is which exists between the people."

"You are most observant, Kat."

"I must ask you something, Marreth."

"By all means."

"Brennan is the first Thane I've met. I've been told a fair amount about Lords, but can you tell me if Thane Brennan possesses Wielder power?"

As they talked, they passed small shops filled with containers of plants, both green and flowered, but the thoughts of Wielders distracted her. She glanced at Marreth, raising her eyebrows seeking an answer to her query.

Marreth blew out a breath. "You ask a large question. Wielder power is generally thought to be only available to Lords of a land. No person knows what this actually means. The history of Wielder power has never been recorded, so we assume there are different ways in which the power is expressed. Some Thanes do appear to show partial power, but then again, non-rulers also demonstrate surprising capabilities as well. I am sure you have been told Deleth displays the power of precognition. Some Masters of arts also show unusual abilities."

"That makes sense." Kat suspected that Deleth, the healer in Shendea, was recruited by Lord Rhognor specifically for her talents. "My friend Liandock, who is the Metal Master in Kaylin, has a unique proficiency with metals, crystals, and stones. His sibling, Irina, is aware of his special skills, but cannot point to what they are."

"Exactly Kat. No person on Pridden truly understands Wielder power, its strength, or in what ways it manifests. The Wielder energy, while spoken of in awe, remains a mystery."

The two women approached the entrance to the arts area, decorated with flags and plants and flanked by two trees, groaning under the weight of magnificent waxy white blossoms spattered with crimson. Kat breathed in the heady and seductive aroma from the blooms. The fragrance reminded her of a combination of night-blooming jasmine and magnolia.

They walked through the market, lined on each side by stalls selling wooden toys for young Glowens, and entered an area replete with shops with masses of flowers creating rainbows of color for their vendors, and foodstuffs in the form of fruit and odd-shaped vegetables. The two paused every now and then when Kat asked about names of various plants and flowers

Fascinated by the toys, Kat picked up a small wooden boat, holding miniature people and oars and a ship's wheel, that turned and moved a tiny rudder.

"Do you have progeny to purchase for, my Lady?"

Kat grinned at the stall keeper. "No, but I wish I had such delightful toys like these when I was young."

The man appeared disappointed.

"I would love to buy some, but a long journey looms in front of me, and I cannot carry excess luggage." Kat stayed a while, while the artist explained the different techniques and woods he used for his creations.

Marreth tapped her on the shoulder. "There is still much to experience, Kat."

"Sorry, his work is wonderful."

Two other stalls caught her attention. At the closest one, equipped with a potter's wheel, a man sat rocking a treadle with his feet, while his long slender hands shaped and guided the clay to create thin, perfectly rounded bowls and cups. At the back of the stall, his kiln glowed hot red, firing the previous day's creations. On shelves along one side, the final results of his labor rested, not only plates and cups, but magnificent and unusually shaped decorative pieces. Kat was particularly delighted by a golden brown bowl, inside of which rested a clay version of a sleeping pyrock.

She stroked the piece and complimented the potter. "You are a wonderful artist."

He raised his head, eyed her up and down, and smiled a lazy grin. "And you, my Lady, would make a wonderful model."

Kat shook her head. *Good grief, he's definitely flirting, but somehow he's not offensive. All the same, I wouldn't trust him at all. Yet others seem to be even more aggressive..* She backed away from the stall as he shrugged and went back to work. *He doesn't even care I said no. What an odd man.*

Kat, followed by Marreth, walked over to the next stall that beckoned her. In the back corner, stood a burly chested man, his black hair pulled back and tied at the nape of his neck, sweat pouring from him, and his upper body clad only in a vest of Rifellan-type armor. From the furnace in front of him, he withdrew a long blowpipe with a large blob of molten glass on the end. He began rolling the blowpipe while breathing down the tube. Slowly the glass began to swell, and when it drooped, he moved the blob of glass to a metal table and restored the shape by continuing to twirl it. He kept returning the glass to the hole in the furnace to reheat it, Kat assumed, so he would be able to manipulate it further. Each time as he lifted the pipe, his upper arms expanded and his chest muscles bulged.

Kat stared at him, as he created a wine glass, astounded by the heat generated. Although standing more than twelve feet away, the heat was so intense she understood why he sweated so profusely. A helper wearing huge protective gloves, held the glass as the blower used what resembled enormous scissors to cut the beautiful piece from the blowpipe. The helper transported the completed glass to a secondary kiln to the right of the main oven. The glassblower closed both the second furnace door and that of the main kiln, and placed the pipe in a tall container. He grabbed a damp cloth, wiped the sweat from his chest and massive upper arms, and used a towel to dry himself. He walked over to Kat who was still standing open-mouthed at the counter.

"Do you wish answers, my Lady?"

"I never observed glassblowing demonstrated so thoroughly before, and you were so clear in your movements, I managed to follow the process easily. Back in my world, I had a friend who worked with glass and gave me a brief demonstration." She patted her forehead. "The heat generated from the ovens is so fierce though. It seems dangerous."

The great bear of a man, his face still flushed from the temperature, beamed at her. "Danger only exists if I were inattentive or careless with my tools. I have blown glass for many paths, and the scars on my arms are from the days of my youth when I failed to pay attention to my mentor. I now revel in the joy of creating."

Marreth stepped forward. "Master Garren pen Darryn, Lady Kat is visiting Thane Brennan on behalf of Lord Eduardo."

Garren extended a hand and clasped Kat's in his large meaty paw and tilted his head. "Well met, Lady Kat."

I didn't expect his hand to be so soft and so warm.

"I suspect you cannot purchase my wares because of your travels, but if you would please accept a small offering, I would be honored." He reached under the counter beside him and extracted a glass ring of unusual design. Two thin bands of glass, one pale pink and one in a deep emerald, rotated around each other. He took her right hand in his and slipped the ring on her middle finger. "Show this anywhere on Glowen and all will know Garren pen Darryn bestowed his honor to indicate you are a welcome guest. All doors will open for you, my dear." He grinned at her and winked.

Taken aback, Kat gulped. "My thanks …er—Master Garren." Although not a Rifellan, Kat found Darryn compelling, and saw his eyes were brown not wolf eyes like the balance of Glowens.

Marreth touched her forearm. "We have spent much time in the market, so let us go for our mid-turn meal. The food stalls are further toward the middle of the market."

"A fine idea. I am ready to eat." Kat glanced back at Garren. He had commenced blowing glass, and once again he glowed in the heat of the ovens.

Kat thought that Glowen men were not necessarily arrogant, but merely confident. They were frank in their desires. *There is something unusual and powerful about Garren. He confuses me.*

CHAPTER 6

Kat held out her right hand, showing off the ring given her by Garren. "It's beautiful. He's a true artist."

Marreth reached over and picked up Kat's right hand. "The pink in the ring exactly matches your bangle. Where did you obtain the bracelet?"

"I bought this for myself in the market at Lord Rhognor's Keep. My friend Walden, sibling to Hesginn, persuaded me to purchase it."

"I learned that Hesginn perished when you were attacked by the Assassin's Guild."

"He betrayed Lord Rhognor and was responsible for the death of the Lady Halfin."

"The people of Pridden have mourned her passing."

"You knew her?"

"I knew of her, Kat. All who met her, loved her."

Both women sighed in unison.

Kat gazed thoughtfully into the distance. "I suspect the gems are valuable. During my walks in Shendea, a man attempted to snatch the band from my wrist. I was fortunate I escaped intact."

Marreth patted Kat's arm. "Glowen is a peaceful land. We enjoy our pleasures too much to spend time robbing others."

"I'm glad to hear this. Kaylin, Shendea, and Rifella showed me many instances of strife and challenge." Kat laughed. “And after the voyage on the boat, I don’t need more trials.”

Marreth patted Kat’s arm again. “You may rest easily.” She sniffed the air. “If my nose is telling me the truth, the food stalls are close.”

Kat inhaled the scents. “The aromas are divine. I detect some familiar ones, but so many are unknown to me.” She smiled at Marreth. “You’ll be my guide through the delicious foodstuffs of Glowen.”

“I suspect you might be surprised. Other lands import a variety of spices and foods grown in Glowen. We do not consume as much meat as most of them, but we do enjoy brantors from Rifella and blicks from Baklai. On rare occasions, we obtain gornog meat, although the Kaylins do not enjoy trading with us. They tend to judge that the people in this land are loose in their morals. A tragedy, in truth. Glowens pity them their rigid conformity.”

As the two women turned a corner of the market, the glorious bouquet of roasting brantor meat, the fragrance of hot spices, and the sweet almost cloying odor of some vanilla-like fruit assailed Kat’s nostrils.

She turned to Marreth and found the woman laughing at her. “What?”

“You resemble the hunting dogs of Kaylin when they sense their prey. They sniff and sniff at the air as if homing in on something exceedingly delectable. You resemble Rifellan royalty, but I suspect you may find much about the Glowens to relate to.” She chuckled at Kat. “We should examine all the offerings before we decide upon our meal. I will help, particularly if you wish to try a new type of dish.”

“Excellent. I want to try different things so I can can be assured of eating dishes found only in Glowen.”

Kat, with Marreth close behind, wandered among the stalls breathing in the aromas and peering at the dishes on display. From time to time, she asked Marreth's advice. After they'd perused most of the stalls, Kat stopped in her tracks. "I know what I would like."

Marreth gazed at her, an expectant expression on her face, and raised her eyebrows.

"I want the blick dish with the hot spicy aroma, topped with the yellow sauce. I can't eat a huge amount, but perhaps also a small serving of the multi-colored roasted Glowen vegetables with the sweet brown sauce. And as to drink, only a substantial mug of the lovely fara tea we had at our morning meal. I enjoyed the flavor immensely."

Marreth led her to a table in the middle of area surrounded by the food stalls, and, as they seated themselves, she motioned to a young waitperson. "Would you please deliver two orders of the blick stew with the roasted vegetables, and two mugs of the fara tea to our table please."

He bowed. "Of course, Healer. Billed to the Keep?"

Marreth nodded and thanked him, and he strode off, but not before smiling broadly at Kat.

Kat waited until they completed their meals before she broached the subject of her nightmares.

Marreth stared in horror as Kat explained about each of the dreams she'd experienced as she journeyed through Pridden. "I have endured these dreams in every land. I'm terrified while caught in the nightmare, but the last two, including the one I experienced during this night, ended with a sense of protection from someone or something." She frowned. "In this one, I woke because Wink returned from her mission to Liandock."

Marreth shook her head with an astonished expression. "I find this most interesting. I wonder if this is a foretelling?"

"Foretelling what?"

"I cannot answer your question. But for some reason, a type of protection seems to be offered. Do you sense something in Glowen which might be protecting you?"

"No." Kat shivered. "Do you think it could be the pendant given to me by Liandock?" She withdrew the stone from beneath her clothing, displayed it to Marreth, and explained how the difference in temperature indicated danger or safety. "I'm only afraid during the dreams."

"Whatever this is, since Wynneth has been the recipient of all the dream information, I suggest you write and tell her about this one too. She does share with Deleth a small amount of prescience."

"I will. But I need your help to write the note. I'm not able to easily express myself in the Pridden language."

"I will." She rose. "Our star is lowering, and dusk descends. I suggest we head back to our rooms. I believe Mouse may have your route through Glowen planned for you."

"You go and attend to your duties. I would like to take another short stroll through the artisan stalls."

Marreth smiled and hugged Kat. "Enjoy. Make sure you see me before you head out on your journey."

She nodded, and as Marreth headed toward the Keep entrance, she walked back toward the artist's stalls, curious to see if Garren was still at his shop.

She strolled among the stores, many of which had the owners bustling about stowing their goods and dropping covers over their wares. Some curtains were tied down and their merchants gone. As she approached Garren's stall, she saw him closing for the night. He had damped the fires for the ovens, and his assistants moved about closing the displays of chalices and glass figurines, sealing them until the morrow.

What about him is so imposing?

Garren had already stored the accessories for glass blowing in cabinets lining the back of the booth. Locking the oven doors, he glanced up and his eyes lit up in a smile as he glimpsed her. "My Lady, welcome back. Are you happy with your ring?"

"I love the colors, and I came back to ask you more questions about your art. However, you appear to be closing for this turn, and I expect your family is waiting for you."

He smiled again. "I would be delighted to answer further questions. I am without a bond mate currently, so I am free to stay here as long as I wish."

That was easy.

He bowed his head. "Would you care to come into the booth and join me in a glass of wine?"

"If you're sure I won't make you late for anything, I would appreciate some wine."

He lifted a section of the counter and ushered her to a small table with two chairs in the middle of the stall.

He held out a chair for her and moved to the counter from under which he brought a beautiful blue bottle with two vibrant blue glasses. "I must admit I water Orenberry wine, because I cannot afford to lose concentration when I am working, so this is quite mild."

"I'm glad, because undiluted, your wine is too strong for me, and I also prefer to keep a clear head." *Particularly around men. Although for some reason, Garren does seem to be one I can trust.*

Garren poured two glasses and handed her one. A tiny electric shock startled her as their hands touched, and Garren's eyes widened.

What the heck was that?

He cleared his throat. "Lady Kat, the Healer mentioned you are in Glowen on behalf of Lord Eduardo of Kaylin. What assignment have you been given?"

"Please, Garren, call me Kat. I have been told Glowens are not formal people, and neither am I. As to what Lord Eduardo requested of me, he simply indicated Pridden was beset by challenges."

"Forgive me, I did not mean to pry." He appeared embarrassed. "But, you said you had some questions for me."

Kat sipped at her wine. "Yes, I do. In the past, as I mentioned, I once attended a glass blowing demonstration by another, but you handle the molten glass differently. The other person made the process appear so difficult, but when you blow the glass, you seem to expend little energy, and I almost think the glass is obeying you and doing your bidding, rather than being forced from the tube."

He seemed taken aback by her words. "You are the first person to mention such a thing." He finished his wine, and poured another glass. He held the bottle over Kat's glass and lifted an eyebrow in query, but she shook her head.

Garren picked up his glass and took another gulp of wine. "My male parent enjoyed a reputation as the finest glass blower in all Pridden. All the lands invited him to visit to reveal his skills. He discovered early in my youth I too possessed a natural ability. Caleesh called for him when I was quite young, and I still miss him." He sighed. "By good fortune he taught me sufficient skills to continue his business. This enabled me to support my female parent and my younger siblings."

I can't help myself. I must ask him. I'm sure I detect something powerful about him. "Garren are … are you a Wielder?"

"What?"

"Do you possess Wielder power?"

"I …I am not aware of any, Kat. I admit I enjoy a special relationship with the glass, but as to Wielder power, I doubt I own such an ability."

Have I blundered again? I blurted that out without thinking. "Forgive me. I was too forward. I hope we may speak again. However, the sky is dark, and I must return to my room at the Keep." She rose and gazed down at him. "You are a most interesting man."

He rose from his seat and stared at her, his eyes almost burning with a hint of … of what?

He's not being sexual. Is he curious? Startled? Kat turned away and hastened to the Keep entrance.

Why did I ask him that?

CHAPTER 7

Kat hurried along the wooden path to the Keep entrance, deep in thought about her encounter with Garren. *Something about him I'm drawn to.* Despite the tingling in her hands, she instinctively recognized the sensation was not sexual, but rather an awareness of intense power and strength. She shook her head, experiencing again the force of his handshake when she first met him and the electric shock when he handed her the glass of wine.

She was paying little attention to her surroundings as she approached the Keep, and only noticed the sudden cold of her stone, when a blow to her back knocked her aside. Someone grabbed her arm. She clutched at fabric on the attacker and it ripped. She yelled at a sudden pain in her wrist. Released without warning from his hold, and unable to keep her balance, she fell to the ground, scraping her arm on the wooden planks of the walkway. Rolling to her side, she glimpsed a figure with dark brown hair and loose inky clothing running toward the market. A scrap of blue cloth remained clutched in her hand. Unsteadily, she stumbled to her knees and, as she began to rise, a strong arm helped her regain her feet. Startled, she recognized one of Brennan's Rifellan guards.

"Are you all right, my Lady?"

"I'm just scraped a little." She held up her arm and, when she inspected the scratches, no bracelet graced her wrist. "Damn, I've been robbed."

"I am Praetor Jagloran. Please let me take you to our Healer, and you can give me the details." He escorted her through the hallways of the Keep to Marreth's door. When the healer appeared, he advised her, he had brought her a patient.

Marreth gasped when she saw Kat standing slightly behind the guard. "What happened?"

"Healer, the lady has been robbed, and needs her wounds tended. May I enter to obtain the details from her?"

"Please, both of you come in. Kat, sit in that chair." Marreth dabbed at the scratches on Kat's arm with an aromatic ointment.

Some were fairly deep, and she winced. "It stings. But it reminds me of the green smell of fresh cut basil."

As Marreth attended to her, Jagloran requested more information.

"I don't know who attacked me, Jagloran. I was distracted. He was a strong man, dressed in dark clothing, but I don't think he was a Glowen because his hair was brown. I never saw his face, but I did rip his sleeve." Kat handed the piece of fabric to the Rifellan. "I am rarely so ignorant of my surroundings, and he caught me off guard." She shivered with the aftermath of the surge of adrenaline she'd experienced.

"Glowen is considered a safe land. People have reported incidents of a few robberies near the docks by a small group of young males, but we suspect they are not from Glowen." Jagloran scowled. "Unfortunately, our group of guards is limited, and as yet we have not located them. We will do our best to recover your bracelet, Lady Kat, but if this group is from elsewhere, your jewelry may already be departing

Pridden." He paced around the room. "It infuriates me when when someone does this to a visitor."

Kat leaned over and held her head. "I'm angry at the thief, and at myself. Could I please have some water."

Jagloran headed directly for the table in Marreth's room, and grabbed a glass and poured water for Kat. He offered her the drink, which she accepted gratefully.

"I can give you a better description of the bracelet. There are fourteen very fine pink crystals set in silver. I suspect they may be valuable because someone attempted to rob me of it in Shendea. I hope the crystals can be recovered, as I'm rather fond of them." She shivered again, and drank more water.

"We will do our best, Lady Kat. I shall request my guard unit to search the market place immediately." He bowed to her and left Marreth's quarters.

Marreth, stared at Kat, and shook her head. "Well, Kat. you certainly do manage to fall into unusual situations."

"Not normally. I'm usually paying more attention to my surroundings. Right now, I'm hurt and I'm angry."

Marreth patted her on the shoulder. "I will put a light gauze over the scratches to keep the ointment on until the morrow. I removed about five splinters of wood from the scratches so they would not fester. The covering will allow swifter healing."

"Thank you. My arm feels much better."

"Now tell me, did your attacker say anything?"

"He never said a word." Kat paused. "I believe he came from some other land, due to the way he moved."

The ointment soothed, and Kat thought about what Jagloran had said about new problems arising from outsiders.

"I wonder why people would come here to cause trouble?"

"I suspect because Glowens enjoy a reputation for being fun-loving people who enjoy life. Perhaps that makes Glowens more susceptible to attacks by outsiders.

"Perhaps." Kat stood. "Thank you Marreth, I feel much better." She rubbed at her cheek. "Now, I should find Mouse, as I did promise to share an evening meal with him, and I should let him know about the robbery."

"An excellent idea."

Kat headed for the exit. As she opened the door, Marreth called out to her. "Pay more attention. Sometimes things happen that are not normal."

Normal? What's normal in Pridden?

CHAPTER 8

Kat traipsed through the halls of the Keep toward the dining hall and paused at the doorway to search for Mouse. He sat at a table with a Rifellan guard, the two of them poring over a series of maps and charts. She approached him from behind, but Mouse turned and waved her over. The guard rose, did the weird Rifellan handshake thing with Mouse and left, heading toward the exit.

Kat still had not been able to duplicate the peculiar hand movements. "Well, Mouse, you will probably not be caught off guard. You knew I was approaching, didn't you?"

"I am always aware of my surroundings."

"Me too. But today I forgot to pay attention and got robbed."

Mouse gasped. "What?"

"I got robbed." Kat held up her wrist. "My pink crystal bracelet. Most of the time, I pay attention to my surroundings, but I was deep in thought, and now I've lost my jewelry."

"Are you all right?"

Kat nodded. "Yup, just a few scratches."

"This is unusual. I am under the impression that Glowen is a safe land."

"The guard who took the details of the robbery said Glowen is regarded as relaxed and safe. But apparently there are a number of unwanted situations which have happened recently. The guards suspect the bandits are from some other land,

and they're not sure why they're suddenly causing problems in Glowen." She shrugged. "It'll be a miracle if the bracelet is recovered, so there is no point in mourning the loss. After all, it is only a thing. Let's order our meal, and you can show me the route we'll take."

Mouse nodded and called a wait-person over to their table.

By the time their meals arrived, Mouse had outlined the initial journey through Glowen. He put the maps aside, and they both dug into their food.

Kat saw him staring at the bandage on her wrist. "I didn't pay attention when the robber grabbed me, so I scraped my arm on the wooden walkway. Marreth had to remove a few splinters, and she also put an ointment on the place where the bracelet snapped and gashed my wrist."

"You always seem to pay attention to your surroundings. Why not this time?"

"I was thinking about the glassblower I met in the market. He's a most unusual man."

Mouse's raised eyebrows mocked her. "A Rifellan?"

"No." Kat snorted and frowned. "He's a Glowen. But … I think he may possess Wielder power."

"Are you sure? Thane Brennan enjoys only a minute amount of power. I am not aware of any in Glowen who possesses more than the Thane."

"I'm almost positive. I picked up the same sensation about him as when I'm around Eduardo. But in Garren's case, the sense of energy is much stronger."

"Kat, I repeat. No Glowen benefits from a possession of much power."

"I'm only telling you what I experienced in his company. There's something else. Garren pen Darren's eyes are not light blue or grey. They are brown, similar to yours."

"Now that *is* interesting." Mouse rubbed his chin.

Kat asked a passing apprentice for a cup of Karri-san. She noticed Mouse staring at her. "I know." She snorted again. "Although I'm not that affected by the Rifellans these days, I have not tasted any Karri-san for two turns, and I think I would be wise to drink a certain amount on a regular basis."

"You are no doubt correct in your assessment. You are aware there are only a limited number of Rifellan guards here on Glowen?"

"Oh, Mouse. Really? Rifellans are some of my favorite people. Don't you think I notice how many there are?"

Mouse sighed. "I did not intend to begin an argument."

"Sorry. I should not assume you were. Things are weird. Why would someone want to steal my bracelet? This is the second time that's happened. The whole thing doesn't make sense."

"The gems may be more valuable than you realize. Were they costly?"

Kat shrugged. "Walden persuaded me to buy the jewelry, and he signed the chit. It may have cost more than I thought, because he was attempting to annoy Hesginn."

"You reported the loss to the guards. Therefore, until they locate your property, you might be best served to forget the bracelet." He pulled the maps toward them again. "Let me complete the information about our initial journey through Glowen. When we leave here on the turn after the morrow, we will head toward the coast to the camping ground at the foothills of Krugg Menyd. They are not nearly as high as Clog Neran in Kaylin and are the only monts in this land."

Kat smiled. "Monts. What I call mountains in my world, you use a different name for in each land. So is mont a word you use in Morden?"

"Yes." He pointed at the map. "The following morrow we will leave the camp and will head for Kadwee through the first of the perfectly laid out forests of Glowen, on the edge of which are the most amazing vegetable gardens." He sighed. "We will certainly eat well in Kadwee, and will probably stay an extra turn." He pointed at a mark on the largest map. "After Kadwee, we near the other coast and will stay at the village of the Keeper of furred stingers."

Kat brightened. "Furred stingers? What are they?"

"The stingers produce another much-prized product, Golden River, that Glowens sometimes export. They live in a type of rounded enclosure where they nest and reproduce. They gather nectar from flowering plants, which they turn into Golden River. The keepers manage them and extract the Golden River on a regular basis, which is then stored in containers and used by the people of this land. Unfortunately for the rest of Pridden, Glowen rarely has an excess of Gold River to sell elsewhere."

"Sounds like honey to me."

"Hunneee? What an odd name."

"Well, honey is sweet and delicious."

"Hmmm. So is Golden River." He shrugged. "Next we will head to Kamerdow, which is a small village at the southern foot of Krugg Menyd. We will only stay one night there and continue our journey through the second forest to Tasik, which lies on the shores of Lake Ufern."

"A lake? Will we have an opportunity to bathe, like we did in Shendea at Lake Glenaddie?"

"I suspect we will, because Tasik is the Glowen equivalent of Roothlan. Tasik is a town with many sights, so we may spend at least two turns there, after which we will return to the Keep by crossing Netht Dowron."

"The trip sounds fascinating, and I am most pleased to hear we will only use a camp one night. I'm sure Arrogol made you aware that I am not fond of camping."

"Kat." Mouse sighed. "The camping situation is a permanent set of wooden cabins settled on raised platforms. Each shelter contains individual rooms with comfortable beds, not as generous in size as those in inns, but still much better than simple cots and blankets. You will not need to use your saddle to pillow your head. Each cabin also contains a small personal and boasts a generous living and dining area."

"Oh, be still my beating heart—luxury camping."

Mouse grinned at her. "Sometimes it seems you are easily satisfied."

"I prefer my creature comforts. Thank you for the brief information. I do believe I will enjoy myself, and particularly since Glowen displays no challenging situations." She smiled at her own words.

"So they say. Shall we meet on the morning of the morrow for our meal? I will bring with me a list for you to pack. Since we will be returning to the Keep before leaving Glowen, you do not need to bring everything."

She nodded and rose from the table. They left the dining hall and headed for their rooms.

Goody, a restful and relaxing journey. Just what I need.

CHAPTER 9

A shaft of sunlight beaming through the open curtains and a loud squeaking woke Kat the following morning.

She slipped from the bed and headed to the pyrock's cage. "Wink, I'm so sorry. I forgot to feed you last night. In my defense, I was tired and you were asleep." She picked up two pieces of food from the dresser, opened the door of the cage and lifted the furry ball of noise from her bed of folded rags. *Poor little Wink. I missed you so much, and here I am neglecting you.*

Her mouth open, Wink accepted two pieces and demanded more. Another two scraps, and the little creature settled back in Kat's hand, waiting, apparently, to be stroked. Two gentle pats on the downy head, and Wink closed her eyes and her head drooped. Kat deposited her in her pen where Wink circled three times, curled up in a ball, and within seconds, the tiniest of snores ushered from the small bed.

Kat yawned, stretched and headed for the shower. Afterwards, dressed in comfortable clothing, she set off for the dining hall. When she reached the hall and searched for Mouse without locating him, she found a table and ordered fara tea.

By the time Mouse appeared in the doorway, she was sipping the hot sweet beverage. She waved at him to join her.

They ordered their food from an apprentice, and while they waited, Jagloran, the guard who helped Kat the night before, approached their table.

"Kat, we managed to capture your robber. However, we did not recover your bracelet."

"If he doesn't have my bracelet, how are you convinced he's the robber?"

"He is from Morden and does indeed possess brown hair, and a rip in his sleeve matches the piece of fabric you gave us. He refuses to tell us what he did with your jewelry."

Kat sighed. "Well, I'll miss the bracelet, but asI told Mouse, it was only a thing." *Don't know what I can take home anyway.*

Jagloran faced Mouse. "Sire, I am aware one of our guards supplied you with maps of Glowen for your journey through this land. However, I believe he forgot to pass this one over to you."

Mouse peered at the map. "This map covers the forested areas on the west side of the island."

"You are correct. The Glowens practice excellent management of their forests, and to protect any of the newly planted trees, they issue these trail maps for people to follow. He apologizes for forgetting to give you this one."

"Thank him for me. I'm glad he remembered."

"I will." He glanced at the apprentice approaching the table. "I shall leave you to consume your food alone." He turned away and left the hall.

The meals arrived, accompanied by the rich smell of cooked grain, and the pair tucked in.

While sipping their fara tea, a young woman bounced up to their table. "Lady Kat, forgive my intrusion. I am led to believe you are on a mission for Lord Eduardo of Kaylin. Am I correct?" Her eyes held an expression of hope, but her voice was too loud and high-pitched. Unlike many of the Glowen women Kat had met, this one was dressed elaborately.

Kat eyed the woman warily. "Sort of."

"How fortunate you were able to spend some time with him. I only met him briefly when he travelled to Glowen to meet with Thane Brennan." She blushed. "He is a most comely man. This is something in which I am an expert. Judging comely men, that is."

Comely? Is she for real? "And who are you?"

"My apologies, my Lady. I am Tessia pen Godron." She giggled and blushed again. "May I ask you some questions about Lord Eduardo?" She flushed an even deeper red and then continued to babble on. "I need to know everything about him. It is most important, and being informed by someone who has met him is perfect, as you are acquainted with him and all the things that he desires as well. As you can tell, all of this is most important to me before I actually meet him." The young woman at last slowed down to take a breath.

Kat glanced at Mouse, but he had an incredulous expression on his face. "Why is this important to you?" Kat was hesitant to discuss Eduardo with a stranger from another land.

The young woman continued to chatter on, ignoring Kat's question. "Well, um. There are many things I need to know. For an example, is there a bond mate in his life?" Poor Tessia's face reflected an almost desperate need to receive the answer to her question. "I need to know this. It is most important."

"Why do you need to know that?"

The tension on Tessia's face increased. "Oh, I would be so glad if he is not yet bonded."

"Er, I do not believe he is bonded, but why?"

Tessia almost wiggled in delight. "Well, I find him most pleasing to the eye, and I am hoping to meet with him. A member of my pod, my male parent's sibling, Emrys pen Godron, is planning to travel to Kaylin. He intends to introduce me to Lord Eduardo as a potential bond mate." She giggled. "I am sure he will find me acceptable, as my pod is important in the production of Orenberry wine. My dowry is a generous one, and I am sure Lord Eduardo will be impressed by the size of it."

"Ah." *I suspect Eduardo might find her overwhelming ... and a bit annoying. She babbles.*

"I wonder, Lady Kat, if I might accompany you on your journey through Glowen. I will be able to learn more about Eduardo." She sighed as she said his name. "It is most important I learn more about him."

Kat glanced at Mouse, who shook his head. "Um, I would need to discuss this with both Thane Brennan and my guide. I cannot promise anything."

Tessia clutched at Kat's hand. "Oh please find a way."

Kat drew back and freed her hand.

A guard approached them, and advised Mouse that Thane Brennan wished to consult with them.

Mouse, a look of grateful escape on his face, rose immediately and almost ran for the door.

Kat faced the young woman. "Leave this with me, Tessia." She followed Mouse with haste from the dining hall.

Hurrying down the corridors, Kat caught up with Mouse and glanced at him. "What just occurred?"

Mouse shook his head as in disbelief. "I have no idea, but I do not wish to bring the child with us."

"I agree, but she's not a child, Mouse. She's a young woman, albeit a most naïve one. However, having her with us would be like playing nursemaid to a puppy." Kat shivered.

Mouse nodded, made a gesture of wiping his brow, and Kat laughed aloud.

ගෙගෙගෙ

Later, seated with Brennan, Mouse went over the route they planned to use through the northern part of Glowen, and he pointed out the protective trail maps they received from Jagloran.

Kat watched the two of them, marveling at the difference between Mouse, who appeared almost diminutive, and Brennan, a tall and powerfully built man. Most taken with his amazing wolf eyes, and much taken by him in general, she still had no desire for a closer relationship. *Some guys are cool, but only for window-shopping.* She gazed at Mouse speculatively. *I wonder if Mouse ever had a relationship with a woman?*

Brennan leaned back in his chair. "I would appreciate it if the two of you would perform a favor for me."

Mouse nodded. "We would be more than willing, Sire."

"I would hope you will agree to take Tessia pen Godron with you on this first journey. Her constant chattering about Lord Eduardo is most trying. We are all anxiously awaiting the day her pod member, Emrys, leaves with her to visit Kaylin."

Kat caught a flash of horror in Mouse's eyes, and she groaned internally but managed to paste a vacuous smile on her face. "If that is your wish, Brennan, we will certainly help you in this task."

By now Mouse's eyes were wide open and horrified, similar to a rabbit in the thrall of a cobra with hood raised.

Brennan sighed. "My thanks. The woman is young and has no concept of the ways of the world. I hope the eventual journey to Kaylin will provide her with some sense of proportion, and she will settle for a Glowen as her bonded mate, rather than reaching for someone for whom she is most unqualified. In the meantime, you will grant me a huge favor by removing her person from the Keep for a short period of time."

Mouse bowed his head to Brennan. "I will contact her later, so we can be prepared to leave after our first meal on the morrow."

Brennan sighed again, this time with obvious relief. "My thanks. I assume this is the soonest you will be able to depart."

Rats. Dragging young Tessia with us may be more challenging than facing assassins. Why does Brennan want her with us?

CHAPTER 10

The following morrow, Kat entered the dining hall of the Keep, and spotted Mouse already seated. He waved her over.

She smiled. "Did you place your meal order?"

"I did, and I ordered groonnan for you, as you expressed enjoyment when Marreth introduced the dish to us."

Tessia came bounding through the doors of the hall and headed for their table. "Lady Kat, I am ready for our trip, and—" she turned to Mouse, "—I packed all you suggested on your list."

"Did you send your bag to the stable?"

"Yes."

"Excellent, because I arranged a gentle horse for you, and I advised the camp leader another is arriving with us."

Tessia's face crumpled. "A horse? I do not like horses. Do you not possess a wagon or a cart to transport me?"

Is she going to complain about everything on this journey?

Mouse shook his head. "The only choice is to travel by horse. We have much distance to cover and a limited number of turns in which to accomplish our journey. To travel by cart or wagon would slow us considerably."

"But Sire Mouse ... a horse?" Tessia's voice took on a whiny tone. "I find them hard and uncomfortable. I am not accustomed to travel by horse." She pouted. "My female parent would never permit me to travel in such a vulgar manner."

Kat snorted. “Tessia, your female parent may consider traveling by horse to be vulgar, but I traveled in three of Pridden’s lands via horse, and nevertheless am referred to as ‘Lady Kat’ ” *Keep your temper, Kat, she’s only a spoiled brat.* “In addition, Lord Eduardo is a fine horseman and much admires females who are well-trained in the saddle.” *Good grief, that sounded like a sexual innuendo.*

Kat glanced at Mouse and caught a mischievous grin on his face. She glared at him. *Rats, he picked up on that. I sometimes forget he’s learning more about my way of speaking.*

Tessia put a hand to her mouth. “Oh. I was unaware Lord Eduardo is so enamored of horses. Perhaps it is good I will have to ride one.” She put on a determined expression. “When we return from this trip, I shall need to spend much time learning about horses so I can be admired by Lord Eduardo.”

Kat glanced to the side and rolled her eyes. *Whew.* “Tessia, perhaps you should order your meal so we can leave on our journey shortly.” She indicated with her head the young apprentice approaching with two meals.

Tessia beamed at Kat. “I consumed my meal earlier. I am so excited about this trip with you, I awoke at star-rise, and am ready to leave.”

“Oh.” Kat scratched at her eyebrow. “If you’ve packed everything you are taking with you on this journey, perhaps you will order some fara tea, while Sire Mouse and I finish our meal.”

“I do have some small items in a pack I wish to carry with me.”

“Fine. After our meal, I must return to my room to fetch my pyrock and a backpack.”

"You possess a pyrock? How exciting."

Mouse cleared his throat. "Tessia, I suggest you return to your rooms, and after Kat and I collect all we need, we will come for you and head for the stables together."

"Of course, Sire Mouse. I shall wait for you both." She rose from the table and virtually bounced from the hall.

Kat shook her head. "This is going to be a long journey." *Was I ever this naïve?*

"She is young, Kat, and Brennan requested our help. You may need to practice much patience."

She stared at the ceiling. "You seem to possess patience enough for both of us." She sighed and proceeded to eat her groonnan.

♋♋♋

Once their meals were over, they returned to their rooms. Kat carefully transferred the sleeping Wink to her travel cage, which she attached to her backpack. She left her room, and, as soon as she knocked on Mouse's door, he appeared, and they set off for the stable.

He advised Kat he had sent word for Tessia to meet them there.

"Fine." Kat glanced at him from under an eyebrow. "Mouse, did you detect a notion that Brennan seemed most anxious for us to leave?"

"Indeed, but I assumed he wanted us to be off with Tessia."

"I sense something more to this. It's almost as if he wishes us to finish our journey, and depart Glowen as soon as possible."

"You may be correct." Mouse stroked his jaw. "I heard faint rumors that Glowen possesses some sort of secret. I only heard this a couple of times and have not since happened upon those who spoke of it." He shrugged. "Rumors arise, remain briefly, and then disappear. I am unable to determine if such a secret truly exists."

"When you consider the Glowens, their lifestyle tends to discourage visitors. Perhaps these rumors indicate some validity." Kat frowned. "But Mouse, if that was the case, why would Brennan allow us to travel through Glowen at all?"

"If you recall, he made a point of telling us Glowen possesses no challenges."

"Yes, he did. Do you think he allows us to travel but is making sure we are accompanied? Can we trust him?"

"Are you suggesting Tessia is a spy and is not as stupid and naïve as she appears?"

"If she is Brennan's spy, she's the best actress I've ever encountered."

Mouse laughed. "I doubt she is pretending. You and I do enjoy a reputation for being truthful. If we stumble upon something, I suspect Brennan trusts we will not reveal Glowen's secret to the rest of Pridden."

"What makes you say such a thing? Why would anyone specifically trust me? And why would I trust Brennan?"

"Kat, you have demonstrated trust in a way. You never discussed the details of what Eduardo requested of you, nor what you experienced in each land, to the leaders of the other lands. You have only ever spoken in generalities."

"I saw no need, and how does this prove I can keep secrets?"

They exited the Keep, and Tessia appeared from nowhere. "Secrets? Who's keeping secrets. Tell me."

"No one is keeping secrets, Tessia. I was telling Mouse, I don't believe I possess secrets to reveal to anyone. But I'm sure if I had any, I would keep them."

"Well, if you do possess a secret, you must tell me. You and I have Lord Eduardo in common, so we are friends." Tessia set her mouth in a firm and determined line. "Friends always share secrets."

Kat sighed. "Should any secrets appear, I will consider this. But, Tessia, we are not acquainted long enough to be considered friends." *Does this child have any ability to filter her words*?

Tessia regarded Kat, eyes wide. "Of course we are, Kat. Lord Eduardo is our link." She peered at Kat. "I see you have eyes of different hues. Did you get the color in Kaylin?"

Kat stared at her. "Get a new color? What are you talking about? They are the color I received at my birth."

Out of the corner of her eye, Kat saw Mouse attempting to hide a grin. She glared at him.

They arrived at the stable, and Mouse brought out the horses for the two women.

Tessia turned to the stable hand. "Come on, help me up on this horse."

"That is Lady Kat's horse." The stable hand cleared his throat and led the smaller animal over to her. "This is the one Sire Mouse indicated for you. She is gentle and will be more comfortable for you."

"But I like the look of that one. I want it." She pointed at Kat's animal.

The young apprentice glanced at Kat, helplessly.

Little brat. "Tessia. This is my horse. Haydar of Kaylin gave her to me for my journey." Kat glared at the young woman, her words clipped. "No one. I repeat, no one rides her but me. Now mount your horse, and we can leave."

The young woman appeared almost frightened of Kat's tone, and hurried over to the horse assigned to her. The apprentice boosted her into the saddle. He seemed to be hiding a grin.

Kat stepped on the stool beside her mount and, gripping the saddle horn, pulled herself up to her saddle, annoyance lending her strength.

She glared at Mouse, expecting him to be amused by the conversation, but, now mounted, he avoided looking at her. He accepted the line for the baggage animal from the stable hand and secured the rope to the back of his saddle. He led the way from the Keep, and Kat motioned to Tessia to follow him.

They rode for a short distance. Kat called to Mouse to stop and rode up beside him. "I paid attention to the maps you presented last evening, and the path is generous and clear. I would like to be in the lead."

"An excellent idea. No dangers exist. However, when you come to a small pool of water in the Yuffern Dowron, we will pause to take refreshment, and the horses may drink their fill."

Kat nodded and set off down the path. This time Tessia rode after her and Mouse brought up the rear.

They followed a well-cleared path with luxurious and colorful vegetation on both sides. The flowers, different from any Kat encountered in other lands, bloomed lush and tall. They exuded scents that reminded Kat of rose and jasmine and plumeria, all jumbled together. She took deep breaths of the glorious fragrances and sat a little higher in her saddle.

Even the presence of the annoying Tessia could not destroy her happy mood. She still thought of home, but admitted that Pridden held some beautiful sights, sounds and smells.

And Liandock.

She heard the sound of water gurgling over stones and stopped her horse. Off to her left the little Yuffern Dowron flowed over and around a number of rocks. She dismounted and led her horse to a side pool in the stream. She watched as Tessia wiggled and squirmed and finally slid off her animal. Kat offered no help. Tessia needed to become more self-sufficient. As the girl walked toward the stream, Kat stopped her. "Take your horse to the stream to drink. She worked hard this morning."

Tessia glared at her but must have read something in Kat's face and obeyed.

Mouse rode up, brought both his horse and the baggage animal to the pool to drink, after which, he tied both animals to a tall bush, and Kat followed suit.

Kat called out to Tessia. "Once your horse has drunk her fill, tie the reins to a bush so she cannot run away."

Again Tessia obeyed, albeit with a sulky face.

Mouse handed out packets of food prepared by the Keep and motioned them to sit on clean rocks near the pool. "This is our mid-turn meal, and we will not be consuming any food until this eve at the camp. Drink from your canteen and refill it from the pool."

Tessia sat, pouting in silence.

Mouse did his best to enroll her in conversation. "How many paths have you lived, Tessia?"

"Twice ten."

"I am aware you are with the pen Godron pod, but what type of wine does your male parent make? I notice the wine that Glowen sends to other lands is always golden in color, but here in your land, I have found wines in a deep red, and one which is pale pink."

"The main wine my parent makes is the golden Orenberry wine, but he also makes the wine called Blud, which is most strong, and even those of us in Glowen need to add water before we drink of it."

Kat chimed in. "So no one drinks Blud without diluting with water?"

Tessia blushed. "Some say a few do consume Blud full strength, but they are shunned, and many believe that Blud drunk undiluted creates strange behavior, and those who do consume it, often depart this world much sooner than most. Many suspect they perform foul practices, and we prefer not to discuss them."

Mouse, one eyebrow raised, probed further. "Knowing this, your father still continues to make Blud?"

"Of course." Pride for her male parent shone in her eyes. "The wine boasts a fine strong flavor and is used in certain ceremonies. All Glowen would miss this wine if he ceased preparation." She almost glared at Mouse. "He cannot help that some abuse it."

"And what is the purpose of the pink?"

Tessia smiled. "Our pink wine is always used for celebrations of bondings and births. Since it is a gentle and sweet wine, none use it for regular consumption."

Mouse nodded, rose from his seat, folded the packets, and walked to his horse to stow the leavings in his saddle bag.

At the sound of a galloping horse approaching them, they all turned.

"Tammyn." Tessia greeted the man. "What are you doing here?"

He slid to the ground. "Tessia, your female parent is most ill and is asking for you. You must come with me at once."

"Oh no. I must go. My parent is ill." Tessia rushed over to her horse, and untied the reins from the bush. The young apprentice helped her on the saddle, mounted his own, and they rode off toward the Keep, Tessia uttering not another word in her haste to depart.

Kat stared at her guide. "Well, Mouse, my thanks to your goddess Caleesh. She removed the irksome Tessia from our company."

"The young woman's female parent is ill, Kat."

Kat sighed. "You don't need to voice your disapproval. It was not a kind thing to say." Kat grinned to herself.

But she did leave.

CHAPTER 11

Free from Tessia's nattering, Kat, smiling to herself, followed Mouse on horseback to the camp he had chosen for their first night in their journey through Glowen. The star that shone on Glowen was bright, the fragrance of the flowers and the twitters of the birds added to her sense of well-being.

She remembered the tune that she, Arrogol, and Bannigus sang during their journey. She began to hum it and added words when she remembered them. She kept her voice low, because she wasn't sure she was able to explain to Mouse why she was singing.

She swayed to the music in her heart. The sun, the sounds, and the sights were joyful. *Liandock didn't want her to leave, but he would help her.* She paused in her singing, breathed in, and lifted her hands in the air and whooped.

Mouse rode hastily up beside her. "Kat what is wrong?"

"Sorry. I am glad to be alive. The warmth of the star and these beautiful flowers. I'm happy, and I simply needed to express myself."

Mouse peered at her, alarm in his expression. "Oh. I have not seen you do this before. I was apprehensive in case something was troubling you."

Kat stopped her horse. *Poor Mouse, I do tend to worry him.* She smiled to herself, but stretched out her hand to pat him on the arm. "I didn't mean to alarm you. Look around.

Glowen is such a beautiful land." She smiled at him, and clicking at her mount, gathered the reins and set off again, singing softly to herself.

♋♋♋

Mouse shook his head and stared after her. She was singing the Rifellan warrior song, and he wondered what memories surfaced for her. Exposed to a side of Kat he had never seen before, he was momentarily stunned. He knew he had not intended to, but had unwittingly spoken the truth to Galdin when he mentioned he suspected Kat possessed some sort of power. *When she touched me I experienced a surge of energy. That has never happened before either.* He prayed it did not place her in additional danger.

He urged his horse to catch up. *I hope Eduardo and I are correct in helping her return to her own world. What would happen instead if she were to remain here and bond with either of us? What abilities could her progeny possess?*

♋♋♋

Kat, in the lead, spotted a series of small structures on the path to the left and stopped her animal so Mouse could catch up. She swiveled around and regarded him over her shoulder. "Is this the camp?"

"Yes. When we enter the grounds, ride past the series of lodges and go to the lean-to at the far end. We will leave our horses in the enclosure for the night. We are fortunate we do not have to build a shelter, but we do need to settle our own horses, and feed and water them after the long day of traveling. I am aware you are familiar with these beasts, and I assume you are able to perform the basics of grooming."

"I am. I guess we'll have to unload our own baggage as well."

"They expect us to. The Glowen who manages this camp will give us some aid, but he is not a stable hand." He pointed to a cabin ahead. "Stop your horse beside the wooden structure on the right, and we will take our baggage inside. Once our bags are stowed, we will head for the lean-to and tend to our horses."

Kat nodded and stopped at the cabin he indicated. Shaped like a hexagon, the cabin reminded her of a cell in honeycomb. She dismounted, grabbed her lighter bags and carried them inside. The wooden cabin contained a communal area and two sleeping quarters stood off to the right side with curtains drawn back. To the left, a small eating area and a doorway led to what was likely a personal.

She settled her load on a table, and headed out to help Mouse remove the balance of the baggage from the pack horse. Once all their bags had moved inside the wooden "honey cell," as Kat now thought of the small building, they walked their mounts to the animal shelter.

Kat struggled somewhat to remove the saddle from her animal, simply because of the height. She placed the saddle on the rack beside the stall and hung the bridle on a hook attached to the wall. Grabbing a brush and a currycomb, she entered the stall and proceeded to groom her faithful companion who had borne her so far from Kaylin. Brushing her animal raised clouds of dust. The mare nickered in obvious pleasure and blew into Kat's hair. "You like that do you?" She brought a container of water and dried grasses for the hay net that hung in the corner of the stall. The mare drank her fill and set to munching on the contents of the net. Kat swung the gate at the front of the makeshift stall closed.

Mouse completed grooming his animal and began to tend to the pack horse. Kat brought a bucket of water and a net of grasses for the creature to eat and, by this time, was sweating with the effort.

"Thank you, Kat, you did well."

Kat shrugged off the compliment, not sure how to react.

Hot and covered in dust, the two headed back to the honey cell. The entire cabin rested on a wooden platform, which must help keep the interior clean. They entered the door, and Kat raced for the personal, yelling "shotgun." The shower was not nearly as fancy as at most inns, but the water was perfect for cleansing a tired, dirty body. Huge towels hung on racks beside the shower and Kat wrapped herself in one, and headed for the room she chose for herself.

As she exited, Mouse was standing near the door, ready to have have his own shower. When he saw Kat wrapped only in her towel, he blushed and dropped his gaze to the floor. "What did you yell when you entered the personal?"

"Sorry Mouse, it was just a silly expression from my home."

She shook her head in amusement and moved to her room, where she chose a long robe similar to those worn in Shendea. This one, though, was cool, light material and slid over her body with silky softness. She entered the general living area and strolled across the room to admire the clean lines of honey-colored wood that smelled similar to pine. She breathed deeply of the fragrance and sank into a long seat in front of a grate. Far too warm for a fire, the grate stood empty. A knock on the door heralded a visitor, and Kat called out "Come."

A tall man, with the inevitable wolf eyes, entered and bowed his head. "Lady Kat, we have been expecting you and your guide. I am Manga pen Yuwen. I will request my assistant bring you a meal and wine. Is there anything you would prefer to eat?"

Mouse exited the personal, and, unlike Kat, was fully clothed in his usual grey robes. He must have overheard the last part of the conversation. "Manga, I believe I speak for Lady Kat as well. Please bring us whatever is intended for this night's meals."

"Very well." He bowed and left.

"What made you order this particular meal?"

"When you are eating in an out-of-the-way place or one which does not receive many visitors, you are always best served to order what they are cooking for the day. Most of these kinds of eating halls cannot easily produce strange dishes from other lands. No doubt you remember well the meal we consumed in Barthon."

She shuddered. "I had hoped to forget. Only on the boat from Orkanna did I feel worse, and never want to feel that way again. I am in full agreement with your decision."

When the meal arrived, they sat at the table to consume their food and Kat asked further questions about the travel route.

They sat for a while longer, and Kat requested they move. "These chairs are not comfortable. Can we take our wine and sit on the sofa. We can continue to discuss the way to Kadwee."

"What did you call this seat?"

"A sofa. Some people also call this a couch."

"Interesting words. I shall attempt to remember at least one of them. We call them long-chairs. They are excellent for allowing two or more people to sit in front of the hearth when the weather is cooler."

"I guess they're also more conducive for creating an intimate atmosphere for a couple intent on bonding."

"I … I suppose so." His eyes opened wide, and he moved imperceptibly away from her.

She stared at him, seemingly horrified by his presumption. "I was not suggesting such a thing between us. You assume too much." She growled her answer.

Mouse blushed. "Kat, I apologize. I was attempting to create a joke."

Kat unable to maintain her stern expression any longer, laughed, shaking her head. "I suspected you might be, so I played a joke back on you."

Mouse stared at her. "You understood I was making a joke, but you pretended to be insulted? And that was also a joke?"

She nodded and her laughter increased.

Faced with the laughter, Mouse attempted a grin.

Wiping her eyes, Kat stood. "That was priceless."

Mouse appeared puzzled. "It was not that amusing."

"You're right, it wasn't, but if you could have seen your face, when you thought you'd insulted me, that was what I found amusing." She regarded him almost embarrassed. "It was also funny that you could make such an odd joke. I'm not used to that. You better warn me next time." She stretched and yawned. "I'm tired and I'm going to bed." She headed to her room and glanced back at him. "Good night, Mouse."

"Good eve, Kat." He gave her a final message. "On the morrow, the manager will arrive with our morning meal after we tug the tassel and are ready to eat."

Kat smiled at him. "Sleep snug as a bug in a rug." She tugged the curtain across the entrance to her room, seeing a final glimpse of Mouse staring at her obviously puzzled by her words.

I wonder if he'll be kept awake attempting to work out the meaning of my expression.?

CHAPTER 12

Kat removed her long robe and prepared to slip into bed. It was too warm to sleep clothed, a single sheet would be lighter and cooler. The thin inner curtains fluttered in the moving air, revealing a sliver of bright moon-light that danced on the floor. She moved to the small window, and before closing the dark curtains that were intended to black out the lights from the night-time sky, she peered out.

The moon hung high in the sky, pregnant with the brilliant light of a thousand stars. *A perigee moon*. The gleaming luminescence always awoke a deep sense of spirituality. As a child after the accident that took her parents from her, she prayed for their return. The fact that they didn't, convinced her that God did not exist. However she remained fixated on the belief that something far greater and more ephemeral did. Something sustained by the moon.

The scents of night-blooming flowers drifted through the window with the faint breeze. She shivered and glanced down at herself. The moon cast silver light on her breasts and on her emerald stone, contrasting against dark erect nipples. She remembered Liandock's touch, shivered again and sighed, and made her way to bed. Wink cheeped as she passed her cage, so she stuck her finger through the bars and stroked the furry little head. As she slid beneath the sheets, she listened to the horses as they nickered and shuffled in their stalls. Somewhere, a night bird called. *The moon has an effect on all living creatures. Perhaps it does possess sentience.*

Her dark and silent room sent Kat drifting into the soothing arms of sleep and dreams. She imagined the moon was breathing, sending life into the world and to all creatures. She sensed the breath on her, gentle and warm. Half awake, she held her own breath. “Is someone here?”

No one answered. Nothing moved in her room.

Only a dream. She drifted back to sleep, surrendering to peace in a now dreamless state.

A sound woke her. She waited, resisting opening her eyes. A barely perceptible scuff of a foot? Perhaps a shoe on the floor of her room? She slit open one eye and gasped. Both eyes flew open. The creature was huge and almost filled the room. It breathed, seemingly leaving scant oxygen for her. She opened her mouth to cry out, but no sound emerged. Again and again, she tried to yell, until at last a high pitched scream tore from her reluctant throat. Her heart pounded in her chest. There was danger. She shut her eyes and screamed once more, and heard the curtain to her room fly aside.

“Kat, are you all right?” Mouse’s voice.

Her eyes flew open as Mouse raced to her side, touching a globe on the wall as he ran toward her.

Kat sat up and seized the sheet to cover herself.

“Kat, what is wrong?”

Unable to catch her breath, she could not answer, just shook her head. At last she stared at him, expecting him to be attacked by the . . .

Mouse stood there. Alone. A dagger in his hand.

“Someone … something was in my room.” She gazed wildly about her. “Not here now. Disappeared. Maybe it’s hidden itself.” Heart still beating wildly, she regained her breath, and her pulse slowed. Her necklace was warm. No danger.

Mouse, clothed in a long grey sleeping robe, searched the room. "Only a few places are available for someone to hide. I believe whatever it was has gone now."

A frantic knocking startled Kat. "Is someone hurt in there?"

"Who's that?" Kat gasped.

Mouse ran to the door and opened it. "Manga. Thank you for coming to check. Lady Kat thought someone had entered her room. We suspect she had an unfortunate dream."

Manga sounded relieved. "Ah, a dream. A dream is possible during our moon's closer phase. People tend to imagine things. If you do need anything, call out, and I will come."

"We thank you for the offer, but all is well now."

She heard Mouse closed the door with a bang and he entered her room again.

"Why did you tell him I had a dream? It was real, Mouse, not a dream." *My stone did not become cold. Why?*

"He seemed frightened, so I told him those words to soothe him." Mouse peered at her. "No one is in your room now, Kat. Perhaps a calming tea will help you return to sleep. I shall make one if you wish."

"Yes. I would apprecciate a tea. Would you wait outside so I may put on a robe."

Mouse glanced at her, barely covered by a sheet, and he blushed. He ducked his head and pulled the curtain across the door as he left.

Kat, shivering with remembered fear, dropped the sheet back on the bed. She was chilled, and grabbed a thicker robe from her luggage. Breathing deeply to gain warmth and some control over her trembling body, she entered the main room and sat in the long-seat.

Mouse brought over two cups of tea. He placed one in front of her and sat at the furtherest end of the long-seat. His face was still slightly pink.

Kat took a sip of the tea. "This is wonderful. Thank you Mouse." *Did he see me naked and he's embarrassed?*

They sat awkwardly, avoiding each other's eyes.

"Mouse, it was real. I did not have a dream."

He finally glanced at her. "I believe you." He rubbed his chin. "Manga was frightened of something, and he was afraid we had seen what he fears."

Kat drank some more tea. "Do you think this might have anything to do with the Glowen secret?" *Surely not a secret about monsters?*

"You know as much as I do. Glowen is proving most interesting."

"And Thane Brennan says they have no challenges here." She snorted. "Sure."

"Kat, do you need more sleep?"

"I doubt I'd be able to go back to sleep." The truth was she was afraid to close her eyes now. "Why?"

"I observe the first light of dawn, and I, too, am clearly awake. I suggest we prepare ourselves for departure, pack our belongings, and head for Kadwee. Once we are almost ready to leave, perhaps you will tug the tassel and order our meal from Manga. After our meal, we can saddle our horses and set off on our journey sooner rather than later."

"I'm all for leaving. I can see no reason to hang around this camp. Particularly since unknown creatures may be about." Kat was convinced the thing was too big for her to deal with. It reminded her of childhood memories of potential monsters under the bed.

Mouse stood and stretched. "If you will get ready and pack your bags, I will feed and water our animals. When I have finished, I will prepare myself while you order our meal. Request Manga fill our canteens with an energizing tea. There are many pools at which we can refill them with water on our way to Kadwee."

"Excellent. I'm eager to journey on."

Mouse left for the stables, and Kat returned to her room. She grabbed her leathers, which she found the most comfortable for traveling, and after showering, dressed herself, and completed packing her bags. She fed Wink, and attached the cage to her backpack.

Mouse entered, went to his room to collect his fresh clothes, and headed for the shower. "You may send for our morning meal, Kat. I shall not be tardy."

Kat tugged on the tassel and piled her bags in the middle of the room.

As Mouse appeared, dressed for the day, Magna knocked at the door with their food.

Kat handed him their canteens. "Would you please have these filled with a stimulating tea, Magna?"

"Indeed. I will place them with your saddles."

Kat thanked him and sat at the table to consume her meal. Mouse brought his baggage to the centre of the room and sat down to join her.

After their meal, the two hoisted their baggage and headed to the stable. Kat helped Mouse load the baggage on the pack animal, and they saddled and bridled their individual horses, Kat with a little help from Mouse.

Once in their saddles, Mouse attached the line from the baggage animal to the back of Kat's saddle. "This section, until we stop for our mid-turn meal, is somewhat difficult. I will lead, and you can take the lead again after the meal, until we reach Kadwee."

Kat nodded her agreement.

What a night. What or who was in my room? Why did my stone remain warm?

CHAPTER 13

Gazing across the long grasses and lush green bushes to her right, Kat glimpsed the sea, a deep azure, decorated with the white frosting of waves. Pridden's star was bright and the day pleasant. She could easily see in every direction, and no large creatures loomed to remind her of the terrifying night.

Mouse was silent, and when she turned to stare at him, he avoided her gaze.

Oh no. He's blushing. He obviously did see me naked. Crap. Being naked in front of Mouse was as bad as being naked in front of a brother.

"Mouse?" He didn't respond.

She called louder. "Mouse."

He stopped and waited for her to catch up, although he still avoided looking into her eyes. "Do you need something?"

"Something simple. I am intrigued by the sight of the sea to our right. Can we stop and move closer?"

"Definitely not. This path is well inside the safe area along this side of Glowen. If we move from this path, we approach closer to the cliffs which overlook the sea. The land is unreliable, and sections have been known to crumble and fall."

"Glowen seems to have many cliffs over the sea from the maps you showed me. Are they all this dangerous?"

Mouse faced her. "No only this section up to Kadwee is a problem. If you were able to observe this area from the water level, you would realize the top of the cliffs extend out beyond the sections at water level. This is because the sea is relentless in grinding away at the land."

"We're definitely safe on this road, right?"

"Yes. Many more paths than exist in our lifetimes would be required before the roadway must move closer to Krugg Menyd." He grinned at her. "You are quite safe, as long as you travel on the path."

Kat sighed with relief. "Excellent." *Mouse is normal. Guess he believes I didn't know he saw me naked. Thank goodness.*

"Do any of your maps hint at the monstrous creature that was in my room?"

Mouse shook his head. "I do not see any indication of it anywhere. Perhaps in Kadwee we might find out more."

Kat squinted at the road ahead. "Perhaps."

They set off, again with Mouse still in the lead.

Kat rode along the portion of the track further away from the sea, and chose instead to view the foothills of Krugg Menyd. The mountains began with gentle slopes rising toward taller crags of rock, which increased in height as they moved toward Kadwee. Soon Kat spied what appeared to be caves in the rock faces and ruins of older stone edifices halfway up the inclines of the Krugg.

Kat rode up beside Mouse. "Can we stop for a few moments and explore those old buildings and perhaps a cave or two? We can eat our mid-turn meal while exploring."

"We cannot spend much time, as I always prefer to enter a village well before dark." He shrugged. "According to the maps, a narrow trail heads toward the Krugg. We can tie the horses to the trees and go on foot."

"Perfect." She followed Mouse as he moved forward. When a rough trail appeared beside the road, he stopped, dismounted, and tied his animal to a bush.

Kat slid off her horse and secured both her mount and the baggage animal. She grabbed the package of food from her saddlebag and, though eager to explore, made sure Mouse was behind her. They set off along the pathway, and when the lush plants on either side of them rustled occasionally, Kat assumed minor creatures lived among the flowering bushes. A sudden thought made her pause. "Mouse, do snakes exist on Glowen?"

"To my knowledge, no snakes exist on this island. However, if you wish, I can take the lead if the movements of whatever lives here makes you uneasy."

"Nope. Not scared at all. Only curious." *She gulped.*

She pointed toward the ruins. "Those ruins are made of stone. How odd, when the Glowens build everything from wood. Do you think these are old?"

"I do not know. I would suspect they were most likely built by some of the first inhabitants to come to Glowen. What is odd is they would build so far from the inlet at the Netht. The inlet would be the easiest place to land."

"But, Mouse, these ruins appear ancient, and I don't think wooden buildings would last long. Perhaps the original settlers in this area needed longevity."

"Perhaps. All the map shows is the word eedhenna."

"I wonder if this is the name for these ruins, or for all the caves on the side of the Krugg?"

Mouse shook his head.

Kat shrugged. "Well, let's examine the ruins anyway." Curious, she entered the nearest one, which sported the broken remnants of a house-sized building, with individual rooms, most simply bare outlines of stone. There was no roof on the structure, and the interior was filled with weeds and odd flowering plants.

She and Mouse walked among two or three broken stone buildings and found the same sort of ruins everywhere. As they exited the last one just before Krugg Menyd, Kat noticed one of the caves was closer than the rest and not so high up the face of the mountain.

"Oh, Mouse, that cave is only a short distance away. We have time just to take a peek."

"Kat I am not sure we should enter them, as—"

A flock of strange birds flew from the cave, interrupting him, screeching loudly and diving at them. Each was about the size of a turkey vulture, and they beat at the intruders with strong wings, which bore few feathers. The entire body of each bird resembled a heavy leathery sack, reminding Kat of pictures she'd seen of pterodactyls. Her stone was bitterly cold. She and Mouse grabbed hefty sticks from the ground and batted at the birds which pecked at them with razor-sharp bills, drawing blood where they struck.

Mouse broke his stick and picked up another. "Run, Kat, run." He set off after her, swinging the stick at their attackers.

She ran for her life back to the ruins, tearing through each one, and headed toward to the roadway. The emerald in her pendant lay like ice on her skin. As she reached the last set of ruins, she tripped over a hidden stone, and crashed to the ground, landing heavily and knocking all the breath from her body.

Mouse, still batting at the birds with his stick, hit a couple and knocked them from the sky, but the rest pursued them with fury. He approached Kat, still gasping for breath, and threw himself on top of her, covering the two of them with his cloak, the material of which offered protection from the sharp beaks.

The creatures ceased their screeching, and the beat of their wings lessened as they retreated. She and Mouse lay silently, waiting for all the vicious fowls to depart.

Kat coughed, fighting for air. *I can't believe how heavy Mouse is. Weird.* "Oof." Her voice was small and muffled. "Mouse, I can't breathe."

He rolled off her, and sprang to his feet. "My apologies, Kat. This was the only thing I was able to think of." He extended a hand to help her to her feet.

How can someone so small weigh so much? "They're gone. Your cloak is amazing. I still felt their beaks, but they didn't touch my skin." She examined the material, but regarded Mouse with astonishment. *He's blushing. Why? He saved my life.*

"The weave is special. Walden of the Magician's Guild designed this fabric. He studied tapestry making before he joined the guild. Unfortunately, he was not given the opportunity to further his studies."

Kat examined the material closely, and wondered if a robe like this would protect her. *It might not be as hot as leathers.* Kat examined her hands. "Mouse, I'm bleeding where those birds found open skin. They're not poisonous are they?"

"I have no idea. We should return to our horses and deal with our injuries. I am only cut on my hands, but your arms and neck are bleeding profusely. You are fortunate you are wearing leathers, otherwise you would be more severely harmed."

They hurried back to where the horses were tied, and Mouse paused briefly to pick up one of the downed birds. He tied the flying creature by the legs to the back of his saddle, but his horse danced backwards and neighed, apparently repulsed.

Kat pulled her canteen of tea from the side of her saddle and washed her arms and neck of blood. The tea soothed a bit. She headed to the baggage animal and removed a small sack, and extracted a tube of ointment. The minute the ointment touched her skin she sighed with relief.

Mouse had washed his own hands. "If you would give me some of your salve for my hands, I will apply some to the back of your neck. You missed some areas."

"With pleasure. It soothes wonderfully." She handed him the container, and sighed again when he spread the ointment on her neck. "Thank you."

After applying the salve to his hands, he groaned with relief and handed the tube back to her. His horse, who was restlessly twisting and turning, attempting to rid itself of the dead bird, nudged Mouse. "My mount is not pleased with the foul avian I tied to him." He removed the bird, and examined the creature carefully.

Kat peered over his shoulder at it. "The beak has got teeth. No wonder they draw blood." She shuddered. "I hope you're not planning on bringing the thing with us." She wrinkled her nose. "Horribly stinky."

"No, I will dispose of it." He shuddered.

The only feathers the bird possessed were on the edges of the wings, and the body resembled a wrinkled pock-marked sack. The head was completely bald and reminded Kat of carrion birds she had seen in Africa. The eyes were huge but had dimmed in death, and a repugnant scent assaulted her nostrils. She paid close attention to the vile thing, attempting to memorize everything about the bird so she would be able to draw a picture for her game information.

"The stink is getting worse, Mouse. Please get rid of it." *I'm grateful video games don't have smell-a-vision.*

"You are correct. Wait here." He strode across the roadway and walked toward the edge of the cliffs, but held back, obviously reluctant to approach too closely. He wound up a swing and hurled the creature much further than Kat thought possible.

He returned to where she and the horses waited.

"Did you manage to throw it in the sea?"

"I believe so. Now we should ride for the pond where I planned we should eat the mid-turn meal Manga packed for us."

ꝏꝏꝏ

A thin stream flowed across the pathway, coming from a tiny pond of water almost surrounded by reeds. Four substantial stones sat to one side, perfect for enjoying their meal in comfort.

"These stones are like seats around a table. How odd."

"The Glowens have, in many instances, tamed their land. Their managers travel around the paths and roadways and groom the rest sites. One of them, many paths ago, brought these stones to this place for the comfort of travelers. According to the Rifellan guards, the Glowens are excellent land managers."

"I'm glad they did. This is comfortable. I guess I should replenish my canteen."

"An excellent idea. Would you kindly refill mine? I wish to consult the maps."

When she returned, he had spread the parchment on the stone beside him, and peered at the chart. "I do believe I missed an important detail. Notice this." He pointed to an illustration and moved the map toward her. "This resembles a bird, but this symbol I now believe indicates dangerous birds. The word eedhenna is the name for these creatures, not the area, as I first supposed."

"I don't believe this. You actually made a mistake, Mouse?

He appeared startled by her words. "I am only Priddanese. I do make mistakes."

"Whoa. I'm simply making a joke. You always seem to be so confident in what routes we take and how I should act, I've begun to rely on you. I'm sorry I insulted you, but I tend to make jokes when I've been frightened by something. Those birds were terrifying." Kat was relieved he appeared relaxed. The green gem in her pendant was warm now that they were free of the vicious birds. She decided she should pay more attention. *Is it cold when Mouse is annoyed?*

He smiled at her. "I understand you. I am not used to the making of jokes. Those of us from Morden tend to be serious people most of the time."

Kat was sorry she'd teased him.. "Perhaps instead of discussing jokes, we should head for Kadwee."

Mouse nodded and folded the map. After completing lunch, he walked with Kat toward their horses.

They remounted their animals and set off in silence toward their destination for the night.

Sometimes, it appears, I only open my mouth to change feet.

CHAPTER 14

On the ride to Kadwee, Mouse suggested that Kat take the lead again. "The forest we are entering is benign, and according to the maps, contains nothing vicious. The trail is well marked, and you should encounter no challenge on the way to the town."

"The vegetation is increasing, and it's so lush. Do they get much rain?"

"When I spoke to the Rifellan guard at the Keep, he did mention this part of the island received rain almost every day in the early evening. The moisture gets time to sink into the soil overnight and, therefore, everything is always green. Some of the plants are huge." Mouse rubbed his chin. "I'm surprised he forgot to mention the eedhenna."

"Remember Jagloran brought you an additional map, which covers this area. He may have assumed you were already warned of those nasty birds by the previous guard."

"I do not remember such a discussion with the previous guard, but what you say makes sense." Mouse waved his hand at the greenery. "Soon you will find more and bigger trees growing in copses among the various plants. Jagloran advised me that the minute flying biters also live in massive quantities among this vegetation. They are not poisonous but their bites are extremely itchy." He dismounted and picked some fleshy leaves from a nearby plant. "Jagloran also mentioned that if the biters appear, rub the juice from this leaf on any exposed skin. They appear to dislike the smell and will refrain from biting you."

"Thank you. We have similar insects on our world. The itch can almost make you go mad." Just thinking of mosquito bites made Kat itch.

As they rode nearer to Kadwee, the biting insects did make an appearance, but the juice, as promised, repelled them. The plant soothed, and further helped heal the areas of the bird attacks.

The roadway wound through a substantial number of trees, and she easily understood how the Glowens managed their forests. A number of stumps, in various stages of rotting, sat next to virile young trees, which had obviously been planted by those who managed the growth of the vegetation.

"Mouse, this is amazing. I'm impressed how the Glowens succeed in keeping their forests continually growing and supplying wood. I am aware they are considered profligate, but they are incredibly organized in how they care for their resources. This is new to me." She stopped to admire the handiwork of the managers. "They've used the broken down wood from the stumps as covering for the road."

Mouse stopped his horse beside her. "The Rifellans are probably the only people who understand and appreciate the care the Glowens extend to their land. There are a greater number of people in a smaller area on Glowen than in the other lands. They deem it vital to ensure all things are sustainable. Glowens are an unusual people. I now understand that the faces they turn to the rest of Pridden are not those they show in their own land."

"They don't seem to encourage people from other lands to live in Glowen. Other than the Rifellans Brennan hires as guards and Marreth, their healer, I don't see any people here from other lands in Pridden."

"Glowens do not encourage visitors. Remember this, because our visit here is a privilege. Thane Brennan respects Lord Eduardo and considers him a friend. This is the only reason we are allowed to spend much time in Glowen."

"Interesting. If only Glowens live here, I wonder why Eduardo thinks this land may be experiencing unrest."

Mouse shook his head. "I am not sure. However, Eduardo rarely makes an error." He clicked at his horse to move forward. "We should be on our way to Kadwee. I suspect Brennan has advised them of our arrival, and we would be impolite to be late for the meal."

"Fine." Kat moved a little faster to take the lead.

♋♋♋

A group of four people waited on the road, apparently for their arrival. As they moved closer, the group smiled and greeted the two visitors.

They descended from their mounts, which three of the men took to the nearby stable.

The fourth man who stepped forward to welcome them, while not as tall as the Rifellans, was nevertheless quite handsome, with his skin a light gold, and his wolf eyes rimmed with midnight blue. He nodded to Mouse but moved toward Kat to take her hand. "Welcome, Lady Kat. Our Thane did not indicate what a beautiful woman we were to expect." He turned her hand over, kissed it, and then licked up the centre of her palm.

Her stone flashed ice on her skin. Disgusted and taken aback by the overtly sexual greeting, Kat jerked her hand from his grasp, not quite sure if she insulted the man by removing her hand. She glanced at Mouse, horrified.

Mouse stepped forward. “Sire, I am Lady Kat’s guide, Mouse. You have not yet introduced yourself, and Lady Kat is not used to such a personal gesture by a stranger.”

The Glowen laughed. “My pardon, my Lady. I am Krogen pen Yuwen, and I am leader of the pen Yuwen pod.”

Kat’s laugh was weak. “I am surprised you are not yet bonded.”

Krogen gazed at her, obviously puzzled by her remark. “But I am, my Lady.”

“Yet you give such an … an intimate greeting to another woman?”

He frowned. “Of course. Why not?”

“Uh. I am not used to this intimacy between men and women who are not bonded to each other.” *No one warned us of these sort of gestures. Ugh.*

“Such a shame you cannot share loving with others. We Glowens enjoy many lovers, but the creation of offspring is reserved for the bonded mate. I find you most pleasing, and would welcome physical knowledge of you.”

Kat stared at Krogen, totally surprised and frozen in her tracks. She turned her head to Mouse. “Help?” Her plea emerged as a squeak. *I would easily handle this at home. But here, if I say the wrong thing, what sort of trouble can I get into?*

Mouse stepped forward. “Krogen, as a man from Pridden, I understand the honor you offer Lady Kat, but she is from another world. She is not used to such lack of formality among men and women. What you ask of her is alien and she is unable to respond.”

"Sire Mouse. How strange a world she must come from. She resembles Rifellan royalty, and we are all aware she is not bonded. She is an extraordinary woman, and I find her eyes most astonishing. To possess eyes of two different colors makes the expectation of physical intercourse even more desirable."

"Please forgive our ways, Krogen. And do ask the rest of your pod to resist the physical pursuit of Lady Kat."

Krogen sighed. "If this will make Lady Kat more comfortable, of course we will not pursue her." He shrugged. "However, you must both accompany us to the evening feast we planned for you."

Kat, the crystal at her throat warm, and more settled now that Mouse had rescued her, bowed slightly to Krogen. "My thanks, we would be delighted to enjoy a *meal* with you." Kat hoped he understood. "May we ask to be shown to our rooms at your inn so we can freshen up before we dine?" *These men are so caught up in sex, how can I trust him to keep his word?*

Krogen bowed and invited them to follow him to the inn.

As she walked beside Mouse, following the pod leader, Kat uttered a silent *whew. I heard of, and have, on occasion, thought of indiscriminate sex, but I've never been confronted with such a weird offer before. Creepy. Not curious anymore.*

CHAPTER 15

Krogen led them down the halls of the inn to their rooms. "We were not sure of your relationship with each other, so we have given you two rooms, but they adjoin. Will these suffice?"

"Two rooms are fine, Krogen. Mouse is my guide, nothing more." *Not sure what words might be misconstrued. Guide should be safe.*

Kat opened her door and began to enter her room, but paused until Krogen disappeared down the hall. As soon as his footsteps faded, she pushed quickly at Mouse's door before he could close it, and slipped inside. "I'm sorry, but I didn't want to use the adjoining door because they might think we lied about you just being a guide."

"If they cannot see you using the adjoining door, how could they possibly think that?"

"You're right they couldn't but, Mouse, these people are beyond weird to me. You have to help me pick my way through this labyrinth of customs. For the first time in my life, I'm at a total loss about men. What do I wear to assure I won't set their senses aflame? How do I refuse their advances without making them angry? Help, Mouse." *I certainly can't trust them.*

Mouse bent his head, shoulders shaking.

"You're laughing at me."

"Forgive me, Kat. I am not laughing at you, but at the situation. I have not seen you so upset before. You always appear most confident around men. Yet these Kadweeans have confused you." He shook his head. "Be yourself Kat. You are well aware of how to refuse a man's advances. I have observed when you have done this before. I believe the only reason you doubt yourself at this point is you found Krogen so extreme in his response to you. Surely other men, perhaps on your own world, have been overly attracted to you?"

Kat inhaled a deep breath. "Not to extent that Krogen was. Men have been too familiar, but not to such a radical measure On my world if a man had made such an advance, I would have insulted him and, quite frankly, been prepared to strike him. I would have no fear of any repercussions, either. In Glowen, I have no idea what the ramifications might be."

"I believe you can relax. Glowens are true sensualists, and I suspect they go after any pleasure they might desire, but I also believe they are not too concerned if one option does not work for them. You were merely one option. I do not expect them to force you to do anything against your will."

Kat laughed. "You're correct. I only panicked because I was afraid to cause a problem with the Glowens. I must admit, you always catch me when I err." She nodded to herself. "I am able to handle men, and it appears the Glowens do not consider their actions reprehensible. Thanks Mouse." She opened the door to leave.

He raised his left eyebrow and smiled. "Relax Kat, and think of the men here in Kadwee as similar to ignorant children?"

Kat humphed. "I suspect they are not that familiar with visitors from the rest of Pridden. This is their problem—not mine. You are right. I must be myself. " She laughed, walked to the next door, and entered her own rooms.

Once inside, Kat unpacked a few things, set up Wink's cage on the dresser, and reached in and removed the ball of fur. The pyrock opened one eye, stretched her wings and each leg separately, and yawned.

"Well, you've enjoyed a long sleep. Are you hungry?"

The little creature squeaked and opened a mouth filled with tiny teeth.

Kat popped in food, and stroked the fine hair on Wink's head. "So when are you going to show me some more flame, little one?"

Wink gave a teeny burp and snuggled back in a furry ball in Kat's hand. She sighed and re-deposited the pyrock in her cage. "You're adorable, Wink, but you are not cuddly."

Kat needed to have a relaxing dinner with the people from Kadwee, so she dressed conservatively. *The Glowens of this town are not dangerous. I was silly to be frightened of their ignorance.* She left her main dagger, but inserted her tiny blade in her left boot.

On her way to the dining hall, Kat knocked at the room next door.

Mouse peered around the door, and ran his gaze up and down her. "I am pleased you are dressed comfortably. You appear to have gained your equilibrium."

"You made sense. I'm being myself again." She grinned at him. "Shall we go to the dining hall?"

Mouse nodded, and they set off down the halls of polished wood.

♋♋♋

Krogen waved Mouse over to the table at which he sat with five other men and two women. Kat remained almost hidden behind Mouse. She agreed to be herself, but still retained a niggling doubt about how to react to these odd people. Krogen patted the seat beside him and invited Kat to sit.

Before she did, Kat peered down at him. “Am I safe from you if I sit here?”

He laughed. “Your guide made things clear you did not wish to receive my advances. I told him I would not do so, therefore the matter is closed.”

“Thank you.” *Hope I can trust him.*

Krogen made the introductions of the people at the table, and while all claimed to be bonded, none of their mates were seated with them. When questioned where they were, vague answers suggested none wished to have Kat or her guide derive anything definite about their whereabouts.

Kat thought how peculiar their answers were, and she wondered why Mouse had a puzzled frown on his forehead.

She gazed around the table at the Glowens seated with them. Eight pairs of wolf eyes regarded her. These were not the ordinary eyes she found so fascinating about wolves at home, it was more like being surrounded by a pack. A pack whose stares were more than curious, and she had an uncomfortable feeling they were penetrating deep into her psyche. She shivered and glanced at Mouse. He was watching them closely and when he turned to her, he raised an eyebrow.

Krogen promised. I'm safe. She nodded at Mouse

The dinner was lush and the food beautifully prepared, but Kat ate mechanically, hardly aware of either the taste or smell. Shifting restlessly in her seat, she was grateful when Mouse after fending off a gesture from one of the women, suggested they retire for the night. "Our apologies, Krogen, but the travel of the day has been long and wearisome."

Krogen leaned forward and whispered something to Mouse, whose eyebrows promptly scrambled hastily up to his hairline. "No, absolutely not. Lord Eduardo made no such request."

Rogen appeared contrite. "Apologies. Pardon my assumption. We shall meet with the two of you on the morrow, and perhaps you will allow us to give you both a guided tour of Kadwee."

"Thank you, that would be most kind." He rose and tilted his head with an almost imperceptible movement, that indicated Kat should leave with him..

Relieved, Kat thanked those from Kadwee, and followed Mouse swiftly from the hall. She moved hastily down the corridor, neither speaking to, nor looking at Mouse.

She had barely closed and locked her door, when a tap on the interior door summoned her. She unlocked it, and Mouse stepped into her room. She raised an eyebrow in query at him.

He walked to the chair at a small table, sat and motioned for Kat to sit in the one across from him. "We need to have a conversation. Things are not what they appear to be in Kadwee."

"They certainly are not. Don't keep me in suspense. What did Krogen say to you?"

Mouse lowered his eyes and gazed at the table top. "I almost dislike admitting what he said. He was most curious to ascertain what sort of a bonding existed between you and me. He believes a male and a female traveling together without enjoying a physical relationship is alien, and Eduardo had requested we needed to be bonded."

"Oh dear. He put you in such an awkward position. They're amazingly single-faceted about sex. So much so, their focus on the subject is almost … almost repellent."

"I thought you found physical interaction pleasant?"

"I do, but I'm choosy, and while I appreciate admiration from males, I do not appreciate unasked for contact. Their admiration doesn't feel genuine." Kat's face flamed. "I am discriminating, but around them, its just as if I'm a thing for pleaure. I almost feel as if they don't see me as a live being."

They sat in silence.

Mouse sighed. "I too find something unnerving about them. They mention bond mates, but avoid talking about them. Why?"

"The expression in their eyes was what I saw when they were at the table. I remember Drainin in Kaylin had similar colored eyes. I call them wolf eyes. But the people in Kadwee posses a sense of the sinister in their stares."

Mouse rubbed his chin. "I would like to suggest we stay over an extra day. I am curious about the mystery surrounding Kadwee and would like to explore this further. You may well discover there is a bigger challenge than you suspect."

"I'm fine with that. Shall we meet for the morning meal on the morrow, and afterwards I will do a little sight-seeing, and perhaps you can figure out what the mystery is?"

Mouse nodded, rose and walked to the internal door. "When I leave your room, bolt this door. I will bolt mine on my side, as well."

Kat stood and waited at the door. "Fine. Are you anxious about this?"

He shrugged. "I feel the people of Kadwee are far too interested in our relationship."

Kat closed the door as Mouse departed, and she shot the bolt. She heard a similar sound from the other side.

Scratching her head, she wandered over to where the py-rock lay curled in a ball of fur in his cage, emitting the tiniest of snores. She reached through the bars and patted the little head.

She undressed, donned a long night dress, and slipped under the covers of her bed. *Somehow I suspect I'll be more comfortable sleeping clothed tonight.*

♋♋♋

Squeaking from Wink and various bird calls woke Kat, and she stretched, ironing out the kinks in her muscles. *I must have slept tensed up all night. Hmmm.*

She dressed in the long loose pants she purchased in Rifella, and a light shirt with long sleeves. *Might as well protect myself from the flying biters, and too much sun.*

She found her way to the dining hall, and scanned the room for Mouse. He was sitting with two Kadweeans, and he glanced up and waved her over. "Kat, I ordered groonnan for you, but you should choose your own drink."

She smiled at him. "Thanks."

A young apprentice approached and deposited her meal in front of her. "What would you prefer to drink, my Lady?"

"Do you have fara tea?"

"We do. I will bring you some shortly." He hurried off.

Mouse introduced her to the two men from Kadwee sitting at the table. "This is Koosela pen Yuwen, and Gaviska pen Yuwen and they are keepers of the many walkways around Kadwee and Krugg Menyd."

"We are well met." *Hope this is a formal greeting and will keep their desires at bay.* "I am so impressed with the order and beauty you create."

Koosela's eyes, not as disturbing as those she'd met the night before, swept her up and down. "You are beauty personified, my Lady." He put his hand out to take hers.

Kat placed both her hands in her lap. "Forgive me if I appear rude, Koosela pen Yuwen, but we are most formal in Kaylin."

He shrugged and withdrew his hand. "Kaylins are more repressed than those of us in Glowen. Sire Mouse expressed the same sentiment when I suggested we enjoy a liaison."

Mouse jumped into the conversation. "I will be accompanying Gaviska and Koosela on a tour of the various centers for which they are caretakers, to learn of the magnificent ways of nature preservation they have developed. You should visit the wild flower reserve. You should be comfortable there."

"An excellent idea, Mouse." *Not sure what he has in mind, but I'll string along, and he does say I'll be comfortable..*

Once they had all completed their meals, they rose, and Mouse headed off with the two Glowens, while Kat, after requesting directions, set off in search of the wild flowers. *Seems Mouse experienced the same challenge as me. He does not allow them to walk on either side of him.*

♋♋♋

At the reserve, Kat met with Skonya pen Yuwen, who gave her a small parchment map showing icons of the various flower types. "Lady, you only need to follow the prepared walkways to arrive at each of the species of flowers. I do not have you listed for a shelter. Do you wish one, and have you brought your own companion? The flower gardens are never crowded. ”

Puzzled, Kat wondered if Skonya meant some sort of assignation. She wanted nothing to do with anything like that. “No, I have no need of a … a shelter.” Kat swallowed. “Thank you for the directions. Will I need to protect myself from the winged biters?”

“No, we surround the fields with the repella, which keeps them away.” Skonya smiled coyly at Kat. “Should you wish a companion, I would be pleased to be of service.”

“Thank you, but no.” *Clever Mouse. He sent me here because without crowds, I shouldn’t run into any challenges from overzealous men. We didn’t consider women, however.*

Kat set off along the walkways, examining the icons of the various flowers as she sauntered along. The breeze was mild, and carried the scents of blooms of all kinds. She was comfortable, even though the exposed rays of Pridden’s star burned on her skin. Kat had only to follow her nose to eventually identify the flower in question. She walked down one path, past a sign for the Scented Rituals, and discovered this particular walkway ended at a section of a jumbled flowers, no longer laid out in neat sections. Beyond the grasses and flowers, she saw the ocean and an island, rising out of the sea like a dark upthrust finger.

Kat stepped out of the neat rows, and into the grasses closer to the top of the cliff.

A man approached from the direction of the town.

Kat, keeping him at a distance, pointed at the finger of rock. “Excuse me. Can you tell me the name of the island off the coast?”

"It is called Pinnacle Rock, Lady."

"Does anyone live there?"

"Some have said strange creatures make their home on the rock. But no places exist on which to land a boat, so we cannot be sure." He motioned her over. "The cliffs are strong here so you may get closer to view the edge of the sea."

"Truly?"

"Yes, it is quite safe here."

She moved gingerly toward the edge and unafraid of heights, was finally able to peer over. *What a magnificent view.* Below her, the sea crashed against the wall of the land, sending plumes of spray many feet in the air. The air rising from the sea was at least, cool.

She sensed the man moving behind her. He reminded her of someone. Who? The sudden stab of ice from her stone startled her. Alarm bells rang inside her head. She whirled around, but he pushed her. She flew over the cliff, and screamed as she fell toward the water. Down, she plummeted through the spray and the waves, and plunged deep in the water with an impact that drove the breath from her and silenced her screams. *I shouldn't have trusted him.* Panicking, time stood still for her. She strove desperately to reach the surface. When she did, she gulped in a huge breath of air, closing her mouth hastily as waves rolled over her. She treaded water, searching for a place to land. Nothing. The area below the cliff consisted of bare rock face. To her left, masses of rocks thrust from the ocean which smashed violently against them. The water was icy and she could not feel her stone. She swam away from the rocks. To attempt to land there would involve serious injury. Fighting water washing over her, her heart squeezed in her chest. The cliffs rose without handholds. She swam beyond the rocks to her left, but once again, only bare cliffs faced her.

She turned and headed for Pinnacle Rock. While no boulders sat at the base, the rock itself seemingly rose from the water in a single sheer expanse. As she neared the Pinnacle, she attempted to hang on to the face, but the entire area was covered in a slippery slimy algae. She was unable to find hand holds of any kind. *The man said there were no landing sites, but perhaps the other side of the rock?* Blood pounded in her ears, and she saw with dismay that this side was also without a landing place. Panting for breath, her arms lead-heavy, and barely making headway, she fought the sea. Without warning an enormous creature rose from the depths and opened a huge mouth, ringed with teeth, blunted and yellow. Kat opened her mouth to scream but inhaled a lungful of water. Coughing and spitting, she backpedaled, but the monster caught her by the arm and dove deep into the black waters. She had time to only grab one lungful of air.

Unable to free herself, she was swept down swiftly, past the pinnacle of dark rock. Despite the frantic need for oxygen, she hung on to life as long as possible. Her lungs burned, and shrieked for air. Terrified, Kat finally surrendered and inhaled water.

I don't want to die!

CHAPTER 16

Pain. Burning. Saltwater seared her eyes and lungs.

Consciousness fading, she was pulled under and then up. Water rushed past as she was heaved upwards through the air. She landed chest down on a hard surface. The impact vomited water from her lungs. The surface of rock on which she had fallen, was redolent with the odor of salt and sea. She lay gasping, like a fish carelessly flung on the shore. She moved her head and saw she was in a huge cavern. *Inside the pinnacle?* Water slapped against the cold rock ledge under her. The sound of waves pummeling against a resistant surface thundered and echoed in the cavern like a hollow drum. *Where is that noise coming from?* She lay, half conscious, caught in the rhythmic pounding of the sea.

At last she managed to roll over on her back and gazed around. The ledge she was on kept her out of the water slapping to the right of her. The roof of the cave loomed far above her, creating an enormous hall, which vibrated with the cannon fire of the sea bombarding the rock outside.

I'm alive. She burst into tears. *I'm alive.*

Every muscle in her body howled in protest as she pushed herself to her feet and staggered against the inside wall of the cave. *Where am I? Where is that monster?* She glanced at the water. The huge creature drifted in the enormous pool beside the ledge. Not a shark, but a formless mass peering at her from one prodigious eye on the side of its head. Her stone warm on her breast, and she was no longer afraid of the beast. Nevertheless, she clung to the wall, as far from the water as possible. She examined her surroundings, and followed the ledge toward a light at the far end of the cavern. As she moved toward it, she glanced back. The creature was gone, submerged again in the depths of sea, she supposed.

The ledge curved to the right, and she followed it to a larger cave, free from water. Kat gasped. Hundreds of beings stood watching her. They all wore long robes with hoods, covering their bodies from head to feet. She had no idea who was male and who was female. She called out to them. "Who are you?"

Silence greeted her, but one being … man? … approached her. *What the ... Liandock? Why is he here?*

"I am the one you think of."

"Liandock?" She blinked to clear her vision. "But you can't be him. He's not here. "

"I am who I am. But this is the one who rests in your mind."

"I don't understand."

"We are Sha-hee. We live in this place and in this time to serve a need."

"A need?"

She stared at her surroundings. Past the great hall in which she stood, buildings, houses and strange edifices stretched before her. *Was this an underground city?* The Sha-hee/Liandock ushered her to a nearby seat. The others retreated from Kat, except for one other who approached with what appeared to be a glass of water on a tray.

Kat gasped as the second being took on the appearance of Liandock as well. She glanced from one Liandock to the other, closed her eyes, and shook her head. "No. Please, not two of you." She only opened her eyes as she heard the server move away.

They were once again the robed androgynous beings of before. With Liandock beside her.

Kat turned to the Liandock being. "How do you do that?"

"We cannot control this. Sha-hee are bound to become those who are strongest in another's thoughts."

"Don't you have any choice?"

"We are not familiar with the term 'choice'."

"Do you not wish to be some other person?"

"Sha-hee only take on the ones in other's minds when we are near them and when in contact with the floor of this world. You have encountered us in the liquid."

"Liquid? Oh, of course, water. Do you mean some of you are like the enormous creature who pulled me under water?"

"Not some of us, but part of us." The voice of this Liandock was unfamiliar, but soothing.

"Part of you?"

"Yes. We are all one. We are also part of the air beings who guard our dwelling place."

"You mean you are also those birds who attacked us near the ruins?" *I'm losing my mind. I don't believe this.*

"Indeed. And the one who threw you to the liquid." The Sha-hee smiled with Liandock's mouth. *It is not Liandock.* Kat shuddered

"Sha-hee wished to meet with you. You are unusual, and not like the ones who live in this land."

Kat's head reeled. "I died in the water."

"Died?" Liandock tilted its head as if thinking. "No, you did not cease to exist. When your inner air sacs filled with the liquid, we understood this was a foreign state for you, similar to those in this land. You are an air being, and we returned you to the air when we discovered this."

Kat shook her head. "You almost killed me, and then you saved me?" She shivered, remembering the fear and horror of water filling her lungs. "Do I understand what you are telling me correctly? These beings in front of me can read another's mind and take on the appearance of whoever they think about. Correct? Can the large creatures in the water and the birds also take on other forms?"

"No, those parts of Sha-hee agree to become either the liquid creatures or the air beings, and they remain so for all their existence."

"So why did you want to meet me?"

"As we said you are unlike those who live in this land. Sha-hee can easily become the ones from your inner thoughts, but your mind is not pliable like the others. We cannot understand how to encourage you to forget."

"And I don't understand why or what you would want me to forget." Kat held her head. "I can barely believe this. My head is swirling. I'm exhausted. This can't be real."

"Sha-hee is aware. You have been through much today, and before we explain further to you, you should rest."

The Liandock being rose, and held out its hand for her. "Come."

Reluctantly, she took the hand, cold but strong, shivering as the sight of Liandock stirred no feelings in her, neither sexual nor platonic, but her necklace indicated no danger. It led her to a small nearby building. As they walked there, the sea of androgynous Sha-hee parted before them.

They arrived at the entrance to the building, and Kat turned to her escort. "What are you named?"

"I am Sha-hee."

"No, I mean what is your individual name?"

"The name of one of whom you think. Liandock." The Sha-hee turned vacant eyes on her. "Please enter and gain your rest."

Kat stared at him and sighed. "Thank you." She entered the small house, flung herself on the bed against the wall, and sleep swiftly overtook her.

Weirder than I ever imagined. I must remember to record this in my notes? But, do I want to?

CHAPTER 17

Kat opened her eyes and yawned. The room was warm and bathed in a soothing red glow. She stretched and felt incredibly refreshed. For a moment, she wondered where she was. The experience in the sea and the sense of horror of her drowning came flooding back. *I've got to find Mouse.* She recoiled at the thought of returning via the sea.

The curtains across the entrance way parted.

Kat sat up abruptly. "Mouse? Where did you come from?"

It couldn't be Mouse.

The not-Mouse staggered. "I am Sha-hee. That was most strange. Your thoughts were of the blonde one from before, but changed, and I became this one. Such a change requires much energy for Sha-hee. And your mind is still filled with all memories from before. We must learn how to be with you. We have never encountered one being who carries so many thoughts. We cannot survive such rapid changes."

"I didn't mean to cause you problems."

"We understand your intentions, but your mind has no discipline." Not-Mouse pointed at a small table. "Sustenance waits for you. We urge you to consume this, and we will return to take you to our gathering. We must discuss how Sha-hee and Kat can remain in one place, without causing such mental energy to endanger us."

Kat gaped at the Sha-hee and nodded. As the being departed, it flickered like a failing light bulb, from Liandock to Mouse and back. *Am I alive? Is this death?* She sat at the table, and ate the food mechanically. Her mind whirled. The Sha-hee said their changes might be challenging. *If I'm alive, they're real. It said they can't survive the rapid changes I caused.*

Kat concentrated on thinking only of Liandock, hoping the Sha-hee would be able to restrict themselves to a single change. *They're my only way of getting back to Kadwee. I can't afford to cause them problems.* She waited, eyes closed, concentrating on the memory of the gorgeous Rifellan Metal Master.

The curtains parted again, and Liandock stood in front of her.

"Excellent. Your mind is strong with this one. Follow me. We are requested to attend Sha-hee." He parted the curtain for her, and they moved down the rock corridors of the interior city to a greater hall that resembled an amphitheater. The theatre was filled with hundreds of the asexual beings, all staring at her with strange, dead eyes. Down in front of the mass of Sha-hee, two chairs were isolated from the rest of the beings. The Liandock being led Kat to one of the chairs, indicated she should sit, and it sat beside her.

She glanced at its vacant eyes. "What now?"

"We confer."

Kat stared at the hundreds of Sha-hee in the circle of seats above her. There was a sense of much conversation, and yet no sound echoed around the cave, nor did the Sha-hee move. *How do I know they're talking?*

Finally the non-conversation ceased. Liandock told her they had reached a conclusion. "Sha-hee cannot destroy a living being, and we are unable to cause your mind to forget. Sha-hee must, therefore, educate you to restrain your mind to protect us from your ability to consider many others at the same time."

"Why is this a problem for you?"

"This land is inhabited by those whom you refer to as Glowens, all need to be with another being to experience a bond. Bonding for the inhabitants of this land is of vital importance to their well-being. However, the land must be limited to only a few offspring emerging from such bonds in order to maintain the balance of the resources of this land. Sha-hee cannot force these beings to abstain from bonds, and thus must provide an alternative. To keep all thriving, Sha-hee must form bonds with individual beings to prevent the emergence of too many offspring coming into the physical. A Sha-hee and Glowen bond does not produce offspring. This is the service that Sha-hee perform for this land."

Kat's head swam with the concepts and challenges of Sha-hee.

Liandock turned to her. "When Sha-hee allows a bond with a being of this land, the Glowen is aware it is mated and is familiar with the face of their mate. That mate appears as Glowen but is actually Sha-hee. We know what is pleasing to a Glowen, and thus we take on an appearance of one who suits. When a Glowen, bonded with Sha-hee, is in their home, all appears normal to them. Sha-hee always remain in the home of their bonded Glowen and is never in the company of any other being, while that Glowen continues to exist in the physical. To the Glowen, this is normal."

Kat shook her head in amazement. "So the Glowens I've met who tell me they are bonded, but whose mates I never met, are bound to Sha-hees. Is this correct?"

"Sha-hee is not plural, but only one, and yes, you are correct. This is necessary to assure the continuance of Sha-hee.

When the bonded Glowen leaves the physical, that part of Sha-Hee is free to re-emerge with the one or to choose another being with which to bond. This keeps the Glowen numbers from increasing beyond the ability of the land to sustain them. Naturally the Glowens who bond with other Glowens are the ones who produce offspring."

"I believe I understand the system."

The Sha-hee continued. "And now we must teach you to be able to conceal your knowledge of us from all others. Are you willing to learn this?"

Once Kat agreed, she accompanied the Liandock being to a training room, where a number of Sha-hee, who made sure to keep back from her physical presence, offered ideas on how to block her thoughts from outsiders. "Why do I need to block my thoughts from others?"

The Liandock look-alike was her primary trainer and handled all direct communication with her. "Kat, some exist, although not many, who enjoy the ability to read other beings' internal thoughts. I do not mean Sha-hee, but other beings in this world. We are not sure what part you will play here, but the capacity to block your inner thoughts from all others will be to your advantage, as well as protect Sha-hee."

The Liandock being encouraged her to experiment mentally to discover a trigger thought that would activate a block. The simple task of imagining a veil dropping over her mind, appeared to work the best. "You will soon learn to recognize when another wishes to penetrate your mind, and the more you practice, the more the veil will automatically descend. I believe you are ready to be tested." He called out to one of the Sha-hee in the room, and although Kat did not understand his words, the other one walked toward her. It came close enough to touch, but did not change into Liandock, or Mouse or anyone else of her acquaintance. "He didn't change, but neither did you change back. Why not?"

"We do not deliberately seek to read your mind. This is something over which we have no control. However, you blocked any thoughts of those in your mind, so while Sha-hee was not compelled to remain in the image of the one most strong in your thoughts, we chose to remain in that manifestation. Our reason was because we discovered when you first came to Sha-hee, you are more comfortable viewing us in this appearance."

"Why can I close my mind, and you tell me others on Pridden cannot?"

The Sha-hee shook his shoulders, which Kat assumed was the equivalent of a shrug. "We are unaware of why this is. You are unique to this world." Liandock's face gave a wry smile. "You are weary from the lessons. We will return you to the resting place, and allow you to sleep. When you arise refreshed, we will return you to Kadwee."

"Thank you. I am tired."

"Rest then, but we must return you soon. The darker one you think of is most likely curious about your absence."

♋♋♋

When Kat woke, the lights in the small room brightened, and she discovered a tray of food and beverage on the small table. She sat and ate the rather bland but nourishing meal, and prepared to wait to be taken to Kadwee.

The curtains parted, and Kat lowered the veil in her mind. The Liandock Sha-hee appeared with five others, and they indicated they were about to return her to Kadwee. As they set off, she thought about Wink. *I have no idea how long*

I've been here. I hope she's not starving. Startled by her own thoughts, she glanced around, but no Sha-hee took on the physique of Wink.

CHAPTER 18

The Sha-hee walked beside Kat answering questions and supplying her with last minute ways of identifying who might wish to gain entrance to the information concealed in her mind.

Kat still shook her head in wonder at the situation. “The more I learn of you, the more I find I cannot call you Lian-dock. You are not him. I shall call you Sha-hee. You tell me parts of you are bonded with some individual Glowens, and yet you are never seen with them in public. Why do they not reveal your presence?”

“We have removed the memory of how they met us and that we are Sha-hee. From their perspective, we are Glowen bond mates of theirs. The Sha-hee who do form the bonds always remain in the familial homes with the Glowens with whom they are bonded. The Glowen beings find this normal. The physical side of the bonding is most satisfactory to Glowens. That Sha-hee must remain undiscovered is vital to our survival. You will be the only living one who will be aware of our existence.”

“Why is the secrecy of you so vital?”

“If the Sha-hee existence is exposed and thus we end up bonding with more than one Glowen at a time because of their undisciplined minds, we become confused and overwhelmed with the mental images of those from the Glowen’s minds. Each mental and physical bonding with a

Glowen requires energy from Sha-hee. If too much energy is required, we burn out. If a part of Sha-hee burns out, their essence is no longer contained in the whole, which is left weaker than before."

"Do Sha-hee live longer than the people on this world?"

"We do. Our existence is eternal. Occasionally a part of the Sha-hee is destroyed or removed from physical existence, but the mind essence of one who was physical is still retained by the whole. When a Glowen leaves this physical existence, their bonded Sha-hee returns to the group and is assimilated once again."

"I'm a little confused. You say the Sha-hee returns to the group. Does this mean when they are in bond with a Glowen, they are not part of the Sha-hee group?"

"No. we are always part of the one. We are Sha-hee. The individual parts may act independently, but ultimately we always function best as part of the whole."

Kat shook her head. "Whew."

She and the Sha-hee began to descend through a rock tunnel, which became colder as they moved downward. Kat needed to swallow to clear the pain in her ears.

"Sha-hee, are we under the sea now?"

"We are, and we must now place a blindfold on you so that you cannot find your way to us. We ask you to refrain from falling into the liquid again, because the Sha-hee from the liquid is only permitted to come to your rescue once."

"But I can now shield my mind from others about your existence, right?"

"We are aware that you now possess a mental protection in place, but how effective this protection is, we have no clear idea. This is for your safekeeping as well as the safety of Sha-hee. Were others to be aware of your knowledge of us, you might be in serious danger."

As he was speaking to her, the Liandock Sha-hee was binding a dark cloth around her eyes. All was now black, and Kat no longer enjoyed the benefit of the dim red light in the tunnels.

"I cannot see a thing now, so you will have to guide me." She put her hands in front of her to prevent any collisions with the rock walls. "You have been on Glowen for many paths, has no one ever discovered your existence before?"

The Sha-hee took Kat's hand and began to lead her forward again. "A few have. However, as we told you earlier, we are not allowed to kill or destroy any creature."

"Wait a minute. Do you mean to tell me those birds would not have killed Mouse and me?"

"No. The Sha-hee of the air would never have destroyed you, only caused pain to frighten you from discovering us."

"But what happens if some do discover your existence?"

"Sha-hee must wipe the memory from their minds. They remember nothing of the experience."

"Am I truly the only living person who is consciously aware of you?"

"You are. The three lords of this world and the leader of this land have knowledge of us, but not in a conscious state. Upon each of them, we placed a light forgetting invocation, so if ever an emergency arose which required our help, the secret of Sha-hee would immediately surface in their minds." Kat felt the Sha-hee move in the equivalent of their shrug. "Such a situation has not occurred in over thousands of paths. And you are the only one we cannot cause to forget."

Kat was guided around a turn, and the passage began to slant upwards again. "This is amazing." *Keeping a secret of this magnitude is almost cruel.*

She and the six Sha-hee continued to walk on but this time in silence. Kat was almost positive the Sha-hee were quiet in their minds, but hers was a roiling cauldron of thoughts and fears and astonishment, and yet she was still able to retain the misty veil over her thoughts.

Occasionally, Kat was steered around a curve in the path, and, at odd times. she climbed some steps. She attempted to keep one hand on the rock wall beside her and once, or twice, encountered only empty space. The path curved to the left and to the right, and by this time, Kat had completely lost her sense of direction. A short time later, she heard the sound of the shrieks of birds. *Are these the caves in Krugg Menyd where Mouse and I were chased by those ghastly birds?* "Sha-hee, can we rest a while? I'm tiring, and I'm thirsty."

"Apologies, Kat. Come over here with us, and there is a seat built into an indentation in the tunnel." He led her forward. "Here, seat yourself." He guided her down to sit and handed her a container of water.

She sighed with relief, drank the water, and thanked them. "How much further do we have to go?"

"Not far now."

They helped her up and again set off on the meandering journey through the under-ground tunnels. The Sha-hee led Kat up another series of steps, and she smelled fresh air and the salty tang of the sea. They led her from the caves, and the heat of the sun beat down on her. *At last, above-ground.*

Guided around and through what seemed like grasses and shrubbery, Kat felt soft earth beneath her feet. Finally, her blindfold was removed. Blinking to focus, she gazed around and only the Liandock Sha-hee was beside her. She had no idea when the other five had parted company.

"Follow the path to your left, Kat, and you will soon come upon Kadwee. May the rest of your journey be well."

"My thanks for saving my life. I will keep your secret."

The Sha-hee bowed his head to Kat, turned, and walked back the way they had come.

She headed toward the road, but when she glanced back, the Sha-hee had completely disappeared. When she reached the road, she turned left and trudged toward the village of Kadwee.

Did I live through all this or simply imagine it? Did Mouse wonder where I was?

CHAPTER 19

Mouse did not expect Kat to join him until the evening meal, assuming she would be enjoying the sight of the flower gardens. But he was concerned when she did not appear. After his meal, he again knocked at her room, but either she was not in her quarters, or she might be involved with someone.

Despite the fact that she rejected the overt advances of the Glowens of Kadwee, she might have found one worth succumbing to. Mouse frowned to himself. *She has never been absent for an entire night.*

He returned to his room and retrieved the maps of Glowen. He had intended that they would leave for the village of the Master Keeper of the furred stingers on the morrow, but he had been unable to convey this to Kat.

He sat at the desk and began to write a note in runes on a piece of parchment. He would at least leave a message for her to contact him so they might plan the rest of the trip back to Brennan's Keep. He added that they should meet for a meal. He folded the note and pushed the parchment under the connecting door between their rooms.

He prepared for bed, hoping to find a reply to his note by the morrow. He was not concerned as yet. Kat did tend to do things spontaneously.

Birds and the sounds of people calling to each other, woke Mouse and he discovered the star had risen for the turn. His night had been disturbed. He woke constantly, wondering if Kat had returned. When he finally fell asleep, the moon had sunk below the horizon. Awake now, he jumped from his bed, completed his morning preparations, and hastily dressed. He knocked on the connecting door, but still no answer.

When he arrived at the dining hall, he scanned the room, but no Kat. However, Koosela and Gaviska were both seated with two others from Kadwee. They waved and invited him to join them.

"My thanks to you both." He sat, and they introduced him to the two other Glowens at the table. Mouse inclined his head to both of them, and called to an apprentice to place his meal order.

After the server left, he was now concerned. "Koosela, you remember Lady Kat whom you met along with me the previous turn?"

Koosela nodded. "She is a fine woman. A shame she adheres to the mores of those of Kaylin. I would be much contented if she were available for pleasuring."

"Er . . .yes. Yet you must be used to the social practices of those of other lands."

Gaviska spoke up. "We do not meet many from other lands, but we are usually disappointed so few appreciate mating as much as we."

Mouse nodded at them. "You must find this frustrating."

Koosela shrugged. "No. Many Glowens are available to us. Why do you ask about your Lady Kat?"

"She is not my Lady Kat. I am merely her guide." The assistant placed his meal on the table, and he began to eat as they continued their conversation.

"You have said this before." Koosela laughed. "We find this so strange you are able to travel for so long with such a compelling and attractive woman, and yet have no physical congress with her." He chuckled, seemingly at the absurdity of the situation. "But you did not tell us why you inquired about the Lady Kat."

"I have not seen her since the previous turn, and am curious as to her whereabouts."

"Did she not say she planned to visit the flower gardens?"

"Yes, she did."

Gaviska laughed at this. "Well, Sire Mouse, this is your solution. The flower gardens are filled with the invigorating scents of many erotic blooms. She no doubt encountered someone to whom she was attracted." He turned to Koosela. "Who might she have met in the gardens?"

Koosela rubbed at his chin. "Skonya pen Yuwen keeps the information about the gardens. I suggest, Sire Mouse, you approach her. She is always privy to what occurs in her domain. A number of shelters were built to be used by those overcome by the fragrances of the blooms. Skonya always is aware of who rests within."

"Thank you for your suggestions. Since I have completed my meal, I will find Skonya pen Yuwen and determine if she encountered Kat." He rose and exited the hall.

♋♋♋

Mouse approached the attractive woman with deep golden skin, and the inevitable eyes of what Kat referred to as wolf eyes. "Are you Skonya pen Yuwen?"

"I am, Sire. Do you wish to make use of a shelter? Have you brought your own companion, or do you wish one to be supplied?"

Mouse blinked rapidly. “No, thank you. I have no such need. Uhm. I believe you spoke with Lady Kat and supplied her with information about the flower gardens the previous turn?”

“I did indeed. I believe she was most impressed with them.”

“This is the only exit from the gardens, correct?”

“Yes, and before you ask me the question. I have not encountered her leaving. I suspect she is still here. You may search if you wish.” She reached back into the hut and removed a piece of parchment from a cubbyhole. “This is the reserved list of those occupying the shelters. If you find one which appears occupied but not on this list, you may search inside.” Skonya handed him the sheet. “Please return this when you leave.”

“I will.” He set off down the paths between the various groupings of flowers. While he admired the beauty and color of the exotic blooms, he was more anxious to locate Kat. He passed a few occupied shelters, but they were all recorded on Skonya’s list. At one point, he came to the end of a path, and the ground beyond was a jumble of wild flowers and grasses, which terminated at cliffs overlooking the sea.

He glanced to his left and a whiff of a heavy, heady and glorious scent assaulted his nostrils. He walked into the section toward a truly erotic aroma. He gasped as his body responded to sensual pleasurable waves of carnal arousal. *If Kat encountered these blooms, I would not be surprised if she sought out a willing partner. I would personally find it difficult to resist any woman.* The blooms were lush, blousy, and pure white. Mouse was convinced they exuded pheromones designed to tempt and seduce any passerby.

He hastened to leave the section. All three shelters here were recorded by Skonya as being reserved for private functions.

Where was Kat?

He headed to the entrance and handed the list back to the keeper. "I found no shelters occupied which did not appear on your list." Mouse felt heat in his face. "Skonya, what is the section with the exotic white blooms called?"

Skonya laughed. "I can determine from your expression you experienced the garden of Scented Rituals." She leaned toward him. "Had I known you would enter the area after detecting the scent, I would have joined you myself." She laughed again. "I often visit that garden simply to enjoy the sensations."

"I understand why you would. A unique experience, indeed." He coughed.

She grinned at him, accepted the list of shelters from his hands and attempted to stroke his fingers, which Mouse deftly avoided.

♋♋♋

He returned to Kadwee and enlisted Koosela and Gaviska to help him conduct a systematic search of the town, which was so lengthy they missed their noon-turn meal. At last, all three, hungry, tired, and hot, entered the dining hall for their evening meal.

Koosela ordered two substantial glasses of Orenberry wine for him and Gaviska. "Will you not join us, Sire Mouse?"

"I am too concerned about Lady Kat to risk losing my concentration. I will refresh myself with tea instead."

"You said your Kat was last seen entering the flower gardens, am I correct?

"Yes. Skonya did not remember seeing her leave the area."

Koosela boomed with laughter and nudged Mouse. "If the Lady Kat entered the garden of Scented Rituals, I suspect she may have forgotten her rigid Kaylin rules and found a Glowen to her liking. I would suggest you relax, because she will no doubt return to the inn by the morrow. The effects of the Scented Rituals blooms invariably last a mere turn or two."

"Your advice is excellent, and we have searched most of Kadwee. I know she would not have ventured onto the cliffs, as we had a discussion about them." He rubbed his brow. "I will take a meal with you both and continue my search on the morrow. Are you aware of an individual who would allow me to send a message via pyrock to Healer Marreth?"

Gaviska supplied him with the necessary information, and, when Mouse completed his meal, he headed for the pyrock owner.

He wrote a note to Marreth, explaining Kat's disappearance, and requested any knowledge she might have of Kat's whereabouts.

The pyrock returned within a few minutes, with Marreth advising Mouse that she would check for news of Kat from her own sources. Mouse reluctantly headed for bed.

♋♋♋

He rose early, grabbed a brief morning meal and set out once again to search for Kat. He walked along the road headed back toward the caves at Krugg Menyd. The star was fully risen when he spied a figure walking toward him. *Kat?* "Kat!" He ran along the road. "Where have you been?"

She sat down on the grass. "I'm exhausted." She was dusty and dripped with sweat.

"But where have you been?"

"It's a long story. Please, Mouse. Take me to my room at the inn and order me some tea and food. I'll be better able to talk with nourishment in me."

"Fine. Come with me."

Why is she avoiding my questions?

CHAPTER 20

Kat sat at the small table in her room, with an edgy Mouse opposite her. *How am I going to explain my absence to him?*

Mouse frowned at her. "Kat you have had tea and food, and now you need to tell me where you have been."

"Why are you so concerned about where I've been? I had a morning meal with you the previous turn, and I'm obviously back."

"You have been gone for two full turns, Kat. You have not disappeared for a complete turn ever before. Eduardo entrusted me with your safe-keeping and I failed him."

"No you didn't. I'm here, and I'm safe."

"But where have you been?"

I've gotta come up with something. "Well, I had a bit of an accident."

"A bit of an accident?" Mouse raised his voice. "What is a bit of an accident?"

"Don't shout at me. I'm so tired, and you make me unable to think clearly."

He held up both his hands. "Kat, I am not shouting. I am attempting to be patient, but you are avoiding my questions." He sighed. "Please tell me what happened."

I should stay as close to the truth as possible, without revealing Sha-hee. "I fell in the sea."

Mouse stared at her. "How did you fall into the sea? The cliffs are huge."

"I didn't mean to go right to the edge. At one point, the land slopes downward, and I slipped, couldn't stop myself, and fell over the edge."

"What?" Mouse's face paled and he stared at Kat, eyes wide.

"Mouse, will you please let me tell you what happened without constantly interrupting?"

He blinked rapidly. "Forgive me, but I am anxious for you to explain what took place."

"Fine, I will tell you all, but stop talking." Kat cleared her throat. "As I said, I walked through the uncultivated portion of the flowers, and when I unexpectedly hit the slope, I couldn't keep my balance and I fell. I rolled down the slope, unable to stop, and dropped over the edge of the cliffs."

"Had you visited the Scented Rituals garden?"

"No, I caught sight of the sign on my left before I reached the untamed section but thought I would explore them later. Why do you ask?"

"I thought perhaps the scent of the blooms had disturbed your balance. I have never seen you be unsteady before."

"Will you stop interrupting?" *I am trying to come up with a plausible story, but his questions keep stopping my flow.*

He held up his hands as if in surrender.

"I tripped on a rock, I think, and I lost my footing. The next thing I found myself sliding down a slope. I grabbed at small bushes and grass, but I couldn't find anything to stop my fall, and suddenly I was in mid-air heading downward."

Mouse opened his mouth, but Kat held up her hand and glared at him.

He gestured for her to continue.

"I couldn't believe how long the fall took. I tried to protect myself by rolling up in a ball so I wouldn't hurt myself too much when hitting the water. I suspect that is what made me plunge so deep. I was stunned, but I guess my natural buoyancy brought me to the surface. I grabbed a breathe of air, and went under again." She breathed in and put her hand to her chest. "I surfaced again and began treading water. I was terrified and I attempted to find a place to land. The cliffs continued into the water, and I didn't find rocks to climb on. So I swam up and down without finding a place to cling to, but luckily, I noticed the peak of an island not far away. I swam over, but those cliffs were also sheer to the water, and were so slippery I couldn't find any place to hang on."

"By Caleesh, Kat, that was more than a bit of a fall." Mouse was still pale.

She glared at him and sighed in exasperation. *Bloody hell, I wish he'd shut up. I'm having trouble coming up with a decent explanation.* "Let me finish. I was frightened. I was unable to find a way of getting back on land, the water was cold, and I was tiring. My arms and legs felt like leaden weights." She shivered. "It was terrifying, Mouse. How was I going to save myself? I did not think I was going to survive." *This is all sort of true, but how to explain how I escaped?* "I could barely keep my head above water when someone said 'Do you need help?' I stared up into the eyes of a man in a small boat."

"What?"

"I know. It was a miracle that he came by when he did. He helped me into the boat, and he took off his jacket and wrapped the warm coat around me. I was so grateful, despite the fact that he lectured me on being so foolish as to approach so close to the cliff edges."

"What was he doing?"

"He was a fisherman, and apparently lived on the coast, alone. I think he was some kind of hermit."

"Her-mit?"

"A word we have for those who live on their own and reject being around other people. He kindly rowed around to where he lived in a sort of cave. He gave me some food and drink and let me sleep a bit. Later, I don't know how long, he took me in his boat to a set of stairs cut into the rock face that led up to the top of the cliff. He directed me to climb up, and, keeping the sea on my left, walk back to Kadwee."

"Your story is too astounding not to be true."

"What do you mean?"

"You seemed to be avoiding my questions, so I thought perhaps you were not telling the full truth."

"Why would I lie? Mouse, I'm exhausted. The swimming all over the place, the climb up the stairs, and the walk to Kadwee, took every ounce of energy I own. I want to sleep. Can we continue our talk on the morrow? I need my bed."

"You do appear to be tired. I will meet you for a meal on the morrow." He rose from his seat. "I will go for my evening meal now and will not disturb you until star-rise."

"Thank you." Kat watched him leave, locked the door behind him, and prepared herself for bed. First she fed a sleepy Wink, who, it appeared, had not suffered from lack of food for two turns. She donned sleepwear, and settled for the night in her bed.

I hope Mouse swallowed that. Gotta keep the Sha-hee a secret.

CHAPTER 21

Kat woke to the sound of knocking on the door to the adjoining room. "Wait a few minutes, Mouse, while I dress."

A muffled "fine" came from the next room.

Kat leaped from bed, thoroughly refreshed. She fed Wink, who chirped gratefully at her, then took a brief shower and dressed. She walked over to the communicating door, and knocked on her side of it.

Mouse opened his door. "You slept too long, and I missed my morning meal, and I am experiencing hunger. Are you ready to attend the dining hall?"

"I'm starving. I'll lock this door and meet you in the passageway." She left her room via the hallway door.

Mouse stood waiting for her, and, greeting her as if for the first time, led the way to the dining room. "I would prefer we sit alone so you can expand upon your adventures of the past two turns. I suspect you may wish to tell me things you would not want the Glowens to be privy to."

"You're right. However, be prepared that when we sit together, the Glowens may decide you are more than just my guide."

"Possibly true, but I wish to know all you experienced. I will have to take the risk they suspect our relationship is more physical than the reality."

Kat sighed and shrugged. "I can't believe how sex-obsessed they are. Not even on my world, where some are addicted to physical interplay, have I met so many devoted to the desire for …for um …mating."

"What is unusual about these people — and I mean primarily the Kadweeans, is that they are so matter-of fact if they are refused."

Kat chuckled. "We have a saying on my world, 'there are plenty of other fish in the sea', but rarely do we act as if it's true. These Kadweeans act as if it is."

Mouse grabbed a table for two and ushered Kat to a seat, while he sat on the other. "We should order, so our meals are delivered before we begin our discussions." He signaled for a wait-person.

Both ordered groonnan and fara tea and waited in silence until the food was delivered.

Mouse waited to pick up his spoon. "You explained a little of what happened to you. I cannot understand why you would approach the cliffs when we had a discussion about them after we left the camp."

"I didn't intend to. I was more curious about the island off the coast. I tripped over something in my path, and then because of the slope, I was over the cliff and falling toward the water."

"Did the soil crumble away? And therefore was the reason you fell?"

"I don't think so. Everything happened so quickly until I began to fall toward the sea below. Then time appeared to slow down." She shivered. "I was terrified."

"I am most surprised you found no rocks or foliage at the bottom of the cliff for you to cling to."

"I'm sure I swam for hours and found nothing. I was certain I was about to die."

Now Mouse shivered. "Thank Caleesh for the appearance of the fisherman. Eduardo would most likely have me banished if you had perished."

"What? Is that the only reason you're glad I survived?"

Mouse looked horrified. "Of course not, Kat. We … we have become friends, and I would miss your company." He blushed and stammered. "I was thinking of seeing Eduardo's face, because I am aware he too would miss your presence." He swallowed. "You mean much, not only to Eduardo and me, but to all Pridden." Mouse stared at her. "You have come to be important in all our lives."

Kat gaped at him, and he dropped his gaze. "Thank you Mouse. Your words mean a lot."

He cleared his throat. "We are behind in our travels by two turns and must depart Kadwee no later than the morrow. I suggest you take the balance of this turn to pack and rest, and we will leave for the village of the Master Keeper of the furred stingers, early on the morrow. We will not plan to stay overnight with the keeper, but will enjoy a noon-turn meal with him. After, we will depart for Kamerdow and will arrive around the evening meal. This way, we will have made up one lost turn."

"Excellent. Tell me, is most of Glowen as hot as Kadwee?"

"Generally, yes. Why do you ask?"

"Well, I've been overheated here, rather like a wilted flower. I want to visit the market to find if I can purchase a couple of lighter and cooler tops."

Mouse lowered his eyes.

"You're laughing at me. Why?"

"I would venture to assume many of the Glowens in Kadwee do indeed think of you as a flower. Your description is most apt."

Kat glared at him. "You don't always have to agree with me." She sniffed. "I'll meet you in the dining hall for the evening meal." She rose from her seat, and left the area.

ꝏꝏꝏ

Back in her room, Kat packed her baggage for the trip to Kamerdow and examined what she still had in her wardrobe. Leathers were too hot to wear in Glowen and she had only two culotte-type skirts, plus one pair of loose pants. She tugged on the tassel in her room, and, when the apprentice appeared, asked if they would launder the loose long pants she had worn for the past two turns.

"We can have them ready for you by the evening meal, my Lady. Will that be sufficient time for you?"

"Perfect. Thank you. I may be at my meal, so can you simply leave them hanging in the closet?"

"Of course." He took them from her and departed.

Sticking a finger in Wink's cage, she stroked the furry head, and the pyrock uttered a tiny peep. Gathering some chits Marreth handed her when they departed Brennan's Keep, Kat headed to the market, making sure she concentrated on the misty veil over her mind.

She only needed to stop for directions once and soon found herself amid colorful stalls of produce. A rumble in her stomach told her it was time for a mid-turn meal. The odors of cooking meats and grilled vegetables led her to the food area. One particular stall displayed meat on sticks grilling on a type of open pit. The skewers were interspersed with various vegetables in a riot of colors of red and green and yellow. Kat requested one, and handed the stall owner a chit. "Can you also give me some fara tea?"

"Yes, my Lady. Seat yourself at a table and we will deliver your meal and your tea to you."

She located a table next to the stall, and within minutes, the stall owner's apprentice placed her meal in front of her. He also brought a pot of fara tea and an enormous cup.

One bite of the meat on the skewer, and she moaned with pleasure. *I have no idea what this is, but it's beyond delicious, and tastes familiar. Yum.* She had to force herself to eat slowly and savor every bite. After demolishing the contents of her plate, she indulged in her favorite pastime of people-watching as she drank her tea.

Two or three men approached her, intent on giving her flowery compliments, but she was firm with her refusals. Unexpectedly, a woman sat down at her table. Unprepared for a solicitation, Kat was nonplussed when the woman kissed her hand. "You are very beautiful, my Lady, and I would make you experience much pleasure."

"I'm sure you are correct, but I am committed elsewhere." *Why do they keep saying I'm beautiful? I'm not unattractive, but beautiful? No way.*

The woman bowed her head. "A pity." She rose from her seat, glided off, and stopped to sit beside a lone man seated some distance away. He, from his actions, was more than willing to accept her compliments and returned the kiss to his hand.

I've sat long enough. This is worse than a meat market. Because this was a food market, Kat laughed at her own unwitting joke. *Better begin my shopping.* She rose and set off for the clothing stalls.

She stopped at a particularly colorful stall, with tops and skirts and loose pants hanging about the display. After fending off the stall keeper's advances, Kat chose a pair of loose pants in a soft dove grey.

The tops were a more difficult choice. So many colors and styles to choose from, but she settled on one in a jaw-dropping fire-engine red, and another in deep emerald green. Both slipped over her head, and flowed loosely, long enough to reach below her hips. Each had a tie at the waist which Kat intended to replace with her own special belt. The fabric of the tops was almost gossamer thin, yet completely opaque.

Pleased with her purchases, she returned to her rooms to complete her packing. A knock at the outside door attracted her attention.

"I have brought you fara tea, my Lady." The tall apprentice at the door was not one she had seen before.

"Thank you, although I didn't order tea. Please put the tray on the table."

"Another ordered the drink for you." As he said these word, the man's appearance wavered, and assumed the likeness of Sha-hee.

As this happened, Kat immediately concentrated on dropping the veil over her mind.

He bowed to her. "Our apologies, but we wished to discover how efficient your mind block is. We are pleased you appear to have perfected this ability, even before you made the concentrated effort." Sha-hee turned to leave her room. "We ask you again, for our safety, do not reveal the presence of Sha-hee. We suspect you are tempted to disclose our existence to the one whom you refer to as guide, and who resides in the adjacent chamber."

"I vowed I would not tell anyone about you, but you are correct I truly desire to tell him. I cannot help but feel he needs to know this. However, I intend to keep my promise."

"Sha-hee thank you, Kat. We believe you are convinced your guide would keep the secret, and we suspect your desire to tell him is valid. We have told you why keeping our secret is so vital to our well-being. We shall leave this for you to decide." It wavered again, resumed the appearance of the apprentice, and departed.

I hate secrets. Keeping them is such a lonely business.

CHAPTER 22

Kat entered the dining room, and scanned for Mouse. He was not yet seated at a table, and she was about to seat herself when she caught Koosela pen Yuwen beckoning her over to a table for eight. Also seated with him were Gaviska and a Rifellan guard. She smiled and joined them, seating herself beside the Rifellan, who turned out to be Jagloran, the guard who helped her after she was robbed.

"Kat, how pleasant to meet you again. I should tell you we have still not been able to locate your bracelet, but we have not neglected the search." He gazed around the room. "I travel around the villages of Glowen on a regular basis to remain cognizant of the happenings in this land."

"Thank you for the update." *Hmm. He's looking rather good.* Kat summoned a waitperson over. "Would you please bring me some karri-san tea?"

"Right away, my Lady."

Jagloran glanced at her, grinned, and raised an eyebrow.

She glared at him. "Don't flatter yourself. It's only pheromones." *I think Rifellans find it amusing they affect me like this. Really, they can be quite annoying.*

He chuckled. "Fair enough."

Koosela waved at someone, and she turned to look. Mouse walked toward them.

He sat on the other side of Kat, as the waitperson arrived with her tea.

Koosela stopped the man from returning to the kitchen area. "Apprentice, I believe we are all prepared to order our meals. Will you fill our orders?"

He complied, and soon the table was alive with laughter and exchanged comments, with all enjoying food between conversations.

Koosela told a story about Gaviska when he first entered the flower gardens. He failed to see the sign about the Scented Rituals, and was lost to all his friends for four turns. Laughing, Koosela pointed at Gaviska. "He does not need the extra benefit of the Scented Ritual garden, believe me."

Jagloran joined in the laughter. "I have a friend in the guards in Rifella who is overly taken by our un-bonded females, and I would never suggest he visit your gardens, either.

Although Mouse had asked both Koosela and Gaviska to refrain from pursuing Kat, they both flirted continuously with her. She was pleased that, at least, Jagloran did not add to her discomfort by further mention of Rifellan pheromones.

Kat, now more relaxed after her discussion with Mouse, handled them both with ease. "You both flatter me outrageously, but I doubt you would respect me in the morning."

Gaviska and Koosela regarded each other with quizzical expressions, shrugged, and continued their conversations.

Kat chuckled to herself. She'd stopped them, and didn't even have to explain the expression.

Mouse rose. "Please forgive Kat and me. We need to begin our journey on the morrow soon after dawn. As such, we must bid you farewell now. Thank you again for your hospitality."

All rose, including Kat, and made brief parting speeches. She and Mouse left the hall and headed for their rooms.

When they arrived, Mouse stopped Kat in the passageway. “Make sure you have packed everything, and I will knock on the inner door to wake you at dawn. When you are ready, order a morning meal for us in your room, and request your luggage be delivered to the stable. When the meal arrives, advise me, and we will eat together.”

Kat nodded her agreement, yawned, and entered her room. After completing her packing, she updated her journal, and practiced some Priddanese writing. She did not write about the Sha-hee in her journals. She needed to think about their secret before she committed her thoughts to writing about them. She finished by ensuring her writing equipment was safely stowed in her diplo bag.

♋♋♋

The following morning, Kat rose early, feeling refreshed, and had fed Wink, when a knock came at the inner door. “I’m up, Mouse, and I’ll advise you when the meal arrives.”

She prepared for her day, and when dressed, tugged the tassel in the corner.

She had tucked all her writings in her diplo bag, when an apprentice knocked at the outer door.

“Apprentice, would you please arrange to have two orders of groonnan and fara tea brought to my room as soon as possible? Oh, and would you also arrange to have my baggage sent to the stable?”

The young man bowed and left, and she attached the pyrock’s cage to her back pack. Her discussion with Mouse the previous turn assured her they would face no dangerous creatures so she packed all her weapons, with the exception of the small dagger in her left boot.

A knock at the door, and the apprentice entered with the meals, at the same time as the stable hand arrived to take her baggage. She thanked them both and opened the inner door. "Meal is here, Mouse."

He joined her, and they discussed the last few items for this part of their journey.

"We will head for the village of the Master Keeper of the furred stingers. We will stop there, only for a noon-turn meal, and then depart for Kamerdow. If you wish to purchase furred stinger items, you may do so there."

They gathered their personal bags, and left via Kat's door.

"Mouse, you left the inner doors open. Aren't you concerned about what the Kadweeans will think?"

"Worrying about their thoughts no longer matters. We are leaving and will no doubt never return to Kadwee."

♋♋♋

By the time they rode toward the Master Keeper's village, the star was fully risen, and generated so much heat that Kat draped her Rifellan scarf over her head and shoulders to prevent star burn. She had worn her latest purchase of loose clothing, which took advantage of the light breezes blowing from the east. "Whew, despite the heat, this clothing allows air to circulate. I made an excellent purchase."

Mouse, who was in the lead, faced back and nodded at her. "You do appear more comfortable. If I were forced to wear leathers, I would follow Jagloran's lead and wear less armor with a cool shirt." He shrugged. "I suspect the Rifellans have had to adjust their clothing for Glowen."

"They manage this heat well, but then Rifella is also hot." Kat patted her forehead with her scarf. "I wonder if we would be better to travel at night when it's cooler?"

He turned back to her. "It is cooler at night, but navigating the various paths is more difficult when there is no moon to light our way. As we near the village of the Master Keeper, we will encounter shade, which will help." He rode on, and Kat hurried to pass him to get closer to the shadows generated by the Krugg.

She stared at the mountains soaring upwards to her left. They were tall enough to spread a substantial amount of shade, and she sighed with relief as the temperature dropped.

Mouse called back over his shoulder. "You will be happy we are almost at the village."

Tucked into protection of the Krugg, a small village appeared, nestled at the foot of the mountains. The wooden buildings were covered with a white coating, and all the roofs possessed a shiny silver overlay, which, Kat supposed, would reflect the star shine early in the turn, and maintain a cool interior in the homes.

Mouse slid off his horse and suggested Kat do the same. He walked his animal and the baggage horse into a lean-to with water and feed for the creatures. He secured both their animals. "We will not be in this place for long, so we need not remove the saddles and bridles." He did, however, remove their baggage from the packhorse and placed it nearby.

As they walked toward the largest home, a man dressed entirely in loose white clothing, and carrying netted headgear came out to greet them. "Welcome to the furred stinger's village. I will give you the tour of their special homes if you wish."

“We thank you, but a tour is unnecessary. I am Mouse, and I am guide to the Lady Kat. We are here to sample Golden River and to enjoy a brief mid-turn meal. We need to arrive in Kamerdow before the fall of night.”

“Please enter, and we will be delighted to serve you a meal, and supply samples of Golden River.”

The two entered the white home of the keeper, directly into a generous eating area, filled with long tables and many chairs. Once seated, an apprentice brought a dish of vegetable stew, and a small amount of a dessert with a dark golden topping. Kat had eaten a similar stew in Kadwee and thoroughly enjoyed the spiciness. The dessert dish was extraordinary, similar to a dark rich honey, but with an elusive flavor.

Kat licked her lips. “Master Keeper, what is the flavor in this topping?

“Ah, you enjoy this.” He placed a dish in front of her with three indents, and from three jars on the table, poured a small portion of Golden River in each of the indents. “This one,” he indicated the lightest one, “is from the furred ones who inhabit the fields of the red flowers to the north of our village.”

Kat dipped a spoon into the liquid and rolled the Golden River around her mouth. She detected a flavor similar to the scent of roses. Unusual but delicious.

“This one, Lady Kat, is from the fields to our east, in which grow our most popular spices.” He pointed to the middle indentation, which contained a bright gold liquid.

Kat’s spoon this time reminded her of the rich tang of basil. Wonderful.

“The third one is the same as the topping on your dessert. These furred ones live inside the forests to our south.”

Although Kat had already enjoyed this one, she took another spoonful. Now she managed to place the flavor. If she closed her eyes, she imagined herself among evergreen trees, with the scent of pine infused in the Golden River liquid. Glorious.

"Your Golden River is magnificent. I would like to purchase a container of each of them." She put her hand in her pocket and drew out a chit, which she handed him.

"I will pack them securely for you so they will survive your travel."

As he went off to pack up her purchases, Kat dipped her spoon back into the indented dish and polished off the rest of the samples. She turned and smiled at Mouse. "What fabulous flavor. But sweet, so I need some water now." She reached for a tall glass on the table and drank deeply.

Mouse rose from his seat. "We must leave for Kamerdow. Retrieve your parcel from the Master Keeper, and we will gather our horses and depart."

The Master handed Kat a well-trussed crate packed with her Golden River containers, which she and Mouse loaded with the rest of the baggage on the third horse.

The three animals set off for Kamerdow and continued around the base of Krugg Menyd, through a forest of evergreens. Although the journey was not as lengthy as she anticipated, they did not arrive at the village until light began to fade from the sky.

Mouse led them toward the stables. "I suggest we settle ourselves, and order a light meal in our rooms. We should meet for the morning meal on the morrow, and you will have time to discover the many uses the people from Kamerdow make of the waxes created by the furred stingers."

"An excellent idea, Mouse. I am not too hungry, but I am tired. The journey to the Master Keeper's village was hot, and the light from your star burned my skin in a few places."

"When you get to your room, use the juice from the plant I gave you to soothe the itches of the winged biters. One of the Glowens advised me it will help relieve star-burn."

Mouse remained at the stable to convey instructions to the stable hands regarding their mounts, and Kat headed toward her room in the inn, lugging her own baggage, rather than waiting for it to be delivered.

I'm so weary, I may decide to skip an evening meal

CHAPTER 23

Kat had ordered tea and cookies when she arrived in her room. She drank half her tea, ate one cookie, but she yawned so often she gave up, and after dousing the globes, snuggled into bed.

ꕥꕥꕥ

Burrowed beneath her comforter, Kat woke to the sounds of children playing in the yard of the inn. She had dreamed of the Sha-hee in the night, remembering the promise she gave to them about keeping their existence secret.

She lay and drifted, imagining the ways in which she might avoid betraying the Sha-hee. It would be easy without the necessity to answer questions.

A knock at her door brought her fully awake. She called out. “Who is it?” *Stupid question Kat, probably Mouse.*

It was.

“I’ll be ready shortly and will meet you in the eating hall.”

A muffled response. “Fine.”

She reluctantly crawled from her bed and headed for the shower. Once dressed, she fed Wink, pausing to stroke the creature a few times, and left her room for the hall.

Mouse sat at a table with three other people, and he waved her over. She recognized Jagloran, the Rifellan guard, and Mouse introduced her to the remaining two. “Kat this is Ebron pen Darryn, and his bond mate Milva. Ebron and

Milva, please meet Lady Kat, who travels here in Glowen at the behest of Lord Eduardo of Kaylin."

She smiled at them. "Well met, Ebron pen Darryn and Milva. Please forgive my forgetfulness, but I cannot remember what the pen Darryn pod is responsible for."

Ebron stood, reached over, and fondled her hand. "My mate and I are artists, and would welcome you to our home for a pleasurable evening, my Lady."

Oh crap. In front of his bond mate? She withdrew her hand swiftly. "Unfortunately, we cannot stay in Kamerdow for any length of time. We have much to achieve."

Milva smiled at her. "Such a pity. We three, no doubt, would experience a fine evening of coupling."

Kat strained to conceal her astonishment, and sat with haste in the seat beside Jagloran. *Are they kidding? A threesome?*

Jagloran grinned at her. "My pheromones and I welcome you, Kat."

She curled her lip and murmured to him. "You are the lesser of two evils, believe me."

"Evil? Lady Kat, I am crushed."

"My apologies, Jagloran. That was rude and uncalled for. You have been nothing but kind to me. It's certainly not your fault I am sometimes affected by Rifellan pheromones. I only wish your people were not so amused by my challenges."

"I must admit Kat, to see an apparent Rifellan behaving like an oversexed Glowen truly is most amusing. However, I now see my amusement is expressing rudeness to you. I will desist in future."

"My thanks. When I am not caught up in pheromone thrall, your teasing is amusing."

Jagloran hit his head with his hand. "Women. How do you expect us to know what you are thinking?"

Kat grinned, patted his hand, and snorted with laughter.

Mouse, on the other side of Jagloran, advised her that he had placed an order for her morning meal. "Oh, and I took a chance and requested karri-san tea as well." He shot her a slight smirk.

Kat chuckled. "Thank you, Mouse. Kind, but unnecessary."

The pen Darryns chattered on about the art in which they were currently involved. Milva proudly announced that Ebron had been given the honor of producing a mural for the outside wall of the village offices. During their discussion, food arrived, and all applied themselves to their meals.

Jagloran reached over and picked up a dispenser. "Kat, you visited the furred stinger village?"

"We did."

"This is a container of Golden River, and a drop or two in any tea enhances the flavors. Do test the taste."

Kat accepted the container from him, dispensed three drops in her karri-san, and drank. She beamed at Jagloran. "Thank you for suggesting this. Delicious." But she twisted her lips in a slight pout. "My challenge is going to be that every time I drink tea without Golden River, I will be disappointed."

"I doubt you would, Kat. The teas generally possess remarkably fine character of their own."

Milva reached out her hand to Kat across the table, which Kat avoided. "Ebron and I must take you to view the works of art produced from the wax of the furred stingers."

Jagloran patted Milva's hand. "You and Ebron cannot afford to spend time away from the completion of the mural."

He smiled at them both. “I am aware you are required to complete the work within the next two turns, so I will give Lady Kat the tour in your stead.”

Kat sighed internally from relief. *If ever I was to take on a vow of celibacy, I would do so in this odd land.* “An excellent idea, Jagloran. I would not want to be the cause of delays in your work, Ebron.”

Mouse chimed in. “Thank you, Jagloran.” He turned to Kat. “While you two are viewing the wax art center, I will prepare for our departure for the Keep on the morrow. We will travel via Tasik.”

They all rose from the table and set off for their various destinations.

ꝏꝏꝏ

Kat followed Jagloran to a section in the village devoted to art. “My thanks for intervening in the invitation to visit the art centre.”

He chuckled. “I do understand the Glowen way of dealing with sexual matters can be quite overwhelming. Most of the people in this land are now used to the fact that Rifellans, when bonded through ceremony, will not indulge in other encounters.”

“They actually accept this from you?”

“They do. When my bond mate, Dayleeya, joined me in Glowen, we held a second bonding ceremony to visibly demonstrate the serious nature of bonding to Rifellans.” He grinned. “They honor our bond, and none pursue us.”

“They do adhere to your wishes?”

“Yes, and Lord Murwenna now sends only bonded pairs of guards to Glowen.”

“Incredible. I never encountered people like the Glowens before. They are the ultimate sensualists. Everything they think is pleasurable, they do, and their sexual habits are quite unusual in that nothing is off limits. In some ways I admire that they can be so open and flexible. However, I do not wish to follow their example. True, sex is a pleasurable experience, but for me, I also need something more."

She gazed upwards. "Sometimes I need an emotional involvement—at the very least, a mutual attraction."

He laughed aloud. "We Rifellans enjoy many physical encounters before bonding, because we are usually seeking our potential mates—and this requires some experimentation. You are correct, though, even this requires mutual attraction. Once we find our ideal bond mate, we no longer need any other physical encounters. Our mates are more than sufficient for our needs, both physical and emotional."

"I can relate to your ways more than most." *Is Liandock the one I want most?*

"I gather Mouse is your guide, and a friend only?"

"A friend, yes. A concept the Glowens seem to find difficult to understand."

Jagloran chuckled.

They approached a building constructed from a stunning golden wood, decorated with magnificent carvings and illustrations of Glowen life.

Kat stared at everything, openmouthed, like a goofy tourist eying the Taj Mahal. "Wow."

"What is a wow?"

"Oh, sorry, simply an expression from my world indicating an extraordinary visual experience."

"Let us enter. We will go first to the room of the waxes, and afterwards, you may wish to tour the rest of the center."

As they entered, Kat was stopped by a huge canvas of a painting of a bee, but it was done in blues and purples. "Oh that's gorgeous."

"Ebron pen Darryn painted that portrait of a furred stinger."

"That's a furred stinger?"

"Did you not see them at the Master Keeper's village?"

"We only had time for a noon-turn meal, and did not take a tour of the village." She stopped for a moment. "Is that the real color of them?"

"Yes, why?"

"We have a similar creature in my world. However, they are yellow and are called bees."

"You may be in for a treat, Kat. Let us enter the wax display, and determine if your bees are similar to our furred stingers"

At one end of the wax room sat a stall selling the various products made from the furred stinger waxes. A young woman sat near a counter, ready to explain the different uses of the products.

Off to the side, sat a small glass case that contained a section of what resembled honeycomb, and inside were furred stingers, supposedly filling the hexagonal comb with pollens and more wax. They were a little larger than the honey bees which Kat remembered, but they were definitely blue, with a purple fuzz on them. They were rather beautiful but seemed more aggressive looking than bees from home.

The balance of the room was taken up with delightful artifacts, molded from various waxes. She admired tiny houses and models of people, wagons and horses, all of which were in three distinct colors. The first, quite pale, showed a creamy golden hue. The second was a fairly bright gold. The final, a deep, almost golden brown color reminded Kat of cinnamon.

Kat approached the assistant. ”Why are these so different in color?”

The young women rose and came over to the display. “This pale one, is produced by the furred ones who live within the forests. The bright gold one comes from the stingers who live in the flower fields to the north of the Master Keeper’s village. The deep brownish waxes are produced by those who reside to the east of the Master’s village. The waxes contain no scent of their origins, so we infuse our products at the stall with appropriate scents from the flower fields of Kadwee.”

“The artwork is eye-catching, but I would appreciate discovering what products you offer for sale.”

The young woman smiled. “Please follow me.”

Kat walked over to the sales stall, followed by Jagloran.

The young woman pointed out the various products on display. “Over here, we have a wax which, when melted into liquid form, is painted on our garments to repel water during our rainy season.” She showed Kat four other products also for general household use. “Our best-selling ones are our scented candles and our lip protectors. The candles are incredibly pure, last at least two turns burning continually, and leave no blackened marks on walls or furniture. The lip protectors are invaluable when used during the greatest heat. Glowens use them most in the area in the southern end of our land. They soften the lips and protect from loss of natural moisture.”

I could have used some in the Great Hellesmouth desert. “Can I try some?”

"Of course. Use one of the applicators, and spoon a little from that container. The container is scentless, so you can get the full benefit of the product alone."

Kat applied some to her lips. "Oh, my lips are so soft. I must have some of this."

"Inhale the scents to decide which you prefer, Lady." The assistant picked up five samples of the scents on sticks. "This one is used for improving the mood and comes from the low-en flowers. This is beneficial for a sound sleep and uses the scents of the koska flowers. While this one, supplies energy and comes from the nerthon blooms. We find this helps to keep one awake, and the flowers used are the difoona."

Kat sniffed scents similar to jasmine, lavender, eucalyptus and peppermint. "Gorgeous."

"Our final one is the scented ritual flower." She handed the sample to Kat.

"Oh my." Heat traveled throughout Kat's body, and caused immediate sensual sensations in her breasts and in her lower body. She was instantly aware of how close she was to Jagloran. *What a gorgeous man. I want him.* She backed away, blushing furiously.

He reacted quickly, and grabbed the sample of koska and held it under her nose. The heat subsided, and so did desire for him.

"Thank you. You gave me the other sample in time."

"Many of us have been caught unaware by scented ritual, Kat. I do understand."

Kat turned to the assistant. "Candles are too heavy for me to take with me, but I'll purchase each of the five lip protectors. But please, double or perhaps triple wrap the scented ritual one so no aroma escapes the package."

Jagloran ordered the same five lip protectors, but also requested the extra wrapping on the scented ritual one. When Kat glanced at him questioningly, he explained, "I always purchase these for Dayleeya. She would be disappointed if I did not come back with them."

"Surely you two have no need of scented rituals." *Aren't they affected by Rifellan pheromones too?*

"No." He dropped his gaze and blushed. "But we do enjoy the extra sensations. Dayleeya swears that particular scent also makes her lips much fuller." He laughed. "She may be correct, but I have never taken the time to observe if this is so."

They collected their parcels, left the wax room, and spent a lengthy and delightful time examining the gorgeous artwork in the primary room. Paintings and sculpture and carvings adorned the room, and each was displayed to show its best aspects. All the lines were smooth and flowing, and conveyed a sensual beauty.

They had viewed all the paintings in the special room, when Kat's stomach growled loudly. "Pardon me."

"I am not surprised, Kat. We have been here most of the turn and missed our mid-turn meal. I suggest we return to the inn, and I will meet you and Mouse for an early evening meal. I wish to leave my parcel in my rooms first."

"Me too, Jagloran. Thank you for the tour. I enjoyed myself immensely."

What a day. I can hardly wait to be with Liandock again and wear the scented ritual lip protector. She shivered in anticipation.

CHAPTER 24

After dropping her parcel in her room, Kat set off for the dining lounge. Mouse and Jagloran were seated at a small table. Happy with her purchases and wearing the lowen scented lip gloss, she made her way to the table and seated herself between the two men. "A fine evening to you both."

Mouse raised his eyebrows. "You are in an excellent mood."

"Well, I've had a marvelous day. Jagloran saved my bacon today, and I'm wearing my happy lip gloss."

Both men were staring at her with puzzled expressions.

Jagloran spoke first. "I saved what?"

"Sorry an odd expression from my world, meaning you rescued me."

Mouse still appeared puzzled. "Rescued?"

"I guess this does require an explanation. Do you remember asking me if I visited the scented ritual garden?"

Mouse agreed.

"Well, the Kamerdow people sell lip protectors, which they infuse with various flower scents. One of them contained scented ritual. Whew. I experienced a much stronger reaction than from Rifellan pheromones." Kat rubbed an eyebrow. "I was out of my depth, Mouse, literally drowning in extreme sensual reactions. "

Mouse murmured. "I do understand."

"Jagloran rescued me by waving the koska scented one under my nose. It's the sleepy relaxing one. Overcame scented ritual quickly." She faced Jagloran. "Just as well, I might have attacked you at any moment." She laughed. "Dayleeya would have had me assassinated if I had."

Mouse regarded Jagloran questioningly.

"Kat speaks the truth, Mouse. The scented ritual is powerful, and yes," he grinned, "Dayleeya would definitely have had Kat assassinated."

Time to change the subject. "Enough of all this fooling around. I'm hungry. Jagloran and I did not partake of a noon-turn meal. Can we order?"

Mouse called an apprentice over to convey the items on the menu for the evening, who obliged by listing everything available.

Mouse raised and eyebrow at Kat. "Which of those will you have?"

"Anything, so long as the dish has no scented ritual in it." She shrugged. "I'll have the same as you. I don't need karri-san. I'll have fara tea, please."

Jagloran also shrugged. "I am hungry. Make that three of the same, please."

Later, orders delivered, all three grew silent, heavily involved in consuming their delicious meals. At last, Mouse pushed back his plate. "I did have a noon-turn meal, so I am well satisfied."

Kat finished cleaning her plate. "I'm still peckish."

Mouse peered at her. "What an odd word. I assume from the context it means you are still hungry?"

Kat wrinkled her nose. "Sorry. I keep forgetting you don't speak my world. I could eat more, and I know what will be perfect—the dessert we had at the Master Keeper's village, topped with Golden Shower."

Jagloran signaled to a server. "I have enjoyed the dessert you speak of. I will duplicate your order."

The apprentice delivered the desserts and said. "Lady and Sires, Kanorang pen Darryn, the song master from Tavollen is with us this eve to provide entertainment. He is a much regarded musician, and will soon begin his concert in our largest hall."

Mouse glanced at Kat and raised an enquiring eyebrow. "A relaxing evening would not be amiss. Our journey to Tasik on the morrow is not lengthy. Shall we attend?"

"I will enjoy the music. Will you join us, Jagloran?"

"Indeed. Let us finish our dessert first."

Mouse resisted dessert, but the other two dug in, and it was so good, Kat longed to lick the bowl. Manners won out, and she refrained, but announced she was ready to leave.

Jagloran stood and offered his arm to Kat, who rose and accepted. She held out her other arm to Mouse, and the three set off arm in arm to the huge hall.

They reached the doorway and Kanorang began to strum a rather odd-shaped instrument in front of him. They entered the hall and found three seats, Kat with Mouse on one side of her, and Jagloran on the other.

How delightful. I have a man I do trust on either side of me, with no desire on my part to take advantage of either. She smiled to herself.

Kanorang was indeed talented. He sang a variety of songs, sometimes inviting the audience to join him in what were well-known tunes in Glowen. In between, he played a comprehensive variety of instruments, including three unusual woodwind types. He switched to two different drums to thump out a rich sensuous rhythm, while his listeners accompanied him with claps and pounding feet.

When the musician took his last bow, Kat rose and attempted to hide her yawn from her two companions. "I do believe I need to head for my bed. Goodnight to both of you."

Jagloran addressed Mouse. "We have been well met, Sire Mouse. On the morrow I must return to the Keep, but will travel around the headwaters of Hewder Dowron, and through the forests directly to Brennan's Keep." He performed the weird Rifellan hand shake thing, and faced Kat. "Kat, we have also been well met. I hope when you both return to the Keep, you will take the opportunity to visit me and Dayleeya at our quarters." He held her hand in both of his and bowed. "Travel well, and travel in safety."

As she and Mouse returned their rooms, she glanced back and waved farewell at Jagloran.

"I'll meet you for a morning meal, Mouse. But only after I've packed everything and sent my bags to the stable."

"I will most likely wake early as is my habit, so perhaps you will knock on my door when you are ready.

Kat yawned again. "Fine."

♋♋♋

Despite being so tired the night before, Kat woke bright-eyed and refreshed, as dawn colored the sky. She carefully stowed the Golden River containers, and the lip glosses, with the exception of the the one scented with nerthon blooms, in her luggage. The nerthon gloss she used leaving her lips feeling smooth and supple, and the eucalyptus smell energized her.

A young assistant arrived to pick up her baggage, and with that completed, she left her room for the dining lounge.

Mouse pored over his maps at a table for two, and as she approached, he raised his head and greeted her. "I ordered groonnan for you and fara tea. I also requested the innkeeper prepare some snacks for us for the journey to Tasik."

"This all sounds perfect. I'm looking forward to a leisurely trip to Tasik and am anticipating a day by the lake on the morrow."

As they ate their morning meal, Mouse briefly covered the ride to Tasik, and what they might expect from the resort town. The meal over, they exited the hall and wound their way to the stables.

Mouse loaded the baggage on the pack animal, and walked to his own horse, which the stable hand had saddled and bridled for him. He put his foot into the hand of the apprentice, and, using it as leverage, vaulted up to the saddle.

Kat used the stool, which gave her enough height to mount her animal with relative ease. "Mouse, these saddles you purchased from Bardu have proved themselves comfortable and easy to ride in. I'm glad you got them."

"Given the amount of riding we have accomplished, I do agree with you." He shifted and settled himself more comfortably. "The roadway is safe from here to Tasik. I suggest you lead."

Kat rode to the path and happily led Mouse and the pack animal.

A safe roadway, cool clothing, soft lips and energy to spare. What more might a woman want? She wriggled a little. *Well ... Liandock, of course..*

CHAPTER 25

Though the heat of the star beat down on them, a breeze from the east and Kat's loose clothing kept the ride reasonably comfortable. Soon they rode through the outskirts of the forest, and tall pine trees supplied much-appreciated shade.

She halted her horse in a clearing within the trees, and called to Mouse. "Let's stop here. The shade is more pleasant, and we can use that log as a seat." She pointed at a hefty log beside a small pool of water.

They stopped their horses, dismounted and tied the animals to nearby trees, after giving them an opportunity to drink from the pool.

Kat, stretched, walked over to the log, and sat.

Mouse, after fetching the snacks supplied by the innkeeper of Kamerdow, joined her.

"Do we have much farther to go?"

"No." Mouse picked up a stick and drew in the dirt. "Almost as soon as we exit the forest, we will come upon the village of Tasik, which lies between the trees and the shores of Lake Yuffern. The inn is located on the east side of the village, close to the lake."

Kat brightened. "Since we will arrive well before the time for our evening meal, can we swim in the lake, and enjoy our meal on the shore afterwards?"

"I have no information regarding this, but as soon as we arrive at the inn, I will inquire about the possibility."

♋♋♋

The two travelers arrived in Tasik, and Mouse arranged for the care and feeding of their mounts, while Kat accompanied the apprentice who carted their luggage to their rooms.

Inside her room, Kat set Wink's cage on the desk and unpacked the clothing she would need for the next two days. She waited for Mouse to advise her about a potential meal by the lake when a knock heralded his arrival.

"Kat, you are most fortunate. We may head for the lake as the innkeeper has supplied us with a ground covering for the shore, and he erected a small hut as a changing place. Before star set, he will have an apprentice deliver our meal to us. If you have bathing clothes ready, we may set out now."

"Perfect." Kat grabbed a bag containing a towel and the clothing she used as a swimsuit. "Lead the way."

They followed a cobbled pathway to Lake Yuffern, a long and narrow body of water, with waves whose ripples danced and glistened in the sun. Lake Yuffern was about half the size of Lake Glen Addie in Shendea. Kat hurried to the black and red hut perched on the edge of the beach so she could change and be first in the lake for a swim. Her suit was more in keeping with Kaylin modes of dress, and consisted of loose leggings and a top similar to a T-shirt, but with long sleeves.

She placed her regular clothes on a hook inside a closet, which she assumed was installed to keep street clothes dry. When she emerged to walk to the water, she noticed two rugs farther along the beach with what she assumed was clothing folded and piled on them. *I wonder why they don't have huts of their own?*

She ran into the lake. *Fabulous. It's beautifully warm.* She dived in and swam for a bit. Unfortunately, when the suit became soaked with water, she felt as if she were plodding through the water. Within minutes, Mouse joined her wearing a similar outfit.

She glanced at him. "The water's gorgeous. But one thing's missing." *Plus these damn suits are so heavy with cloth.*

Mouse frowned. "What?"

"Shade splashing us."

He smiled. "Ah, yes. Your invisible cat. The visit was amusing, but I prefer not to be splashed, so I do not miss her."

"This is intended to be the equivalent of a resort, and yet I see signs of only two other visitors. They also don't seem to use change huts."

"Well yes. The landlord told me how most Glowens use the lake. They do not use huts because they do not change into suits for swimming."

"What do you mean?"

"They … they wear no clothing to swim."

"Oh Mouse, why didn't you tell me? I could've swum without this darn suit, which is incredibly freeing." Freed from bulky clothing she'd be able to breathe, without being trapped by all that cloth.

An expression of horror twisted across Mouse's face. "Such a thing would be inappropriate, Kat. You and I do not—" He sputtered. "The people who swim in this way are bonded, and we most certainly are not."

"I wasn't intending to be naked in front of you, I would take precautions."

"I do not think, it would be wise at all." He still appeared horrified.

"How silly. Look down the beach. That man is emerging from the water, I can barely tell he is totally without clothing, and I'm not bonded with him either. If I take off this costume in the water, he'll never be able to see me."

"Kat, you cannot. You cannot appear without clothing in front of me. I am your guide."

"Mouse, I said I would not expose myself to you. I will take off my costume, but in the interest of propriety, you only need to face away from me. Let's be real. Since I'll be underwater you won't see me anyway."

"By Caleesh, I beg you not to remove your clothing."

"Too late." Kat had wiggled out of her costume and remaining submerged, held the pile of clothing out of the water. "Better turn around now, because I'm just going to throw my clothes on the beach, so I may have to jump a little. As to the other couples in the lake, they're so far away, I'm sure they can't see I'm not wearing clothes."

Beet red, Mouse turned away from her.

Kat leaped up slightly and threw the bundle of clothes at the rug. "Mouse, I'm submerged again, so you can safely face me. I promise to warn you if I need to stand."

Kat wiggled luxuriously in the water. *This feels glorious and free. The sensation of water on me is so delicious. I only wish LIandock was here instead of Mouse*. She swam around, delighting in the freedom of the water around every part of her body.

Although Mouse was facing her, he was still blushing and had increased the distance between them. "Kat, I would suggest you leave the lake and don your clothes now. The star is beginning to set, and the apprentices will soon be here with our food."

"Fine. Can't you get them for me?"

"Yes. Wait. I will leave the lake and get your swimming costume and bring it back so you can don it under water."

"Fine."

Mouse exited, reached the rug on the beach, and tossed Kat's wet swimming wear to her. He hurried to the hut to change back to his street clothes.

Kat struggled to pull the soggy bathing costume back on, bounced up and down in the water to get all the sand off her, and waited for Mouse to exit the hut. Once he did, she left the lake to change.

Dried and clothed, she stowed her wet bathing costume inside her bag, and walked down to the beach. Joining Mouse on the mat, Kat made herself comfortable and sat cross-legged, waiting for their food.

Two apprentices appeared from the direction of the inn, laden with dishes and serving platters. Mouse sitting opposite Kat, glared at her.

She sniffed at him. "I'm aware you're unhappy I swam without clothes." She grinned. "C'mon tell the truth. You never saw even a glimpse of me unclothed, so no one else could either."

Mouse opened and shut his mouth several times, but no sound emerged. Finally he found his voice. "You are being outrageous." He seemed unable to find a way to meet her eyes.

"Mouse, forgive me. I am teasing you a bit. Your world is so discomfited by brief attire, and bodies and customs, except in the case of the Glowens. And, to me, they go overboard. On my world many cultures have areas where they may swim or walk naked with each other, and it is not considered sexual." She shrugged. "I'm sorry if I embarrassed you."

Mouse regarded her closely. "You are such an odd woman. I can never anticipate what you will do or think of next. You are not an easy person to be with."

"I'm pretty normal for a person in my world: I enjoy life, I am strong and healthy, I find sex pleasurable, I delight in new experiences, I love to learn new things or to do them, and my body is just my body, and is nothing of which to be ashamed. I actually quite like it."

Mouse began to eat. To Kat, he appeared to prefer to keep occupied without talking.

He's being unreasonable. She was sure no one had glimpsed her unclothed. Kat stabbed at her food, annoyed at his apparent indifference. At last she rose and sniffed loudly. "I'm not terribly hungry. Excuse me, I'm going to my room. I suspect I'll eat my morning meal in private."

Still no reaction from Mouse.

She glared down at him. "If you wish, I will meet you for the mid-turn meal."

Mouse did not raise his head to her. "Fine."

Kat turned on her heel and walked back to the inn. She could not understand Mouse's reluctance to speak to her. She knew if he had been abler to see her, he might be embarrassed. She was convinced he had not.

Why'd he lose it? I didn't expect that of him. Maybe if Glowenr had seen me, I would've understood his annoyance.

CHAPTER 26

Mouse glared as Kat stomped off along the path toward the inn. He rubbed the area between his brows and growled. She claimed she wanted him to help her avoid socially awkward situations, and this turn she made the worst mistake ever. *Swimming naked. I am positive the Glowens will be convinced we are bonded.* He shook his head in frustration. *She seems convinced no Glowens saw her unclothed, but I am not.*

He rose from the mat, and picking up the bag containing his swimming gear, slowly trudged to his room. He was positive if the Glowens had seen her naked, they would assume Kat lied about her aversion to physical contact because she followed Kaylin customs. They are aware that Kaylins avoid contact between males and females before bonding.

He wondered what the actual outcome with their hosts would be. He entered his room and pulled at the tassel in the corner.

While waiting for the assistant to appear, he hung his wet bathing attire in the personal. The suit would dry overnight and could be re-packed on the morrow.

Mouse answered a knock at the door. "I would appreciate some tea with calming abilities. Do you have such a beverage in this inn?"

"Yes, Sire. We have kossil-kweth tea, which is distinguished for its calming and collected properties."

"Excellent. Would you bring me a container with enough to serve three people."

"I will. Do you wish three mugs as well?"

"No, only one."

The young man bowed and left.

Mouse walked around his room, clenching and unclenching his fists. He had assumed that at last Kat was becoming adjusted to Pridden customs, but she was as willful as ever.

A knock indicated the arrival of his tea, and he directed the assistant to set the tray on a table accompanied by two chairs.

"Thank you, apprentice." He locked the door once the young man departed.

Mouse sat at the table, poured a generous cup, and drank. He pinched the bridge of his nose, and breathed, aware of the relaxing effects of the beverage flowing through his body. He had almost finished his first cup, when a moth flew through the window and fluttered about his head. He reached up and captured the creature in his hand and brought the moth close to his ear.

Galdin's voice issued from the tiny messenger. "I understand you are now in Glowen, and I have received reports of the debacle in Rifella. The routing of my assassins, and the capture of my two allies was unforeseen and interfered with my plans. You are fortunate you are not in my presence. I am sorely tried by your incompetence. However, your are also fortunate I do not wish you to focus at this time on bringing the woman to me. To attempt to transport her to Morden from Glowen would prove to be foolish."

Mouse took the creature away from his ear. *By Caleesh, he continually rages at me.* He listened again to the moth.

Galdin continued. "I assume you will be traveling to Baklai next, and that would be a much easier place from which to bring her. Something has arisen which holds greater importance. I have been informed Glowen conceals a vitally important secret, which may be of more use than possession of the women. You are to concentrate on discovering the source and essence of this secret. Fail in this, and your days are numbered."

After delivering a message of this length, the moth fluttered and died in his hand. *Galdin has never been known to be brief.* He removed the bag of moths given him by Galdin and extracted another, which he brought to his mouth. "My Lord, Thane Galdin, I heard rumors of one, but as yet no one I have questioned is aware of such a secret, except they fear some thing or person. I will do everything in my power to learn the details." Mouse took the moth to the window and threw the creature into the air.

As the moth fluttered off, he followed its path with much trepidation. *I have no idea as to the actual secret, and as I told Kat, I am sure I do not wish to know anything about one either.*

He returned to the table and poured a second cup. He needed the tea twice as much as before. *I am not pleased with Eduardo. He is responsible for my disquiet, having saddled me with Galdin threatening death and Kat reverting to her stubborn refusal to obey Pridden's rules.*

He drank the tea and took another deep breath. Gradually, his anger about Kat's actions, and his fear for her, dissipated. Mouse pursed his lips. *What to do?* There was only one logical step. He would seek her out and explain he had become angry with her because he was worried about the ramifications of her actions among the Glowens.

As for Galdin, he would make a few more inquiries regarding the secret, but would not pursue the matter with too much depth. If Galdin wanted knowledge of what the Glowens were hiding, surely they would be in danger if he found out.

Mouse poured himself a third cup of tea. His mind now at ease, he yawned, and headed for his bed. He would need his sleep this night. He was not looking forward to the confrontation with Kat on the morrow.

Thank Caleesh. At least Galdin does not wish me to travel to Morden as yet.

CHAPTER 27

Kat rose early, and, after feeding Wink, showered and dressed for the day. She was up too early to head for the dining lounge, although she was hungry. Still frustrated from her argument with Mouse the evening before, she packed everything for the following morning. The ink was now dry on all her notes on the table, so she gathered her journal pages and stowed everything in her diplo bag. Aware Mouse intended them to leave on the morrow, packing now would be one less thing to do later on.

She wished they could leave this turn, because she was not looking forward to meeting with her angry guide. She wondered if they would continue their argument. Hunger forced her to obtain her meal in the dining lounge as opposed to waiting for one in her room. If Mouse was also there, she would have to deal with him sooner, rather than later. Steeling herself for the possible challenges, she exited her room and set off for the dining hall.

She paused at the doorway, but Mouse was not in the room. Conversation stopped when she entered, and all eyes turned toward her. Kat caught her breath. With a roomful of wolf eyes facing her, she headed for the nearest small table and sat. Their stares were more than unsettling, and she felt a frisson of fear crawl up her spine. An apprentice approached, a smirk on his face. "Do you wish a meal?"

It worried her that he was being so informal. "Yes, please. Groonnan and fara tea."

He nodded and swaggered off.

A Glowen approached, sat across from her, and attempted to take her hand, which she placed in her lap abruptly.

"You are a most pleasing woman. After your meal, you should join me in pleasure."

She shoved her chair backwards. "No." *What's going on?*

He sighed. "A shame. I seem not to be what you are looking for." He rose and walked away.

No sooner had he left when another took his place. He too attempted to take her hand and requested her presence for pleasuring. This time, she just shook her head, although, her insides twisted and she recoiled from him.

When a third Glowen reached out for her, tendrils of fear enveloped her. "Why can't you people leave me alone?" *It's too hot for my leathers, but they might have made me less enticing to these lechers.*

The man regarded her with astonishment. "You did not present yourself accurately. You claimed you adhere to Kaylin customs, but you bathed unclothed with the man you insisted was your guide. You would not have done so were you and he not bonded."

At this point Kat found she was surrounded by wolf eyes all staring in her direction, and the sense of entrapment was all encompassing. *How do they know?* She wished she had a concealing robe similar to what Mouse wore.

The man across from her stood. "Because your bonded one remained clothed, clearly you had not spoken the truth to us. We find it is now evident you do wish to join in our pleasuring, and the man you stated was your guide has stepped aside to allow this. The only option we see, is which of us will be fortunate enough to be the one chosen?"

Kat, unable to reply to this weird logic, rose from the table and ran for her room. *They could not have seen me unclothed in the water? It's impossible.* When she reached it, she slammed her door shut, and almost at once, a knock sounded. "Who is it?"

"Mouse."

She let him enter and closed and locked the door behind him.

"Kat, I have come to offer my apologies. I should not have shown such anger toward you."

"Please, you do not need to apologize. You were right." She shook her head and avoided looking at him. "What I cannot understand is how they know? How did they see me? I was positive they couldn't. You would think I would have learned by now your cautions regarding Priddanese customs are always correct. But I truly thought they could not see me unclothed in the water." She stared at his eyes. "I'm the one who should ask your forgiveness. I made a terrible mistake the previous evening."

Mouse blinked rapidly. "Why do you think that now?"

"Because of what just happened in the dining hall." She explained what the Glowens had done and said. "I became afraid." She paced the room. "From their words and actions, I began to believe they might force me to take part in what they refer to as pleasuring. It appeared I was not going to be allowed to have a choice except for which one." She stared at him again. "No women wishes to be the object of sex without her consent. I can handle myself, as you are well aware. But against thirty or forty men and women who were in the dining lounge? I was seriously outnumbered."

"I do not believe they would force you."

"Mouse, they said I had made the decision to be pleasured, and my only choice was with who. I still cannot understand how they knew I wore no clothes."

He rubbed at his brow. "Perhaps the situation is more serious than I believed." He barked out a demand. "How much packing do you have to accomplish?"

"I've packed everything. I sensed we might need to leave sooner than originally intended."

"After what happened to you in the dining lounge, we do. I too am packed. We must carry our own bags and go straight to the stables without informing anyone. I will obtain mine and join you."

After he left for his quarters, Kat gathered all her bags and joined Mouse as he exited his room, laden with his own baggage.

Silently, they hurried down the hallways, exited the inn and headed without pause to the stables. Luckily, no stable assistants were about. Once they arrived, Mouse loaded the baggage on the pack animal while Kat fetched their saddles and bridles. Mouse helped her saddle her animal and did the same for his own horse. They both put the bridles in place, and using a step stool, mounted, both panting with the hurried effort.

With Mouse in the lead, the packhorse attached to his saddle, and Kat following, they rode with haste toward Tavollen. Once Tasik was out of sight, Mouse stopped. He slid off his horse and indicated that Kat should do likewise. "We are in a most compromising situation. I would request we make use of Wink to send a message to Thane Brennan. Only he can help our situation."

"Fine. I'll get her cage."

"While I compose the note, perhaps you would fill our canteens. A trail to the left leads to the south edge of Lake Yuffern. Make sure you are not seen by anyone and return quickly."

Kat did as he asked, and when she returned with two full canteens, he requested she bring out Wink, along with a tube to hold the message. Mouse handed her the note, which she inserted in the tube and reached for the furry pyrock. "Wink, we need you to take a message."

The pyrock opened sleepy eyes, stretched, and held out a foreleg.

Kat attached the tube and gave her instructions. "Take this message to Thane Brennan please."

Wink stretched again and raised her wings. She leaped up, and popped out of existence.

Mouse breathed a sigh of obvious relief. "The message to Brennan should be of help. However, you have not eaten a meal, and we may not be able to enter Tavollen to assuage our hunger. The people there may be as angered as those in Tasik. Luckily, I have dried journeyklim in my bags. The flavor is pleasant, and the klim is filling." He dipped his hand into his satchel and brought out what appeared to be bread. He broke off a piece the size of his hand, and passed it to Kat. "Place this in your saddle-bag so you can reach it while you ride. We can pause here no longer."

Kat did so, and retied Wink's cage to her backpack.

Mouse held out his hands for her to place her left foot on. He threw her up as if she were weightless, and she landed perfectly in her saddle. *He never looks strong enough to do that.* She raised her pack from the saddle horn and fitted her arms through the straps, so that they rested without chafing on her back. When she glanced around, Mouse was mounted.

Before he took the lead, he turned to her. "We are headed for Tavollen, but I am not sure we will stop at the village. If Thane Brennan has not yet interceded on our behalf, Tavollen might prove unpleasant. My intent is to bypass the town and cross the Netht Dowron and proceed straight to the Keep."

"Do you think the people in Tavollen will know what I've done?"

"I am not sure, but news seems to travel quickly in Glowen."

"I will not argue with you. You are my guide and I truly do trust you."

Mouse chuckled.

"Why are you laughing? You should be pleased I trust you."

"I am. I am simply wondering how long this will last."

Kat held her tongue. *The problem is, he doesn't trust me. After last night I'm not surprised.*

CHAPTER 28

After a long day in the saddle, Pridden's star was perched on the horizon, ready to disappear for the night, when Mouse finally led them around the village of Tavollen. They rode directly for the bridge, clattered over the Netht Dowron, and down the road curving toward the Keep.

Wink popped into existence, and they stopped for a moment. Kat extracted the note from Wink, and placed her back in her cage. "I'll feed you when we arrive at the Keep. Be patient."

She handed the note to Mouse.

They rode on as he read it quickly. "Brennan says he will indeed intervene on our behalf with the citizens of Glowen. His wording indicates that he is not too pleased with us. I believe we have caused him much extra work."

"You mean I've caused him extra work."

"Your behavior has, yes, but I was not forceful enough to prevent you from the actions you took. I had no idea how seriously the Glowens would react, but I did suspect your actions would be observed."

"How did could you possibly know that? I did not see anyone who was in the position to view me."

Mouse shrugged and sighed. "I did not see anyone either. But I suspect that one is rarely unobserved.

"Do you think Brennan will eject us from Glowen?"

"I do not believe he will. He is aware how his people behave when confronted with the opportunity for pleasure.

He has learned to be more moderate because he does have to deal with the leaders from other lands."

"Mouse, I am so sorry I ignored your warnings. I should have suspected your concerns might carry danger. I promise I will make sure Brennan is aware the resulting situation was not of your doing."

"Despite what you may think of me from time to time, Kat, I am man enough to admit when I have made a mistake. I do not need you to attempt to protect me."

Oops, I think I stepped on a toe.

He shook his horse's reins to hurry it on. "Enough discussion for now. Brennan will meet with us on the morrow. We had best head for the Keep as soon as possible."

The star sank lower and lower, and was almost completely below the horizon as the two travelers approached the stables of Thane Brennan's Keep. The thudding of hooves on the packed ground of the stables must have roused the master, and he came out to greet them as Mouse slid from his horse.

"Sire Mouse, we received a message from our Thane you would be arriving. I will arrange for your horses to be fed and watered. My apprentice will deliver your baggage to your rooms within the Keep."

"My thanks, stable master."

Kat dismounted, backpack in place, and grabbed her diplo bag and long bow. "I'm truly exhausted. I assume we are still in the original rooms they provided for us?"

The master of the stable overheard her. "You are, Lady Kat. As you enter the Keep, Healer Marreth will meet you both to confirm everything for you."

"My thanks." Kat yawned and headed toward the Keep, her various bags were flung over her shoulder. She was tired, and everything felt heavy to her.

Mouse followed close behind, with his map bag slung across his chest, and he carried his own baggage.

Kat was only too glad to wait for hers to be delivered.

At the entrance, Marreth hurried toward them. "Welcome back. I gather you have had some challenges. I will escort you to your rooms. Have you had the opportunity to enjoy a meal?"

"Not a proper one. Mouse had some dried journeyklim with him, which proved filling. I don't need to eat, but I would like tea." She glanced back at him. "Do you want food?"

"I too have had sufficient journeyklim, but I would most certainly appreciate tea. Marreth, can we obtain kossil-kweth in the Keep?"

"Anything found anywhere on Glowen can be found in the Keep. I will stop in at the dining hall and request some be sent to your rooms. I am sure you can find your own way, since you are in the same rooms as before. I will meet with you both for the morning meal, and we will discuss your challenges during this visit through Glowen. Thane Brennan will be anxious to meet with you as well."

Mouse yawned. "We will see you on the morrow."

They continued down the halls, and Marreth left them at the entrance to the dining hall. Both gave her a wave, and Kat yawned again, this time so widely her jaw creaked.

As they arrived at their rooms, she and Mouse grunted at each other as both were so tired. No sooner were their doors open when two apprentices appeared bearing the tea they had requested, plus Kat's baggage.

Once in her room, Kat shoved a couple of treats through the bars of Wink's cage which she placed on the dresser. She took a gulp of tea, and then undressed and threw her clothes on a chair. She had a brief shower to wash off the dust of travel before sinking into her bed, too tired even to unpack to obtain a night-dress.

I hope Brennan will forgive my error and not report me to Eduardo, who would probably ...

♋♋♋

Kat woke in the middle of the night, aware that something was on her head, tangled up in her curls. She froze, not daring to move a muscle. Whatever the weight on her head, it did not move.

When she heard faint snores, she breathed a sigh of relief, and gingerly raised a hand and patted something furry and soft. When she touched the creature, a squeak emerged. "Wink. Way to give me a heart attack." She reached up and carefully extracted the pyrock from her hair, sat up in bed and examined the ball of fur in her hands. "What are you doing there? You can't be cold."

Holding Wink in one hand, she slid out of bed and walked over to the dresser. "Oh bother. I forgot to lock the cage door. But why would you want to sleep with me? I could roll over in the night and squish you."

Wink flapped her little wings and squeaked and chirped a few times. Sighing, Kat fed her a few treats, and placed her back in her cage, this time firmly locking the door.

The tea still sat on the table, the cup almost full. She drained the contents. "Only lukewarm, but it'll help me go back to sleep."

She burrowed in among the covers, and dropped off.

If Brennan reports me to Eduardo, how will I get home? Why do these people make things so difficult ...

CHAPTER 29

Sounds of the Keep coming to life woke Kat the next morning: voices and hammering from somewhere, heavenly smells coming from the kitchens, axes chopping at wood, further off, the clattering of horses hooves on wooden walkways, and bits and pieces of conversations.

She was stiff because they rode a fair distance the turn before without the opportunity to walk and warm her muscles. She stretched and groaned contentedly, and this helped loosen her body. Luxuriating under warm water, and some more stretches aided in restoring her normal fluid self.

Finally, fully awake and dressed in clothing suitable for meeting with Brennan, she proceeded to the dining hall. As she passed Mouse's quarters, he appeared, and they walked to the lounge together. Mouse entered without stopping, but she hesitated a moment until Marreth waved at them and Kat followed Mouse to the table.

Marreth stood and gave Kat a hug. "You both appear well rested, so shall we order our meals before we discuss your journey?"

"Yes please. I'm starving, since I didn't eat anything last evening."

Mouse nodded his agreement.

Marreth called over a serving assistant, and placed an order for the three of them.

Kat eyed her curiously. "You hugged me. Won't the Glowens decide you are indulging in some weird pleasuring?"

Marreth laughed. “Not at all. They are well aware I am a healer. They have also accepted all healers are required to use physical healing techniques which have nothing to do with pleasure. I began a rumor to suggest hugs are a most important and effective healing application.”

Kat chuckled. “In truth, they are. On my world when someone is sad, a hug is beneficial. How clever of you though to turn your knowledge of the Glowens’ ways into a benefit for your calling.”

“The Glowens have a very rigid idea of what pleasure should be, and as you and Mouse have discovered, if you are not conversant with the exact ways in which they apply their logics, you will run afoul of their ways, in the same way as you ran into trouble with the Kaylins when you accidentally exposed your legs.”

Kat laughed. “I assume Wynneth told you about that.”

“She did. Wynneth knows everything that happens in Kaylin.”

A young serving man delivered their meals, along with a huge pot of fara tea and three mugs. Talk ceased while they dug into their food.

Kat finished first and turned to Mouse. “Shall I tell Marreth what happened?”

“Yes. I am almost finished, so I will fill in details.”

“Initially, I was taken aback by the way the Glowens, more often the men than the women, took every opportunity to touch me and suggest sexual liaisons. They apparently had difficulty in understanding I have Mouse as my guide, not a bonded mate. To them, that a man and a women might have a platonic relationship, appeared unthinkable. Mouse explained to them I was sent by Lord Eduardo of Kaylin, and I had accepted Kaylin ways.”

The healer did her best to hide a smile.

"Marreth, I understand I don't adhere to Kaylin ways, as you pointed out when referring to the 'leg' scandal. I'm not a prude, but constantly being harassed by these people was neither flattering nor pleasant. However, they seemed to be determined I would be part of their sexual scenario whether I wished this or not. My only choice appeared to be who."

Marreth grimaced. "I should have warned you. The Glowens in the northern area are overt in the extreme. Perhaps we should have sent out an announcement about your arrival, and that you are in Glowen on behalf of Lord Eduardo of Kaylin. Our only defense is we are not accustomed to people from other worlds, and those from other lands are not accustomed to the Glowens."

"The announcement might have helped."

Mouse chimed in. "I did my best to explain to them that Kat was not one to indulge in indiscriminate pleasuring, and I had been assigned a job to guide her by Eduardo. Initially this appeared to help."

"Mouse did an excellent job. The number of sexual advances reduced. I unwittingly exacerbated the problem when we arrived in Tasik, and I decided to bathe in Lake Yuffern without clothes."

"Oh dear, what happened?"

Kat explained to Marreth. "The other people were so far away, I twas convinced they couldn't possibly know I was naked. I thought I was safe."

Mouse interjected. "I explained to Kat that I suspected only bonded couples, or those who had accepted another for pleasuring, were allowed to swim unclothed. I now understand she was absolutely convinced we were far enough away from the others in the lake so they would be unable to catch sight of her."

Kat sighed. "Of course, I couldn't stay in long, because apprentices would be delivering our meal. Mouse bought my suit to me which I put on under the surface. From then on, I was dressed. How could anyone have seen me unclothed?"

Mouse shook his head. "I admit, Marreth, I was furious with Kat. I was positive she had placed us in an untenable situation."

"Mouse is right. I had dumped us squarely in a huge pile of excrement, because on the following morrow, I was cornered by Glowens seeking pleasure with me, and when I refused, they became angry. They said I had lied to them, and Mouse and I were indeed bonded. I fled to my room, told Mouse what happened, and we left without hesitation."

Mouse scowled. "We stopped briefly to send a message via Kat's pyrock to Thane Brennan asking for his help."

The healer regarded them with worried eyes. "No wonder you fled. Well, Brennan wishes to hear your story from the two of you and has requested you meet in his private dining room for a mid-turn meal. I will come for you when we need to attend him."

They all rose, and Mouse headed for his quarters.

Kat held back. "Marreth may I come to your room? I have something to discuss with you."

"We can go now, if you wish."

"Yes, this is important."

Marreth led the way to her rooms, unlocked her door, and ushered Kat inside. She tugged on the tassel and, when the apprentice appeared, ordered fara tea. She and Kat sat at the small table in the corner. "While we are waiting for the refreshments, Kat, tell me what do you think of your experiences in Tasik?"

"I'm confused. I was out of control from the constant pressure of all the men to desire everyone as sexual companions. A few women also approached me—but both the males and to a lesser degree, the females made me feel I was being coerced. I rarely talk about it, but I have problems trusting men at the best of times, and these were not the best of times. Now I'm less likely to trust males than before."

At this point the apprentice delivered their tea and cookies, and Marreth poured them each a cup. "You wanted to talk about something. What is on your mind?"

Kat cleared her throat, and shifted awkwardly in her chair. "I'm pretty sure I have knowledge of the Glowen secret."

Marreth backed her seat away from the table. "No Kat, do not put any thought into this, and absolutely never talk about it. I do not wish to have any notion of this, if one exists. Please, do not tell me anything."

"I wasn't intending to tell you, but I was considering I should tell Mouse since he has been my guide through four lands. I believe I have an obligation to share the secret with him."

Marreth stared at Kat, horror etched over her face. "Do not tell Mouse. Do not do him such a disservice. If such a secret exists, admit this to no other person. I have seen other Glowens disappear if they mentioned the words 'Glowen's secret'. This is something Glowens never discuss. Something about these words heralds danger." She leaned toward Kat. "I beg you. Keep any knowledge of this locked away."

Kat raised her hands as if to ward off Marreth. "Stop. I promise not to speak of this to you again." She rose and headed to the door. "I will return to my rooms to prepare to meet Brennan for our noon-turn meal."

As she was exiting the room, Marreth called out to her. "Remember do not speak of any of this. Keep your thoughts and words to yourself, and your knowledge unspoken."

"I understand what you're saying, Marreth."

Nevertheless, she is wrong. He deserves to know. The Sha-hee hinted I might consider telling him. I'm convinced it's not right to keep Mouse in the dark. He would never reveal what he knows.

CHAPTER 30

Kat left Marreth in a state of dismay, fled to her own room, and locked herself in. She understood the Sha-hee wished to keep their existence a secret, because of the potential challenge to their lives. But had they not hinted she might tell Mouse? What was so curious was how Glowens managed to be unaware of them. What was even odder was that the word secret was synonymous with danger.

She walked down the hall and stopped at the entrance to Mouse's quarters. She knocked, and he opened the door, and seemed surprised at her appearance.

"Kat? What can I do for you?"

"I was hoping we might have a talk before we meet with Thane Brennan. I want to make sure we are consistent in our stories to him." *An excellent excuse to speak with him.*

"Fine, I will come to your room, since my maps and instructions are spread all over. We can discuss this if you wish. However, provided we both relay the truth, I can distinguish no reason why our recounting of the incidents should not be consistent." He followed her to her room and entered and prepared to seat himself at the small table in the corner. "Let me first call for tea, so we can relax while we review what happened." He tugged at the tassel in her room.

Almost immediately, an apprentice appeared, and Mouse ordered tea. "I believe we should be dressed in comfortable and casual clothes. I am not sure how Brennan will react when we give him the details of what occurred, but I do believe he will be less likely to be angered if we refrain from being formal."

"I agree. Marreth told us before our first meeting with Brennar, the Glowens are not formal people. The people in Kadwee and Tasik confirmed that."

"I am still a little surprised you took such offense at their attempts to seduce you. I had assumed you were not a stranger to such efforts from men in general."

A knock at the door indicated their tea had arrived. The apprentice placed the pot and mugs on the table and left silently.

Kat poured two cups, took a sip from hers, and placed it back on the table. "To answer your question, I am used to men flirting and acting seductively toward me. I am young, not unattractive, and I'm a in a profession on my world that consists primarily of males. This can be flattering. But to have every single person, even the women, in an entire room staring with obvious lust at me was not flattering." She grimaced. "On my world, when a man makes a comment about his desire for a woman, with open admiration, the words or gazes he imparts are pleasant and make the woman feel admired. But the Glowens, when they stared at me with their wolf eyes—their gazes are almost feral. and I sensed I was more like a victim, which is not a usual sensation for me." She shuddered.

"I had no idea you experienced their attentions in this way. I only knew you were uncomfortable, but I did not realize the depth of your emotion. I apologize for the misunderstanding."

"Mouse you don't need to apologize. How might you understand what was in my mind at the time? The weird thing is I was not wearing seductive clothing in any way. I had considered wearing my Rifellan leathers, but the temperature was so high, I would have drowned in my own sweat."

Mouse rubbed his forehead. "You might consider wearing your leathers for the rest of the trip through Glowen."

"An excellent idea. I'll adjust them in the same way Jagloran did. Except I'll wear the cool shirt under the armored top. And instead of wearing the leather leggings, I'll wear loose long pants. I'll appear to be wearing full leathers, but I'll still be able to keep relatively cool." She cocked her head at Mouse. "You wear your long grey robes in all weather. I am sure they are warm enough when it's cool, but how have you fared in our trip around the northern area of Glowen?"

"The only time when my robes were not warm enough, if you recall, was the trip to Lord Rhognor's Keep. As for keeping cool, you might remember from our clash with the birds near the caves on Krugg Menyd, the cloth in my robes is strong. However, the fabric still breathes and allows air flow. Plus, because of the volume of my robes, I am protected from the burning rays of our star."

"Had I known how comfortable you are able to be in your robes, I would have requested them from you. They would have kept me cooler and also might have protected me better from the lascivious advances of the Glowens. Is it possible to obtain a robe like yours?"

"If you will give me permission to send your pyrock to Walden, I will request if we can have a set of robes fashioned for you. One thing, grey is reserved only for me. They will need to be a different color."

"I don't want to use any color used by the Shendeans, and black reminds me too much of the Assassins' Guild. Perhaps a golden brown?"

"Brown should be fine. Can you call your pyrock to come to you here?" He prepared a note for Walden and placed it in a tube.

"I think so." Kat closed her eyes and concentrated on calling Wink to come to her. A sudden squeak and a fluttering of wings, confirmed the little creature had come at Kat's bidding. "Wink, thank you for coming. We are going to give you a message to take to Walden in Shendea." She took the tube from Mouse to affix to Wink's leg. Once tied in place, Kat thought of Walden and tossed Wink in the air. The little creature flapped her wings and disappeared with a pop.

Mouse sat back. "You wished us to confirm what we would pass on to Brennan. Give me your thoughts."

"I think you should handle the actual interview, but make sure you place the blame for my nakedness firmly on my shoulders."

Mouse grinned. "I do not believe your shoulders were what caused the challenge."

"Don't start with me, Mouse. Please convey a little of what I've explained to you today about what I experienced from the Glowen's pursuit of me."

"I am aware of what you wish me to say. I will do as you ask. Are you complete? I ask because I wish to meditate before we meet with Brennan."

"One more thing." Kat leaned on the table and placed her chin on her clasped hands. "I believe there is something you are entitled to be privy to."

Mouse gave a puzzled frown. "Indeed?"

Kat opened and closed her mouth several times and finally blurted out what she was attempting to say. "I know what the Glowen secret is."

Mouse jumped to his feet, his chair falling over as he rose, and backed away,. "Stop!"

Kat stared at him open-mouthed.

Mouse kept backing away from her. "Do not say another word."

"But —"

"I said not another word. I do not wish to be apprised of this."

Kat held out her hand in confusion. "Mouse —"

"You must not say anything more, nor mention the word. I wish to be kept in ignorance." His voice had lowered to a hiss, and anger flashed from his eyes. "I mean it, Kat."

Kat closed her mouth and swallowed. "What —"

"You must not mention this to anyone, and if you ever … ever mention this to me once more, I will abandon you in this land, and you will never set eyes on me again."

At his words, Kat's stone in her pendant turned icy cold. She clutched at her chest, afraid of what he was suggesting.

He turned and strode from her room, slamming the door behind him.

Kat rose from her seat and stood in shock staring at the door. *What the? I've never seen Mouse so furious. He was like a wild beast. And my stone confirmed danger.*

♋♋♋

Mouse strode down the hall, entered his room, and slammed and locked the door. He shook from the surge of adrenaline, caused by fear, not anger, which hit him when Kat uttered her words. He would not be able to explain to he that her knowledge contained the potential to place her in abject danger. He regretted that he had exploded like the Burning Rock Mountain in Shendea, instead of explaining the peril in which she had placed herself.

Kat, Kat, Kat. I must now cause myself to forget I ever perceived the word secret linked to your name.

He paced the floor in his room, slowly willing the fear to drain away. He had to protect her from Galdin. Galdin not only wanted her for some foul ritual, but he knew, now he would want her for the Glowen secret.

Marreth will be coming for us to join Brennan for a mid-turn meal. I must calm myself and clear my mind of what I have experienced.

He pulled the upholstered chair to face the window, and grabbed the padded cover from the bed. He wrapped himself in the comforter, settled in the chair, breathed to clear his mind, and drifted through the higher realms.

Peace. Peace.

CHAPTER 31

Kat, beside herself after the clash with Mouse, needed to calm down. First, she indulged in a warm comfortable shower, massaged herself with essentials oils of lavender, and dressed in her comfortable but conservative clothing, ready to meet with Brennan.

To assure her thoughts were calm and collected, she settled down for a meditation in an overstuffed chair in front of a well-padded footstool. This allowed her to concentrate on calming her mind and put the veil in place, knowing she would be ready when Marreth came for her.

The knock at Kat's door roused her from the soothing state of mind. She concealed her dagger under her belt, and covered it with a colorful scarf she'd purchased in Rifella. She knew she would be safe with Brennan, but she was uneasy now in Glowen.

She greeted Marreth and walked through the hall to the room occupied by Mouse. A knock by the healer, and he exited his room to join them.

As they approached the entrance to Brennan's private quarters, Marreth stepped forward to announce them to the guards.

Mouse turned and looked at Kat for the first time since meeting them again in the hall. "Kat, my apologies for losing my temper in such a severe manner after our morning meal. I did so because I worried so much for your safety, I lost my sense of balance. I do beg of you, never mention the word again, to me or to anyone else. I fear for the danger this might cause you."

"Thank you for your apology. Your rage surprised me, and scared me a little. I have never seen you lose such control before. I'm persuaded your warnings are justified. I had no idea it put me in danger. I give you my word, my lips are sealed." *I'm still burdened with the secret on my own.*

Mouse exhaled in apparent relief. "This eases my mind. I thank you."

Marreth came walking back toward them. "We are invited to enter." She led them into Brennan's private room, and bowed her head to the Thane. "Sire Brennan, I bring you Lady Kat and her guide, Sire Mouse."

Uh oh, she's being most formal. Mouse and I are in trouble.

"Thank you Healer Marreth. You are not required to stay." Brennan's mouth was firm, but his eyes twinkled.

What's going on? How did he make his wolf eyes seem like they're laughing?

Marreth bowed again and exited.

The Thane clapped his hands, and two apprentices appeared carrying jugs filled with a clear beverage. "Orenberry wine will serve us while we discuss your predicament. I have arranged for the meal to be delivered once our discussion is complete."

The apprentice poured a mug of the beverage for Brennan and deposited one jug on his left. The other apprentice placed a jug beside Mouse's mug and another next to Kat's. Both silently left the room.

Brennan lifted his mug and gulped a huge draught of liquid. "Drink."

Mouse wasted no time and poured wine into his mug.

Kat poured hers and took a cautious sip. Though not strong, the wine flavored with something like strawberries tickled the palate. Relieved the wine was well watered, Kat took another sip. She needed to keep her head clear and her mind focussed.

Brennan took another gulp of his wine and leaned back in his chair. "I must be told the exact details of what occurred in both Kadwee and Tasik. Please relate everything to me, clearly and with precision, Lady Kat."

"Um … wouldn't this be better to get the information from Mouse, since he is my guide?"

"On the contrary. I suspect, because he is your guide and Eduardo assigned him to protect you, he would shoulder the blame for all that happened. I want your report."

A trickle of sweat ran down her spine. She had counted on Mouse taking on much of the responsibility without her having to shift the cause to herself. *Damn, damn, damn.* "Well, the residents of Kadwee, particularly, are quite forward in their intentions. I felt backed into a corner." She shivered, remembering, and explained the details to Brennan. "Luckily Mouse explained to those in charge, I adhered to Kaylin mores, and Glowen overtures upset me."

"Did this solve the situation?"

"Generally, yes, although the people were unable to understand how two might travel together without a bond between them. The concept of guide appeared foreign to them."

Brennan leaned on his elbow, his hand covering his mouth. "I understand."

Puzzled, Kat stared at him. Was Brennan smiling?

He cleared his throat a couple of times, rubbed at his forehead, and raised his eyes to Kat. "Explain what happened at Tasik."

Kat lowered her head in embarrassment. She told Brennan how she had decided to swim in the nude, despite Mouse's warning against it. "Mouse threatened to leave me if I did anything so foolish again."

"So what happened?"

Kat relayed how the Glowens expressed anger toward her, and because she felt unsafe, she fled to her room and met with Mouse, and, they left for Tavollen immediately.

Brennan eyed Mouse. "Is that when you sent me the pyrock message?"

Mouse nodded.

Brennan continued to regard Mouse. "Is what Lady Kat told me accurate?"

"Yes, but—."

Brennan cut him off with a gesture. He looked from one to the other, and roared with laughter.

She and Mouse gaped at each other. Had Brennan gone mad?

At last, Brennan stopped laughing, wiping the tears of mirth from his eyes. "This is one of the funniest stories of outsiders falling afoul of our way of life. Unfortunately, your challenge was instigated by your actions, Kat. I will send out information that you flouted our unsaid rules, because you thought you were required to swim naked to honor the Glowens. You will be at the base of a number of humorous stories, but you will no longer be subject to my people's desire to couple with you."

He chuckled, shaking his head. "My people are bound in their ways, and like those in other lands have difficulty changing their outlook. In one way, you gave our people a clearer example of how the lack of knowledge that outsiders have for the Glowens can cause problems. No doubt, this will serve us well in the future, and despite what you thought, you would never be forced to enter a relationship with anyone. You have uncovered one minor challenge. The theft of your bracelet. However, I am sure we will eventually solve this ourselves." He clapped his hands, and two apprentices entered bearing platters of food and more jugs of wine.

The smells arising from the dishes, and the flavors resembled ambrosia. During the meal, the three enjoyed funny stories of others who made assumptions of the Glowens, and all three asked questions of each other to add to their knowledge of Pridden. Most of Brennan's questions centered around the world Kat claimed as home.

The meal over, Mouse requested they head for their rooms, because they planned to continue on their journey through the southern part of the island.

Brennan, still chuckling occasionally, agreed they should set out on the next part of their journey on the turn following the morrow.

Kat returned to her room and updated her writings. She made sure to record the situation she unwittingly created by swimming naked in Lake Yuffern. When she perused her unusual word list, she realized she had not added anything since leaving Rifella.

She pinched the bridge of her nose, thinking hard to come up with an interesting word. She rubbed her wrist absentmindedly, missing her pink bracelet. "I've an idea. Purloined. The perfect word." Her bracelet had been stolen, and purloined meant something looted. She hardly intended to use the word, because she thought of it as old-fashioned, but it was a good addition to her list. She added some words in Priddanese to her list, so that she could ask Mouse how to write them correctly in the language of Pridden.

Although she wasn't that hungry, she decided to call on Mouse to join her for a light evening meal. She left her room and strolled down the hall to Mouse's quarters.

"Excellent idea, Kat. I considered coming to ask you the same question. I will obtain the map for the southern part of the island, so I can show you the route."

They walked to the dining lounge, entered, and found a table.

They had almost completed their meals when a voice called out, "Kat."

Kat glanced toward the entrance to the lounge. *Oh no. Tessia.*

The young woman, accompanied by a familiar Glowen man, rushed over to their table. "My female parent is well again, and I checked with Thane Brennan, and he gave me permission to travel with you to our family village of Godron House. But I must tell you I am most unhappy with you."

Mouse, rose and invited the two to sit at their table. His face remained blank, completely free of expression. *Poor Mouse is not happy with the appearance of Tessia either.*

She peered at the Glowen, ignoring Tessia. "We've met before, haven't we?"

He smiled and, reaching for her hand, bent forward. "We met when you disembarked from your sailing vessel. I do apologize. I misinterpreted your challenges after a rough trip from Rifella. I am Emrys pen Godron, and am sibling to Tessia's male parent." He lowered his head and kissed the back of Kat's hand.

Before he might attempt to take a further liberty, Kat removed her hand from his.

"Yes I remember, but I was still quite ill from the effects of the voyage."

Tessia flounced into the seat beside Kat. "I said I am unhappy with you."

Kat sighed. "Oh, why?"

"You indicated to me only a slight acquaintance with Lord Eduardo, but from what I was told about your conduct at Tasik, obviously you and he enjoy a much closer relationship than I imagined." She frowned at Kat. "Do the two of you possess an agreement to bond at a later date?"

Kat sniffed in annoyance. "Tessia, I told you before. Eduardo asked me to perform a chore for him. Nothing more."

Tessia opened her mouth to speak again.

Kat held up her hand. "I said, Tessia, Eduardo and I are friends. I do not wish to speak of this again."

Emrys patted Tessia's arm and shook his head at her. *At least one person is listening to me.*

Kat rose and addressed the young woman. "There is much to complete on the morrow, so kindly excuse us. We will no doubt meet with you so we can finalize the details of our journey to Tavollen and Aythin."

Emrys rose and bowed to Kat. "Indeed, we look forward to seeing you on the morrow." He turned to Tessia. "We should order our own meals now."

Mouse followed Kat from the dining lounge. "Well handled. Although, do remember that for some reason,

Brennan favors Tessia." He shrugged. "I suggest we attend to our packing and any last-minute details on the morrow, Kat."

"I plan to. I will consume my morning meal in my rooms, and then I must deal with some items in the market. I suspect Tessia may track me down and will want to have a mid-turn meal. I will spend the time after the meal packing and preparing to leave. I assume we will meet for the evening meal to discuss anything else?"

"I do understand some challenges will arise when traveling with Tessia, but she is of obvious importance to Brennan, and I suspect we will only need to spend about seven turns in her company. Do your best to tolerate her."

Kat laughed at him. "You are attempting to tell me to be patient. Correct?"

Mouse nodded. "I am. But please do take note, I am not lecturing you as you once complained about." He smiled and opened his door and went in.

Kat crossed the hall and unlocked hers and slipped inside.

No matter what Mouse says. The girl is tiring.

CHAPTER 32

An emphatic knock woke Kat. She blinked, and yelled out, "Who's there?"

A rather piercing voice called back, "Tessia. I have come to take you to your morning meal."

"One moment." Kat jumped out of bed, grabbed a robe, and tromped over to the door, which she opened a sliver. She squinted at the young women. "Tessia, I'm not planning on consuming my morning meal in the lounge. I shall order what I need in my room. Afterwards, there are some items I need to attend to. But I will, if you wish, join you for a mid-turn meal in the market."

"That would be excellent, Kat." She hesitated. "Could we perhaps enjoy a tea in your rooms now?"

"No." Kat wafted her hand toward her clothing. "I am still attired in my nightwear, and I must spend some time alone. I will meet you at the market for the mid-turn meal."

She closed the door firmly, and heard Tessia scuff her feet down the hallway.

Kat fed Wink, stroked her, and placed her back in her cosy bedding. She indulged in an invigorating shower, and dressed in long black pants and the top of her Rifellan leathers, covered by a light black shirt.

She tugged at the tassel and, when the apprentice arrived, requested a small amount of groonnan and tea.

The young apprentice delivered her meal quickly.

After eating, Kat wrote briefly about the Sha-hee, without naming them, in her journal and finally, departed for the market. Leaving the inner part of the Keep, she headed for the section where the artisans displayed their wares. Garren pen Darryn was setting out glass objects in his display cabinet.

He waved her over, a beaming smile on his face. "Lady Kat, welcome. Can I supply you with tea?"

"Good morrow, Garren. I would enjoy sharing tea with you. But should you not be blowing glass?"

"Our market is closed one turn out of every seven, which was the previous turn. I always shut down the kiln during such a time, so now I am waiting for the oven to re-heat." His eyes twinkled at her. "I cannot imagine a better way to wait than to enjoy tea and a conversation with you." He reached for her hand, led her through the split in the counter and seated her at the table for two inside his booth. Before he released her, he gave her hand a feathery kiss.

Whew. Something is so compelling about him. He has a definite effect on me in some way. She grinned at him. "Glowens are so outrageous in the way they amuse themselves with women. But you, Garren, are far more adept at how you tease me."

He laughed. "On the contrary, my Lady, the only person I am teasing, is myself. You are a most compelling woman and one with whom I would be delighted to enjoy many things. However, sadly, I am aware your heart leans in a different direction."

She stared at him, astonished. *Did he read my mind?* She imagined the veil slamming shut over her thoughts.

"You possess an interesting talent, Kat."

Uh Oh. "Talent?"

"Yes. A moment ago, you clouded your senses even more from me. I am aware of no others who possess such an ability."

She put extra effort into the veil. *Who and what is this man?* "Garren, can you read my mind?"

"No one can read minds. I simply received sensations from you of someone of importance in your life. But oddly, you managed to cloud those senses. I am not sure if you did this deliberately."

"No one can do such a thing any more than you can read minds." She chuckled. "I must ask you something."

"Ask me anything you wish."

"You resemble most Glowens, except your eye color is different. Yours are brown, not like those of a wolf."

He wrinkled his brow at her. "What is a wolf?"

"They are animals from my world, similar to the hounds on yours. But they are bigger and stronger, and they hunt in groups. Many fear them, but if left alone, they avoid people. They truly are magnificent creatures."

"They sound almost dangerous."

"They can be."

"To answer your question. My male parent had brown eyes, and his parent also. As far as we understand, the males in our family have always possessed brown eyes."

"Interesting. I asked you when we first met if you are a Wielder."

"I said at the time, and repeat myself, I have heard the word, but I am not familiar with what a Wielder is, and I doubt I am one."

"No matter what you call this, Garren, you posses a power of some sort, and I wish to ask you a favor."

"I will do whatever I can for you, Lady Kat."

"I am here on a mission for Lord Eduardo, who has promised to help me return to my own world if I uncover certain challenges in Pridden. I also need to find in the lands of Pridden, those who are powerful enough, when combined, can help me to return home. Will you be one of those who will help me, Garren pen Darryn?"

"I am not aware if I can supply the power you wish, but for you, I am willing to try."

"Thank you." Kat glanced out at the market and spotted Tessia wandering among the stalls. *I don't want her seeing me with Garren.* "Please excuse me Garren, but I see someone I am attempting to avoid. Hopefully we will speak later before I leave Glowen."

"I anticipate, with pleasure, our meeting again."

Kat rose, took his hand in both of hers and smiled at him again. She slipped out from the booth, and wandered toward the food section of the market.

Tessia called her name.

Kat stopped, turned, and, waving at the young woman, waited for her.

As soon as she caught up, Tessia began chattering. Kat barely listened her, so involved was she in her contemplation of Garren and his possible power and the charisma he exuded as a strong commanding male.

"—so do you agree?"

"I'm sorry, Tessia, I got distracted by the glorious aroma coming from the booth to our left, and I missed what you said."

"I want you to tell me when you will be in Lord Eduardo's company again. I am not sure you and he are only friends. Such a thing is so difficult for us Glowens to believe."

"Tessia. What more can I say? You are aware Mouse and I are friends. I believe he and Eduardo are friends."

"You never use his title when you speak of him. I suspect that is more than friendship."

"You Glowens are not that formal. In other lands, when people become friends, they drop formality as well. I'm telling you again, Eduardo and I are friends. Only friends." Kat shook her head in frustration. She sniffed the air. "I like the aromas coming from that stall. I will order from them. What about you?"

"Fine."

They ordered and sat at a nearby table to await delivery of their food. When the meal arrived, Kat, who had only consumed a small amount of food in the morning, applied herself with gusto to the delicious concoction, once again not cognizant of what Tessia chattered about. Hearing the odd word, she answered in monosyllables and the annoying Tessia hardly noticed Kat's inattention.

Finally, their meal completed, Kat rose. "Tessia, I need to prepare so much for us to leave on the morrow because we will not be returning to the Keep. I am obliged to complete enough chores to keep me busy until after the evening meal. However, I will meet with you on the morrow for our morning feed, and I'm sure Mouse will supply some final instructions for you. Emrys will be accompanying you, am I correct?"

"Yes. Emrys and I are returning to Godron House, and we will be preparing there for our eventual trip to Kaylin."

"Excellent, we'll meet again on the morrow." Kat hurried toward the Keep, and set off for her quarters.

When she gained entrance to her room, she packed everything. After feeding Wink, she knocked on Mouse's door, to ask for his help in sending a note to Merrindock of Pakanna, the prefect in charge of armor creation. She wished to ask Merrindock to deliver her amor to the harbor master in Baklai.

He invited her in and wrote the note for her. Mouse pointed out the Pridden words and what they meant.

Kat thanked him and headed back to her quarters. She placed the note in a tube, attached it to Wink and sent the little creature on her way.

Kat added the words Mouse had shown her, to her translations of Priddanese writing. Still amazed at Brennan's reaction to their challenges with the Glowens, Kat pondered his words. *Come to think of it he is correct, that I may not have been in danger. My pendant never grew cold as cold as it might have. Perhaps I would not have been forced.* She rubbed her forehead, and thought how old experiences still haunted present happenings. She shivered when she remembered the actions of her husband's cousin, Maxwell.

She considered all that had occurred since arriving in Glowen, and realized her stone had not truly warned her of danger with the Sha-hee either.

I haven't been paying enough attention to the pendant Liandock gave me. She drew the stone from her clothing and inspected the necklace in the mirror. Instead of a glorious brilliant emerald, the poor stone hung lifeless and pale green around her neck. *I've neglected you. Liandock told me how to reenergize you.*

She treated herself to a warm aromatic shower, and when finished, she massaged her entire body with silky scented creams.

She tapped the globes in the room to dim the light. From her largest bag she withdrew the lip glosses, unwrapped with care the one that contained scented ritual, and applied a small amount to her lips. She rewrapped the gloss up again as the sensual waves of arousal hit her. She sank on her bed, naked—ready for pleasure.

I'll imagine Liandock is here.

♋♋♋

Languid and limp, she drifted into sleep. A knock at her quarters roused her. "Who is it?"

"Mouse. Would you join me for an evening meal?"

She called back to him. "Yes. I needed a nap, so I will meet you in the dining hall after I change my clothes."

"Fine."

Kat sat up and stretched luxuriously. *I feel terrific.* She rose from the bed and sauntered over to the mirror. The stone glowed a brilliant emerald, deep and achingly beautiful. Kat stared at her own reflection. Her skin shone, and beamed with health.

She grabbed another quick shower to wash off the remnants of the scented ritual aroma and hummed a tune to herself as she dressed in the long black pants and soft silky shirt. She brushed her tangled curls, applied the nerthon lip gloss, and set off for the dining lounge.

The moment she walked through the entrance, Mouse hailed her from a table for four, with Jagloran seated beside him.

She smiled and sauntered to the table. Both men regarded her with puzzled expressions.

Jagloran stood and held a chair for her. "You appear well rested."

Mouse peered at her. "More than well rested. I would add, most energetic."

"I am. I used the lip gloss with nerthon scent. It's intended to supply energy."

Mouse caught the attention of an apprentice and ordered for the three of them.

Jagloran leaned over to Kat. "You used the scented ritual, did you not?"

"What makes you say that?"

"The aroma no longer lingers, but your lips are fuller. I remember telling you my Dayleeya appreciates this particular result from it."

"Please let this remain between us."

Jagloran chuckled. "I am bonded. You and I are friends. And I do not gossip."

The three spent a delightful time at the evening meal, but eventually Mouse rose. "Kat, we must leave early to be in Aythin before dusk. We should complete our packing so we can depart soon after the morning meal. I will send a message to Tessia and Emrys to meet us early."

They left for their rooms. Once inside, Kat completed her packing, making sure the scented ritual was well contained. In the closet, she hung her clothes for the morrow, and attached the pyrock's empty cage to her back pack. Everything was now ready for an early departure.

Peering in the mirror, she admired the stronger bronze color of her face and decided makeup would not be needed for the next few evening meals. She detected a faint remaining aroma of the scented ritual gloss, and felt a stirring in her body.

Tonight I will dream of Liandock.

CHAPTER 33

Ssarff, as head of the Assassins' Guild, rode up to the entrance to Galdin's Keep, grumbling to himself that Galdin had demanded his appearance. He delighted in the knowledge that Galdin was unable to read the minds of Assassins. *We would be so vulnerable if he were able to penetrate my thoughts.* The ride from the Assassins' Guild to the Keep had been swift and hard, and Ssarff ached from riding with only brief stops for the past turn and a half.

He approached the black iron gate, heart sinking at the foreboding appearance. *What is he going to want now?*

The guards at the gate, usually surly with most visitors, recognized him and bowed their heads in obeisance.

Ssarff kept his smile hidden from them. *Thanes may come and go, but Assassins are forever. Even in this Keep, the guards are aware of those who possess power.*

Ushered through the gate where assistants waited to take his horse from him to lead it to the stable, Ssarff kept his council. Unlike Galdin, the guards honored Ssarff and always gave him his due.

He walked the cobbled path toward the inner keep and made his way to Galdin's meeting room. He snorted to himself. If Galdin were able have his way, he would name the room a throne room. Keeping his thoughts as unruffled as possible, he stopped at the huge iron door and waited for the guard to announce him. He ordered himself to maintain a calm demeanor. While Galdin could not read his thoughts, he could interpret expressions on Ssarff's face.

At the door, a guard bowed slightly. "Assassin Ssarff, Thane Galdin awaits you inside. Please hold while I announce you." He threw open the metal doors, "Thane Galdin, Guild Master Ssarff attends you."

Galdin nodded and gestured for the guard to admit the assassin.

Ssarff strode with purpose toward the man hooded in black and tilted his head the bare minimum. "Thane Galdin, I trust I find you well?"

"Yes. I am most well. How fortunate you arrived so quickly at my order."

Order? He wishes.

"I have a most important mission for you, Ssarff." Galdin waved his hand to indicate Ssarff should seat himself. "While the woman continues to elude me, she is with my servant in Glowen, and to bring her to me at this time would be difficult. They will next be traveling to Baklai, and she will be much easier to capture there. rather than to transport her to my Keep at this time."

"If you do not wish us to bring the woman to you, Thane, what do you wish from the Guild?"

"What do you know of Glowen, Guild Master?"

"Little. While they travel to promote their Orenberry wine, they are not given to simply touring, and, to my knowledge, they never hired any of our Guild."

Galdin fixed the black pinpoints of his eyes on Ssarff's face.

I always feel such unease when he does this. Ssarff was well aware that he and his assassins held more power than

Galdin, but he also knew only too well Galdin commanded the army within Morden and, the army held mastery by fear over the majority of citizens.

Ssarff and his Guild would not encounter an easy time should they ever attempt to wrest control of Morden from Galdin's greedy claws. *The time will come. I pray to Ssayleese, the time will come.*

"Some interesting items about Glowen have come to my attention — things of which few are cognizant."

Ssarff raised his eyebrows, and he perked up his ears. "Glowens possess something you covet?"

"I am not sure. Recently a rumor came to my attention of a secret which the Glowens go to extraordinary lengths to conceal."

"What is the secret?"

"Unfortunately, this is something which I have not been able to discover. Underground whispers of a secret arise from time to time, yet no name or form is mentioned. However, part of the rumors state that the fortunate one who understands the secret will benefit from fortune and power never seen on Pridden before."

"My Thane, it appears most unlikely such a secret exists about which no one has been aware."

"I have been apprised of this from three different sources."

"Were the sources all from Glowen? And why did they tell this to you?"

"Let us say, I encouraged them to speak to me."

No doubt he tortured them. "Was one of these sources your servant who accompanies the woman?"

"No. The fool is ignorant. In this regard, he is useless."

"I assume you wish us to travel to Glowen?"

"I do. I will make this truly worth your while to bring back this secret to me." Galdin named a sum that caused Ssarff to gasp.

"My Thane, your payment seems more than fair. However, while we need only send a small party, the journey is lengthy and costly. I assume we may count on receiving half the fee in advance?"

"I will dispense one third the fee upon your acceptance of the assignment, and one more third when you contact me from Glowen to say you were able to obtain more information and concrete evidence that the secret exists. The final amount you shall receive when you appear again in this room with the details."

Ssarff was impressed that Galdin was willing to pay a fortune for the information. "What happens if we discover that no secret does exist? What if it is only a rumor?"

"Then you shall keep the amount given for the acceptance of the assignment. No further amount will be paid to you, because the assignment cannot be completed. However, I doubt the secret is only a rumor. The three sources from Glowen were loathe to speak of this until persuaded. They resisted until the very end."

He did torture them. Whatever the secret is, this must be most valuable. Galdin stops at nothing to obtain more power. "Thane Galdin, I find your terms acceptable, and we will undertake the enterprise on your behalf. One further question. Can we expect any help from within Glowen?"

"I do have an ally in Glowen. He is not from Morden, so I am not sure how much he can be trusted. But in this instance, he is the only one with enough avarice to recruit him.

He believes I will share with him the secret and the power it conveys. Obviously you are not required to share anything with him."

"Who is this man, and what is his position in Glowen?"

"He is called Emrys. Glowen possess a familial system called pods, and Emrys is the leader of the pen Godron pod, who control the wine making on Glowen. Since so much Orenberry wine is exported, they are an influential and wealthy family. Emrys, however, desires to rule all Glowen and is convinced the power imbued by the secret will allow him to do so."

"I have been advised that Thane Brennan is a potent force in Glowen, and is also well regarded by his people."

Galdin smiled. "For now."

The expression on his face sent ripples of fear and horror down Ssarff's spine. "I understand why you do not wish to share the secret with this Emrys."

Galdin shrugged. "If necessary, eliminate him. Although without his exact knowledge of the secret, removing him may not be wise. One other thing. He is planning to travel to meet with Eduardo, the Lord in Kaylin. He is attempting to arrange a bonding with Eduardo and his sibling's female progeny. You may discover using the young woman, Tessia, as the conduit to Emrys, to be to your advantage."

Ssarff rose. "I do believe I have all the information I need for our trip to Glowen. We will keep you informed as to our progress, my Thane."

"Excellent. Visit my advisor about your initial fee. I also suggest you carry with you a series of messenger moths to contact me about your progress."

Ssarff bowed his head and backed out of the room. Outside the doors, he headed for Galdin's advisor and later the dining hall to partake of a much-needed meal. After a brief rest, he made his way to the stables.

The purse attached to his belt was well weighted. *One thing about Galdin, he pays in gold rather than chits. This trait alone almost makes up for the evil surrounding him.*

CHAPTER 34

After Galdin's Keep disappeared behind the forests, Ssarff paused to prepare a messenger moth for his second-in-command. Holding the creature in his hand, he brought it up to his mouth and whispered, "Ssestin. I received a lucrative assignment from Galdin. I shall be back at the Guild in two turns. Be prepared to meet and discuss plans to journey to Glowen."

He urged his horse on. He planned to stop near the foothills of Mont Zumbis, among the trees of the Froodhow Forest. Plenty of small pools nestled among the trees, so both he and his horse would receive enough water for the journey.

By the time Pridden's star slid halfway below the horizon, and the colors in the sky turned from red to orange, interspersed with streaks of purple and blue, Ssarff yawned and searched for a suitable place to rest for the night.

An animal pathway to his left beckoned, and he followed until a small clearing appeared. He dismounted and allowed his horse to drink from a minute pool at the edge of the clearing and tied the reins to a nearby tree so that the animal could crop the fresh grass.

Removing the light saddle traditionally employed by assassins, he placed it on the ground to serve as a pillow. He then cut leaf-laden branches from bushes nearby and covered the ground next to his saddle to cushion his sleeping area. Hungry, he retrieved journeyklim from his saddle-bag, and drank from his canteen, which he refilled from the pool.

Ssarff stretched and yawned again, wrapped himself in his black cloak, and lay among the leafy branches with his head supported by his saddle. Within minutes he slept, although, like all the assassins, his sleep remained augmented by an awareness of all surrounding him.

The first faint tendrils of dawn light wakened him, and he stood, shook out his robe, stretched, and saddled his animal. Using the cut branches, he swept the area free of footprints, leaving the resting place pristine once again. He mounted his horse and set off for the Guild.

♋♋♋

By the time he arrived at the Assassins' Guild the following turn, the evening meal was almost over. Ssestin arranged for a meal to be brought to Ssarff's quarters.

"Did you find your journey pleasant and incident free, Guild Master?"

"Indeed. While I eat, give me a list of any things which occurred during my time away. When I am finished my meal, we will discuss the assignment Galdin asks of us."

Ssestin nodded agreement. He removed a parchment list from his pocket, and advised Ssarff that the newest recruit had failed to pass the test to join the Assassins, so Ssestin had sent him home. "You will be pleased to know, that I procured an assignment from Lord Rhognor to cleanse the inner passages of his Keep of a band of undesirables. We have already seen some success, and Lord Rhognor paid us handsomely."

When pleasantly full, Ssarff put his dishes aside and drank tea from his mug. "You have done well. Let me now tell you about Galdin's latest quest for us."

Ssestin appeared glum. "Please do not tell me he wishes us to go after the annoying woman again."

"No, she is not the target. But why do you say she is annoying?"

"I am not sure that she is. What is annoying, however, is Galdin's obsession with her."

"You are correct. He is obsessed." Ssarff rubbed at his eyebrow. "Perhaps he is also correct, and she does possess a certain amount of power. She has certainly managed to elude him until now." He shrugged. "No, she is not the target. Galdin appears to have knowledge of a secret concealed by the Glowens. One which he believes demonstrates the ability to bestow power and wealth on those who are the owners."

"Is the secret what he desires?"

"Yes. He assigned our Guild to track down the source and learn what the secret is and what is given to those who are aware of the existence of it. Finally he wishes us to bring the details back to him so he may pursue the powers which this so-called secret conceals."

"If he is not aware of what it is, how does he expect us to recognize it, much less capture it?"

Ssarff shrugged. "I cannot tell, Ssestin. But his offered fee is much larger than any paid to us before." Ssarff held up two hands with nine fingers extended to indicate the size of the reward.

Ssestin gasped.

Ssarff continued. "In gold, not chits. The value must be high indeed."

Ssestin breathed out a huge lungful of air. "Master Ssarff, such an amount would make us the wealthiest Guild in all Pridden."

They both sat, staring at each other, engrossed in their own thoughts of the riches involved.

Ssestin spoke first. "Will there be any allies in Glowen to help us?"

"Galdin informs us that we may obtain help from one of the wealthiest men in Glowen, Emrys pen Godron, who is the head of the wine maker's pod. He is a man of much power in Glowen and is also well known throughout Pridden. The other contact is this man's sibling's female offspring, whom he wishes to bond with Lord Eduardo."

"Lofty aims, indeed."

"You are correct, and if the man succeeds, Galdin benefits more. The bonding with the young woman will help bring Eduardo closer to Galdin's clutches."

"I must ask you, Ssarff. If you do discover the secret is particularly valuable, will you turn it over to Galdin? This might benefit the Assassins' Guild far more than the fee Galdin offered."

"The thought does not escape me, Ssestin. Daily, Galdin becomes increasingly difficult to deal with. His desire for power and wealth grows stronger every day, and his edicts grow more onerous to live under. We are fortunate he cannot penetrate the minds of the assassins to read our thoughts."

"How many assassins do you wish to send to Glowen?"

"Only fourteen, Ssestin. Fourteen is the most powerful number declared by Ssayleese. Make sure they lighten their hair and darken their skin so that they can pass as Rifellan merchants. We will ostensibly visit to obtain Orenberry wine. Make sure you choose assassins who are most built for combat. That way they will fit the expected bodies of Rifellans. Plan on departing with your group in two turns hence. Remember to take with you a supply of messenger moths so we can enjoy prompt communications."

"I will begin preparing recruitment on the morrow, Guild Master."

"You truly are my second-in-command, Ssestin. I will rely on you to be aware of a secret which speaks of power and wealth, and to decide upon the value of this secret to our Guild."

"I will serve you well, Guild Master."

He is my trusted aide. He will find what needs to be found.

CHAPTER 35

Kat woke to a knock. Half awake, she staggered from her bed to the door and called out, "Who's there?"

"Mouse. I thought you might wish a wakening call. Are you packed?"

She called back through the door, "Yes, all prepared."

"I will give you time to dress and meet me for the morning meal."

"Fine."

Kat rushed to shower and dress for the day. Her silky shirt and the loose grey pants would keep her cool, and the upper part of her leathers would perhaps help restrain the ardor of the Glowen men.

Mouse sent an apprentice to take her bag to the stables, and, as he left to deliver them, she carried the rest with her and set off for the dining lounge.

She joined Mouse at the table. Few people occupied the room. She hung her bags over the back of her chair and greeted Mouse.

"I ordered groonnan for you and fara tea."

"Perfect." She yawned.

"Are you still tired?"

"No, I only need some exercise to air out my brain."

Mouse blinked a couple of times, but before he could say anything, the server delivered their morning meal.

As they ate, Mouse placed a folded map on the table and pointed out the initial route to her. "We will stop at Tavollen to arrange food for a mid-turn meal when we arrive at the midway point to Aythin. Tavollen is where the pen Cadno pod live who are in charge of the shipyards, while Aythin is where the pen Iselon pod reside, and they are important on Glowen, because they are the ones primarily responsible for maintaining smooth relations with other lands." He rubbed his brow. "Incidentally, Tessia and Emrys will meet us at the stable. After I contacted them the previous evening, Emrys advised that they would consume their morning meal in their rooms."

"Fine by me." She shook her head. "I must admit I still find the Glowens so weird. They possess an excellent and logical way of managing their land, but their adherence to pleasure above all things is beyond weird."

"I do not believe you will find the Glowens in the southern parts are quite so overt in their pleasure seeking. Since the pen Yuwen pods are the primary residents of Kadwee, Kamerdow, and Tasik, they are, from what I have learned, the most fanatical about pleasure and, in particular, sexual pleasure. Marreth said she suspects they are like this because they are constantly exposed to flowers and plants which arouse the senses. Likely this is the cause of their extreme behavior."

Kat breathed a sigh of relief. "Seems we got off lightly."

"An odd expression, but I do understand what you mean. And, in hindsight, I agree with you."

"I only wish we were warned sooner of the potential problems."

"Kat, perhaps we may find we have been of more value because we received no prior warning."

"Whoa. What do you mean?"

"While our challenges were severe, perhaps Brennan will need to implement some changes among his people. He, and especially Lord Eduardo, are attempting to create a more harmonious relationship between the lands. We, unwittingly, may have pinpointed an area which requires much improvement. Remember, Glowen is not visited by many others."

"Perhaps. All I can tell you is my lack of trust in men has increased substantially."

"You are making a statement that is not entirely true."

"What?"

"There are many men you trust considerably." He rose. "We should leave for Tavollen now." He gathered his maps and his bag, and walked toward the exit. He glanced back. "Think about those who you do trust during the rest of our journey."

She furrowed her brow. *Trust men? He doesn't know what I've been through.* She grabbed her bags and followed Mouse.

As they approached the stables, Tessia called out to Kat, "At last. We thought you were never coming."

Kat frowned. "Tessia. We said we would meet you at dawn, and your star is only now peeking over the horizon. We are not late."

"Well, we have been waiting forever."

Kat raised an eyebrow at Emrys. "How unfortunate." *I wonder if the stupid girl understands sarcasm?*

He smirked and shrugged his shoulders. "Tessia tends to be impatient."

Kat regarded Tessia and shook her head. "You are going to need to learn to be patient on this journey. Remember, Tessia, you asked to accompany us. My guide, Mouse, will set our pace, and our intention is to observe. One cannot be observant while rushing to arrive anywhere early."

Tessia had the grace to appear embarrassed. She mumbled. "I understand."

Mouse ignored them all and began methodically loading his and Kat's luggage on the pack animal.

Kat watched Tessia pacing. Despite her words, she did not understand about patience. Kat sauntered over to Mouse, patted him on the arm, and murmured to him so Tessia would not overhear. "Don't allow her to rush you. Take your time, unless, of course, there is an urgent need to leave quickly."

"Do not concern yourself. I find myself inexplicably slowing down." He grinned at her.

"Ah, of course." Kat hid a smile.

Kat's mount, saddled by a stable hand, stood waiting, and the man now attended to Mouse's horse.

She double-checked the cinch. She did not intend to travel by hanging under her horse's belly. She regularly attended to this, ever since, as a new rider in her early years, she forgot do so, and suffered the ignominy of viewing the underside of her mount. She became convinced the damn animal had snickered at her.

Mouse retrieved their bridles, and handed Kat hers.

As she slipped the bit into the mouth of her horse, she glanced toward Tessia, pacing faster and appearing stressed with impatience. Kat leaned into her horse's neck, hiding a smile.

Unless she possesses particularly fine breeding credentials, Eduardo will never consider her as bond material. Her hidden smile broadened.

The stable hand brought stools for Mouse and Kat, and they both mounted. Again, the agility with which he gained his saddle astonished Kat. *He never fails to amaze me how he can mount an enormous animal with such apparent ease.*

When she looked at Emrys, he was mounted and had already helped Tessia onto her horse.

Mouse suggested to Emrys that he lead the four of them, placing Tessia and Kat behind Emrys, and with Mouse and the pack animal at the rear.

The four set off and soon clattered across the bridge over the Netht Dowron on the way to Tavollen, which was located close to the Netht.

As they entered the town, Mouse called to Emrys to stop. He needed to make one call at the inn, and then they would be able to leave for Aythin.

Kat's job was to obtain a noon-turn meal for the two of them from the inn, which they would consume at the halfway point to Aythin. She assumed Mouse would be inquiring as to when they could depart Glowen by boat for Baklai. When they returned to Tavollen to catch their boat, she would be able to enjoy time to tour the market. Brennan had arranged to meet them there before they finally departed his land.

She completed her chore, and returned to their horses. She handed Mouse the package of food and drink, which he stowed with care on the baggage animal.

Tessia and Emrys waited for them, mounted on their horses.

Kat dragged a stool beside her horse and stretched to put her left foot in the stirrup, hauling herself up using the saddle horn. *I must be getting stronger, 'cause mounting my animal is getting easier.*

When she turned to glance at Mouse, he too was saddled.

"Kat, I suggest you take the lead this time. The way is easy to follow, and there are no vicious creatures to contend with. Emrys, will you follow Kat, and Tessia will ride between between you and me. It is always best I bring up the rear, as the baggage animal is affixed to my saddle."

Before she took off, Mouse sidled his animal beside her. "This will force Emrys to slow down. Our horses will be traveling much further than his, and we do not need to push them beyond their limits."

She smiled at him and set off in the lead toward Aythin.

Keeping a steady gait, she turned back to Emrys. "Did you both order a noon-turn meal from the inn at Tavollen?" Kat hid a smile. *It would have been kinder if I'd asked him this before.* "I picked up the order Mouse arranged for us, because we will be stopping to rest and feed ourselves halfway to Aythin. The stop will be brief."

Tessia called to Emrys with a horrified babble, but he slowed his horse to walk beside her and patted her hand. "I did, Tessia. I did. You will not starve."

Kat faced forward, and grinned to herself again. *What a pair. Tessia is a spoiled child, and Emrys is the one who spoils her.*

They continued on, Kat admiring the lush fields of various plants, some tall, some short but all replete with strange shaped fruits and vegetables. When the star stood directly overhead, Mouse call to Kat to halt.

She stopped and glanced back at him, past Emrys and Tessia. "Yes?"

Mouse called, "To your left, you will notice a minor path, which will lead us to a clearing. We should stop here for our noon-turn meal. There is also a pool close by, which will enable us to fill our canteens and allow our mounts to slake their thirst."

Kat peered forward and caught sight of the small path. She turned back to Mouse. "The path is here, and I will head for our rest stop."

When she reached the area, she halted, and the rest filed into the clearing. Each dismounted and, except for Tessia, tied their horses to trees surrounding the cleared patch. Mouse released a blanket from the pack animal, and spread it on the ground. He pulled packages from the baggage horse and handed half to Kat.

Emrys helped Tessia from her horse and took her reins and attached them to a tree. He detached a similar number of food packages from his horse and gave some to Tessia.

"Thanks Mouse. How clever that you brought a blanket." Kat grabbed her canteen and sank cross-legged on one corner.

Emrys sat in the opposite corner and called back to Tessia. "Bring your canteen because you will want something to drink."

Tessia pouted a bit but grabbed at her canteen and settled herself with a flounce close to Emrys.

They all sat quietly, munching on the substantial meal the innkeeper at Tavollen packed for them. Kat attempted to work out what the flavor of the meat in the bowl reminded her of. She didn't feel like asking questions, so she enjoyed the food and kept silent.

Once he finished his food, Mouse rose. "As soon as you have eaten your meal, take your horses to drink at the pool, and fill your canteens." He placed the wrappings in a bag, and secured it to the pack horse's baggage frame. As soon as Kat watered her horse and filled her canteen, Mouse stepped up to her and clasped his hands together so she was able to use them to mount. He pushed at the same time, which threw her upwards into her saddle..

She smiled down at him. “Thanks.”

Emrys helped Tessia into her saddle and, with his foot in the stirrup, hauled himself aboard his own horse.

Mouse set off in the lead, with Emrys and Tessia behind, and Kat remained last with the pack animal attached to her horse.

Kat humphed to herself. *Tessia didn’t even say thank you. Spoiled brat.*

CHAPTER 36

The four traveled together until the star reached the horizon.

Emrys stood in his stirrups and called to Tessia. “There is Aythin at last.” He spoke to Mouse. “You two may wish to travel slower to preserve your horses, but we are almost home, so we will go on ahead.” He waved at Tessia to follow him and rode past Mouse, urging his horse into a canter.

Mouse paused, covering his mouth to avoid breathing in the dirt raised by Emrys’s hasty departure. He glanced back at Kat. “Do not hurry, or you will be inhaling the dust from their horses.”

“I already am, a bit.”

As the airborne soil died down, Mouse moved forward again. “We will not be far behind, and Thane Brennan sent word ahead to request rooms for us.” He snorted. “Their actions will not interfere with our reservations.”

Kat shook her head. “Tessia is a spoiled brat. but I don’t think much of him either. Perhaps this is a trait of their pod.”

“I do not believe so. You and I met traders from the pen Godron pod in Shendea and Rifella. They were not unpleasant people.”

“You’re right. A polite and happy people. Not in the least bit arrogant.”

By this time, the two riders plodded along the roadway to the Aythin inn. As they neared the stable, an apprentice ran to take the horses' reins, to allow them to dismount. Kat always slid down the horse, hanging from the pommel. Awkward, but easier than attempting to step down from the saddle.

The young apprentice led both horses to stalls, while another unloaded the pack animal and guided it in as well.

The master appeared and welcomed Mouse. "Sire, Thane Brennan advised us you would be arriving this turn. We have placed your mounts in the stalls we reserved, and will send your baggage to your appointed rooms. You will be here this night and the night on the morrow. Please do not hesitate to contact me should you require anything else."

"Thank you, stable master." Mouse gestured to Kat. "Shall we go to our rooms? We can settle ourselves, and then obtain a meal."

Kat, her backpack with Wink's cage attached, on her back, hung her diplo bag over her shoulder. Carrying her long bow, she followed Mouse to their rooms at the inn.

She put the key in the lock as Mouse called out to her. "I'll come for you once you are settled, and we shall dine."

"Thanks. I'll only be long enough to wash the dust off me, which the pen Godrons stirred up."

Kat entered her room and placed Wink's cage on the dresser, still-empty. She had not yet returned from the armor producer. Kat pulled out fresh clothing from her baggage and nipped into the personal to free herself of dust. Refreshed and dressed in clean clothing, she opened her door and found Mouse approaching. "Perfect timing."

As they walked down the hallway to the dining lounge, a thought crossed Kat's mind. "Do you think Emrys and Tessia will want to join us for the meal?"

He gave a wry smile. "I suspect so."

His words were prophetic because the other two sitting at a table for four, waved them over. Kat glanced at him and returned his wry smile.

They sat at the table, and the server announced that the meal of the day was musserel in a thick stew with a spicy Baklai condiment. Kat recognized this as the scent she smelled before, much like a broiled steak, except with a sweet spicy odor to it. The stable hands and the master also exuded the same scent. When she ordered, she asked the server the contents of the dish. Astonished to learn the meal consisted of only thick slices of broiled musserel with spices and a few additional vegetables, she inhaled the aroma eagerly. "But what kind of meat is a musserel?"

The server giggled. "Musserel is not a meat, my Lady, but is a vegetable which grows underground. A delicious one, yes?"

"You will find musserel is most filling, Kat." Emrys explained the reason for the small serving amounts.

Tessia was the one who yawned this evening. She did appear tired, with faint blue circles beneath her eyes. Emrys shot a concerned glance at her. "You, young one, should be abed."

She yawned again. "I am tired, Emrys. This has been a long turn. I need to rest." She simpered at him. "Please do not wake me on the morrow. I will need to catch up on my sleep."

"We will leave you abed, Tessia, and you will awaken refreshed."

Kat rose, hiding a yawn of her own. "A long turn indeed. I'm exhausted, and I'm heading for my bed as well." She faced Mouse. "I might skip the morning meal, but I'll inform you if I'll meet you for the noon-turn one. May the night be kind to both of you."

Kat ignored the outstretched hand offered by Emrys, and almost staggered from the dining lounge toward her room. There, she doffed her clothes, grabbed a night dress from her bags, and stumbled for her bed. Halted by a flutter of wings and peeps from an excited pyrock, she caught the creature and extracted the tube from her foreleg. "Here." She trust three treats at her, watched her gobble them down, and deposited her in her cage and secured the door.

Once more she stumbled to her bed, slid under the covers and drifted off to sleep. *I'll ask Mouse to read the note in the morn...*

♋♋♋

Kat lay drifting in a dream halfway between sleeping and wakening. Someone delicately caressed her face. *Liandock?* The dream was too delightful to open her eyes to gaze on his face. This was always her favorite part of sleep. The halfway dream — warm, comfortable and safe. She sighed luxuriously. The hand that caressed her face squeaked. *What?*

Her eyes snapped open. "Wink. How did you sneak out of your cage? I know I locked the darn thing." She raised her hand and caught the furry pyrock. Stroking the little head, she rose and sauntered over to the cage. *Locked!* "Did you jump from your cage over to me?" Wink had never done that before without being called, and, as far as Kat was aware, pyrocks normally stayed in their cages until removed for message service. Wink butted her furry head against Kat's hand, so she fed her and tucked her back in her cage. The tiny creature curled up in a furry ball and emitted faint snores.

I must ask someone about this. Who would understand most about pyrocks? Kat wandered over to the window and peered out, catching the first light of dawn coloring the sky.

Showered and dressed in comfortable clothing, she decided there was no need to wear her dagger, but she always tucked the small knife in her left boot. Remembering the attack by the birds near Kadwee, she wondered if she should wear the dagger when they were on the road. However, the Sha-hee had said the birds would not have killed them.

She returned to the window and stared out at the beautiful scene, with lush greens all around, and the star barely risen, glowing on the trees. Her stomach growled, so Kat left her room, pausing at Mouse's door to knock. When he answered she asked if he would like to join her for a morning meal.

"Your timing is excellent, Kat. I planned to head for food myself."

He locked his door, and the two walked down the hallways, following the mouth-watering smells of cooking.

"If possible, Mouse, can we eat alone? Without Emrys and Tessia?"

"I would prefer this myself, but we cannot be rude. I do believe Emrys and Tessia enjoy a unique relationship with Thane Brennan."

"Oh rats."

Mouse glanced at her, his brows wrinkled. "Rats?"

"Sorry, Mouse, just an expression indicating I'd rather not meet with them."

When they walked through the doorway, to their pleasure, Emrys and his relative were nowhere to be seen. They headed to a table for two, when a voice stopped them. "Lady Kat?"

Kat turned to the woman who called her name, puzzled because she had never seen this particular Rifellan before.

"Yes? Please forgive me but I do not remember meeting you before."

"You haven't, but I recognize you from the description given to me by my mate, Jagloran. I am Dayleeya."

Kat smiled delightedly. "I'm so glad to meet you. Jagloran is a kind and helpful man. And … he adores you."

"Would you and your companion join me?" She addressed Mouse. "Jagloran mentioned you are Sire Mouse, Lady Kat's guide."

"We would love to join you Dayleeya, but please, neither Mouse nor I stand on ceremony. Forget the Lady and the Sire bits."

They sat and called to a server for a morning meal, and Kat ordered Karri-san tea.

Dayleeya grinned. "That is the one thing which tells me you are not Rifellan. Karri-san."

"I think your mate said the same thing."

Dayleeya's face lit up. "Speaking of him, he appears as if called."

The Rifellan guard walked up and sat beside his mate. "Are these two telling tales about me?"

"You are fortunate, Jagloran. They were both singing your praises."

Two apprentices delivered four meals to the table. Kat regarded the dishes and Jagloran with a puzzled frown on her face.

He smiled. "I ordered on my way over to this table."

Kat sniffed the air. "This is also made from musserel, correct? It has the same distinctive scent."

Dayleeya nodded. "The people in Aythin eat vegetables, and the only food they consume is musserel. If you met them on the road, you would notice they also exude the same odor."

"This is such a fascinating land. Even though Glowen is smaller than any of the others, I find more variety in this small island than in any of the other lands we visited so far." Kat queried Mouse. "Do you agree?"

"I do."

Jagloran nudged his mate. "You need to visit the market. Why not take Kat with you, and give her the benefit of your experience. She may find something she wishes to purchase."

Dayleeya turned to Kat. "Would you enjoy a trip to the market?"

"I would love to go. I only need to finish my tea and we can head off."

Jagloran clapped Mouse on the shoulder. "We can spend time at the small guard hut outside of the village and I can give you a more detailed view of the route you two will be traveling."

They all rose, and Kat and the Rifellan woman set off for the market while the other two headed for the guard hut on the outside of the village.

"Kat, I need to stop briefly at the wine stall that carries Orenberry wine." She beamed. "I am the official person who places all orders for Glowen goods for Rifella. A new male is in charge of receiving orders for wine in Dornish, and I need to procure his name."

"It sounds like fun."

"Once I possess the name, we can tour the marketplace, and by the time we finish, we can pause for a noon-turn meal. Musserel will be prepared in another unique way."

The two women spent the morning visiting the market stalls, and Kat, relieved she found no items she was compelled to purchase, carried no packages.

Their noon-turn meal was indeed musserel, this time cut in slabs and roasted over flame, similar to steaks. Spiced and browned, the air crackled with the scent of fired meat, and a flavor so similar to steaks Kat had back on her own world, she was struck by a momentary pang of homesickness.

This is amazing, but I miss my real life. Will I still return if given the choice of Liandock or home?

On their way back to the village, Dayleeya asked about Kat's ring. "Is the ring made of glass? How beautiful. Where did you find it?"

Kat told her about meeting Garren pen Darryn and about his talent. "The odd thing about Garren is he doesn't have wolf eyes. They are brown."

"Wolf eyes?"

"Yes, the pale color with the deep blue ring around the outside of the iris. All other Glowens I've met are blessed with those kind of eyes." Kat explained why she called them wolf eyes. "Garren is the exception. He claims that all his ancestors possessed brown eyes."

"I am familiar with the man you mean. I have seen his work, and he is incredibly talented. He claims that all his family come from Glowen, but some of the older females whisper of strange beings who merged with the original line."

"This might be true, Dayleeya. I sense a feeling Garren possesses a power, which he denies."

"In Glowen, who knows what things are hidden."

At the door to the inn, Dayleeya took her leave of Kat. "Mouse mentioned that you two are headed for Dornish as well. Let us meet for the morning meal and head for our destination together."

"I would love to travel with the two of you. Now I need to do some writing, so I will head for my room. I will definitely see you on the morrow."

So Garren may be the resultant progeny of some strange being. Surely not the Sha-hee. But while they can mate, they can't breed with Glowens, can they?

CHAPTER 37

Kat arrived at Mouses's room to tell him about her morning with Dayleeya. "She and Jagloran are also heading to Dornish, where they need to settle some business. She suggested we meet on the morrow in the dining hall."

Mouse smiled. "Jagloran suggested the same."

"I like them. They remind me of Bardu and Irina in many ways." Kat held out her hands. "Would you mind if we skipped the evening meal? My noon-turn meal proved substantial, and I'll order something light in my room. I also need to make sure I'm packed before I sleep."

"You make sense, Kat. You are comfortable with the routine now. This will give me the opportunity to bring Eduardo up-to-date on our travels. Would you allow me the use of your pyrock to send the message to him?"

"Of course. Come to my room when you are ready. If you don't mind, would you also read the reply I received from the armor maker?"

"I will, and my thanks for the loan of Wink."

Kat made her way down the hallway to her room and pulled out her journal and other writing materials. She spent the afternoon bringing the journal up-to-date, and added the question about Garren and the possibility of a strange being among his ancestors. She closed her journal slowly, still pondering her thoughts about the talented glass blower.

I wish I could request help from the Sha-hee about returning me home. But since I can't tell anyone about them ... She sighed.

She completed practicing her Priddanese writing and adding to her list of words, when someone knocked at her door. She admitted Mouse and offered him a tube for his message. She took Wink from her cage and tied the tube to her foreleg. "Wink, please find Eduardo and deliver this to him." Wink squeaked at Kat. "Of course, you want food first." She gave the pyrock three treats. Wink butted Kat's hand with her furry head, flapped her wings a couple of times, and popped out of existence.

Kat turned to face Mouse. "If she returns in the middle of the night, I'll bring you the reply on the morrow."

Mouse nodded. "I have already consumed my evening meal, but I shall meet with you for the morning one."

"One last thing, Mouse. This note from Merrindock. I believe it is an agreement to deliver my armor to Baklai. Am I correct?"

He glanced at the note. "You are correct. He has agreed."

When he left for his own rooms, Kat pulled the tassel in the corner. Soon a young apprentice appeared, and Kat requested kossil-kweth tea and some cookies, which he delivered within minutes.

After she drank her tea and nibbled at the cookies, she walked over to the window and closed the curtains, aware nightfall was upon them. She completed her packing, and once clean, she slipped into a warm comfortable bed. Sleep closed her eyes and folded her in its gentle arms.

♋♋♋

Crackling from outside her room roused her. She crept to the window, peering through a gap in the curtains, and gasped. A tall creature strode toward her, malevolence in every movement of its body. A dark hood hid the face. A glint of polished black nails protruded from bony hands, which clawed toward her as it reached the window.

She shrank back, but the creature appeared unable to touch her through the glass. A line of cold sweat tricked down her spine. All she could do was stare at the horror, mesmerized by pinpoints of light from beneath the hood. She closed her eyes to block the sight of the evil before her. A scratching noise from the glass forced her eyes open again, and a thin finger melted through the glass. It reached toward her, and ran a line down her cheek.

She cried out, opened her eyes and sat up, dislodging Wink from her shoulder, who squeaked in alarm. *A dream*! Kat picked up the little creature and rushed from the bed to the window. The curtains were still drawn, but she whipped them open. Nothing there. Kat's heart pounded. Wink's fur stood on end, and she hissed as a pencil line of flame issued from her to bounce harmlessly against the glass.

"You see something I can't? I thought this was just a nightmare."

Wink chirruped, her fur now flat against her body, and she settled comfortably in Kat's hand. Wink held out her foreleg, and Kat removed the tube. She fed the creature a couple of treats and placed her in the cage. The tube, she left on the table to discuss with Mouse on the morrow. With his help, she would also report the foul dream to Wynneth.

Kat left the curtains apart so the light of dawn would wake her, if she could fall asleep again.

♋♋♋

While the first fingers of dawn did help, the faint snores of a furry body pressed agains her ear brought her to consciousness. *Wink jumped again. I should also question Wynneth about her behavior.*

Kat moved Wink back to her cage and she dressed for the trip to Dornish. Leaving her room, and taking with her the tube Wink brought to her in the night, she crossed the hallway to knock on Mouse's door. He answered, dressed and prepared for the day. Kat held up the tube.

He smiled. "Ah, do come in."

They sat at the small table in his rooms, and he read the brief note. "Well, Eduardo is pleased with your progress. He received reports from both Rhognor and Murwenna, and they confirm what we reported."

Kat stopped him as he began to rise. "Before we head for the morning meal, can you help me send a note to Wynneth?"

"I will." He fetched a pen and parchment and asked her to dictate what she wished to say.

Kat gave him a quick précis of her dream.

He wrote the note, and then regarded her with a frown, mouth open. "Kat I had no idea these dreams plagued you. Why did you not tell me?"

"Not necessary. I reported most of them to Wynneth or to the other healers. Sometimes too many suggestions of how to handle challenges can be confusing."

"You may be correct, but Wynneth receives no contact with the dark nature of those who oppose Eduardo. I do. Knowing about these things is important to me."

"If knowing about my dreams is necessary, I will advise you in the future. I need to add one more thing to the note."

Kat told him about Wink's weird tendency to leave her cage in the night and sleep with her.

"You choose wisely. Wynneth knows much about the pyrocks, and I am lacking in this area. If anyone can explain their behavior, Wynneth is the person best able."

Mouse completed the note, which he handed to Kat, who rolled it and placed it inside the tube.

"I'm going to put this tube on Wink and send her to Wynneth. I'll be brief, and will meet you outside my door so we can go eat."

After Wink flew off, she collected Mouse, and the two walked briskly along the hallways to the dining lounge. When they entered, Mouse headed for a table for six.

Kat frowned. "Why six?"

"Well, you confirmed Dayleeya and Jagloran will be joining us. You may have forgotten we also expect Emrys and Tessia."

Kat grimaced. "I did forget. Thanks for the reminder."

Jagloran and his mate joined them. Only moments later, Tessia and Emrys stood at the doorway for a moment before heading to their table.

Emrys greeted both Jagloran and Dayleeya and introduced Tessia to them as his sibling's progeny. "I do not believe either of you met Tessia prior to this. She led a sheltered life. My sibling Gwindon, is the manager of the wine makers and controls the quality of our wines. I am in charge of the sales of our wine throughout Pridden. Our positions are much valued in Glowen, and between us, we desire a worthy mate for her."

Dayleeya smiled at Tessia. "There must be many honorable males in your land who would welcome a bonding with her."

Emrys sighed. "Unfortunately, Tessia glimpsed Lord Eduardo when he visited Glowen a number of paths ago, and she desires him alone as a bond mate." He shrugged. "This means that later, I need to travel with her to meet with him. Although this is an onerous journey, her parent and I admit the union would be advantageous for Glowen."

Kat watched Tessia with curiosity. The young woman sat quietly, staring at Dayleeya and Jagloran. *Tessia hasn't said a word, and she's regarding the Rifellans with awe.*

The rest of the group chatted and laughed as they consumed their meals.

At last, Mouse announced that he and Kat needed to leave for Dornish to arrive in time for a tour of the winery itself. All returned to their rooms to arrange the disposition of their luggage.

As Kat walked with her guide down the hallway to their rooms, she asked, "Mouse, did you notice how quiet Tessia became at the meal?"

"I did. I considered that if we had but known, we might always travel with Rifellans when Tessia is in our presence."

Kat laughed. "Our journey with her would have been so much easier if we were aware of this." She rubbed at her eyebrow. "I wonder why she is so speechless in their company?"

"I doubt you can inquire from Tessia herself. However, you and Dayleeya appear to be friends. Perhaps you should ask her I would like to be familiar with the answer myself."

"I'll ask her on the journey to Dornish."

Kat unlocked the door to her room, walked over to the tassel and tugged, in order to request her baggage be delivered to the stable.

Once they were one their way, she picked up her smaller luggage, and met Mouse in the hall. They headed to meet with their companions.

I must remember to ask Dayleeya about Tessia.

CHAPTER 38

Once mounted, with baggage loaded, the six set off for Dornish. Kat and Dayleeya dressed similarly, loose, cool pants, topped with silky shirts, and covered by Rifellan leather tops.

Kat wore her dagger tucked beneath her belt and the small knife inserted inside her left boot. Dayleeya and Jagloran, she saw, both wore a daggers at their waists. Their knives blended in as part of their normal uniforms.

As they rode, Jagloran slowed his mount to ride beside Mouse, who, with the pack animal attached to his saddle, brought up the rear. They began what appeared to be an animated discussion, although Kat realized neither man took their eyes off the group.

Mouse acts like a warrior, similar to Jagloran. Never saw that before. Kat kneed her horse to ride beside Dayleeya. "Jagloran never lets his guard down, does he?"

Dayleeya grinned at her, pride in her expression. "He is a Rifellan warrior."

"He is a fine mate, Dayleeya. I've never given thought to having only one man in my life before. But if I find myself in that position, I hope I am as fortunate as you." She shrugged. "But finding a man worthy of trust is difficult."

Dayleeya peered at her, a puzzled expression on her face. "I do not think you find this as trying as you maintain."

Kat shook head in confusion. "What I really wish to learn from you is the odd situation about Tessia. Why does Brennan view her as valuable? And Emrys appears to dote on her. I don't understand this, since I find her quite trying, and I often wish the child would cease talking."

"Well, you stumbled upon a most unusual situation. The first thing you must realize is, the pen Godrons are the most important family on Glowen, and their wine-making abilities brought acceptance of Glowen as a valuable part of Pridden. Although the Kaylins refuse to deal with them personally, the wine is still appreciated in their land. Kaylin as you are aware, perceive the Glowens as inferior and wanton."

Kat laughed. "I am aware of the view by those who live in Kaylin."

"You may not be knowledgable about this, but Lord Eduardo, in the interests of reducing formalities between the lands, has been slowly, but inexorably, moving toward less formal relationships between the Kaylins themselves."

"I wasn't aware of this. But he is less formal than many of his people."

"Thane Brennan agrees with Eduardo that Pridden will be stronger when the lands form firm bonds with each other, and formalities do tend to exaggerate differences."

"I admire Eduardo's strength and diplomacy. I now understand that Brennan shares this view with him."

"Which is why Brennan considers a mating bond between Eduardo and a female of the most important pod in Glowen to be of great value."

"Is this why Tessia is so adored by her parent's sibling?"

"I suspect she is more important than we realize." Dayleeya stretched in her saddle. "A dearth of females were born in the pen Godron line for many paths. When Tessia birthed, multiple celebrations occurred, and they spoiled the child enormously. Of course now, with the potential of a mating with Eduardo as a possibility, Tessia is almost considered the one who will solve all of Glowen's challenges with the rest of Pridden."

"That's a huge load to place upon the head of one young woman. And, I do believe I know Eduardo fairly well. I cannot see him wishing to be mated with Tessia."

"I only met Eduardo a few times, and I tend to agree with your assessment. However, Kat, remember, sometimes politics outweigh our own desires."

Kat rode in silence as she pondered what Dayleeya suggested to her. *Eduardo is a strong, handsome leader. His future mate would need to be an unusual woman.*

"I have one more thing to ask you, Dayleeya. Tessia is very quiet around you and Jagloran. Do you know why?"

"I too noticed her reluctance to speak in front of us. I have no idea why this is so. All I suspect is that she is not used to warriors. Her family are tradespeople. I do believe she sees Rifellans as more powerful and stronger than her pod, and she is not sure how to be in our company."

"That sounds logical. Tessia is naïve to a major degree."

Jagloran came trotting up to Dayleeya. "We have traveled well. Rather than stop for the mid-turn, Mouse suggests we wait to partake of a meal until we reach Dornish. I must admit I prefer to wait, because while journeyklim pieces are nourishing, I would much rather consume some freshly cooked dishes."

Kat thanked him. "I'm able to wait for my meal. Perhaps you might convey the information to Tessia and Emrys."

Jagloran smiled. "I planned to."

As the six continued on their way, Kat dropped back to ride beside Mouse, and the Rifellan guard joined his mate.

ஒஒஒ

The party arrived at the Dornish stables, and arranged the care of their mounts for two turns. When Mouse said he had booked rooms at the inn, Emrys offered them an alternative. "Since you are all here to view the wines, I suggest you join us at Godron House. We will tour through our largest winery, and offer a second tour of our own private wine production. On the morrow following, you can set off for Deon House and tour the actual berry farms."

Kat glanced at Mouse. "Is there time enough for us to do so?"

He nodded at her. "Our thanks, Emrys. We appreciate your offer."

Jagloran stepped forward. "A most generous idea, Emrys, but we are dining with another mated pair from my guard unit, so we will stay at the inn." He turned to Mouse. "We will cancel your booking for you."

"My thanks, Jagloran."

The Rifellan smiled at Mouse. "It makes sense for us to handle this for you. On the morrow we travel across country for Tavollen and return to the Keep." He smiled at Emrys. "We do not possess the luxury of touring further."

Emrys bowed his head to Jagloran. "Of course. You need to maintain a certain position for our Thane. We will no doubt meet again at some future turn."

Kat intervened. "Men, you forget we did not consume food this noon-turn, and I need to eat. Might we locate our rooms at Godron House first and afterwards meet in the dining hall of the inn so we can join with Dayleeya and Jagloran?"

They all agreed, and the two Rifellans followed the apprentices who carried their baggage and led them to their rooms.

Emrys arranged for rest of the bags to be transported to rooms at Godron House. Dining at the inn suited him well, because he was needed to aid Jagloran and Dayleeya to choosing the wines for delivery to Rifella.

After an assistant led her to her room in Emrys's home, Kat refreshed herself and set up Wink's empty cage on her dresser. As Kat was about to leave her room, squeaks and chirrups heralded the arrival of her pyrock.. "Wink you're back. You were a long time." She caught the creature in mid-air and took her to the dresser, where she removed the tube, fed her, and placed her carefully in her cage. Kat tucked the reply from Wynneth in her pocket and left her rooms for the inn's dining lounge.

As she walked the hallways of Godron House, she admired the paintings of the winery and the people. The illustrations, beautifully done, with bright, living colors entertained her as she headed to the inn.

Her stomach emitted a series of growls when confronted by the delicious odors of spices and cooking meals wafting from the building beside Godron House. The other five, already seated at a table, waved at her to join them when she appeared at the entrance.

"Forgive me for being tardy." She faced Mouse. "Wink returned with a reply from Wynneth. We can view the note later, but at this moment, I'm so hungry, I could eat roadkill."

They all stared at her, and Tessia piped up, "What kind of animal is a roadkill?"

Damn. Damn. Damn. Explaining this would be inappropriate. "Roadkill is not an animal, merely a foolish expression from my home world."

"But what does the expression mean?"

"There truly isn't one, Tessia. The expression is meaningless."

Mouse attracted Kat's attention. "Kat, the innkeeper recommended their version of musserel. The spices in this area of Glowen are quite different from those of Kadwee."

Mouse to the rescue again. "My thanks for the suggestion. I will try it."

They all ordered the same dish, and Jagloran declared it as his favorite when visiting Dornish.

The meal finished quickly, and the two Rifellans rose, explaining they needed to place their wine orders for Rifella.

Emrys rose with them. "I must accompany you to make sure the order is correct, and I wish to show you a new wine we created." He addressed Tessia. "My dear, will you take Sire Mouse and the Lady Kat to meet with Trevalynn so he may conduct a tour of the primary winery for them?" He explained to Mouse. "Trevalynn is my second-in-command at the winery."

"My thanks to you, Emrys." Mouse did the weird Rifellan hand-shake thing with Jagloran, and bowed his head at Dayleeya. "We have been well met, and hope to meet with you again."

Kat hugged Dayleeya and patted Jagloran on the arm. "You both are well met." In her peripheral vision, she caught Emrys eyeing her with suspicion. "Dayleeya took beginning healer lessons with Marreth." *Not true, but he won't be aware of my lie and hopefully will keep his hands off me.*

His face cleared, and he nodded. "Ah."

The party broke up, and Tessia held out her hands to Kat and her guide. "Come. Follow me."

ꝏꝏꝏ

Near the entrance to Godron House, the three approached a small office, attached to a number of buildings, but separated from Godron House itself.

Tessia greeted the man inside. "Trevalynn, Emrys wants you to take the Lady Kat and her guide on a tour of the winery."

"Fine." He smiled at them. "Welcome to our winery." He led them through a series of rooms — berries arrived at the winery, washed in clear water, and moved into a room containing huge open vats. Men and women, wearing what appeared to be white silk socks, tramped on the berries in the vats to release the juices. One small vat contained those of a deep red color. Two others were filled with light pink berries. The balance of the open vats held clear golden globes, plump, and almost translucent, with the sheen of pearls.

Trevalynn directed them around the vat room. "All these juices run into canisters set around each of the open vats. The containers carrying the raw juices are strained before being stored in the massive enclosed wooden vats you will see in the next room."

Trevalynn turned to them, eyes shining, which made him appear more wolf-like than before. "We are about to enter the most exciting of all of the winery rooms. The wine in these vats is fermenting to create the final products. We prepare three different wines in there: the Blud wine, which is the strongest, and Glowens themselves water this one down to be able to drink it; the pink, which is often used in celebrations; and the white, which all Pridden calls Orenberry wine. The white is the only one sold outside of Glowen, while the other two are retained for our consumption solely."

Trevalynn opened a huge wooden door, and an ominous sound issued from within. As they entered, the noise increased a thousandfold. The room, lined with three rows of massive barrels, one marked with a dark red symbol, two marked with a pink symbol, and the balance unmarked, stretched the length of a tennis court.

The incredible sound was the most extraordinary characteristic. The round barreled vats groaned and moaned like scores of huge trolls in agony. They creaked and muttered and almost appeared to move. It seemed like the room, filled with living giants, suffered the throes of anguish and trauma. The heady aroma of wine sat thick in the air, and Kat's senses reeled, almost drunk on the fumes. The room held power and pain and the redolence of creation.

She almost staggered when Trevalynn ushered her and Mouse physically from the room.

He secured the door behind them. "Please sit down in the fresh air." He brought them mugs of water, which they drank gratefully.

Once they recovered their wits, Trevalynn led them to the tasting room. "We have lined up the three basic wines in our cellar. Please take a small amount in the glass and savor the wine. Roll it around in your mouth, but do not swallow. Spit the wine in the bowl provided. If you do swallow, combined with the effect of the previous room, you might become most inebriated. If you test the Blud wine, make sure you mix it with plenty of water first. Once you complete the tasting, the mugs of water on the table are for you to clear your palate."

Kat, while willing to try the wines, was reluctant to imbibe the Blud one. She tested the white. It was a pleasant dry wine, but, as she experienced before, it was too strong.

Spitting the liquid into the bowl was awkward. The pink was also strong, but was fruity. If she were forced to come up with a word to describe it, it would be pretty.

She stepped up to the Blud wine sample, poured a small amount into the glass, and diluted it with two-thirds of water. The wine was still too strong, and she spat it out with haste. The only word that came to mind about it was death.

Mouse stared at her. "Are you well?" He turned to Trevalynn. "Our thanks for the opportunity to taste the wines. I do not know how Kat fared, but although I spat out what I tasted, I'm affected by the fumes of the vat room and the wine itself. I do believe I will retire to my room and indulge in a brief sleep. Kat, will you wish to do the same?"

She glanced at Mouse with gratitude. "I do want a nap."

They thanked Trevalynn again and walked to the separate structure of Godron House.

They strode down the hallway to their rooms, and Kat stopped at her door. "I will not attend a meal this evening. We ate our noon-turn meal late, and I feel the effects of the wine. I shall meet you on the morrow for the morning meal."

"You mentioned you received a note back from Wynneth. Do you wish me to read it to you?"

"Not now, Mouse. All I want is my bed."

CHAPTER 39

Squeaking from Wink roused Kat from her nap, and she raised a bleary head. Assuming the pyrock needed food, Kat dragged herself from the bed and staggered to the desk, popped some nuggets in the small waiting mouth.

Wink butted at Kat's hand until she stroked her, and she quieted and curled up in sleep once more. Kat wondered if she should call for a meal. Her stomach grumbled a loud 'no'.

She ran her tongue around her mouth. *Ugh My mouth is furry and horrid tasting. Reminds me of the awful Blud wine.*

She tugged at the tassel, and, when a young assistant appeared, asked for kossil-kweth tea. While she waited for him to return, she removed a few items from her bags. A knock at her door heralded the arrival of her tea, and the assistant placed a generous pot and a mug on a small table. He bowed and left, and Kat poured out a cupful at once.

She sat sipping at the kossil-kweth, and experienced the calming effects, but when she checked the inside of her mouth again, it still tasted nasty. She brushed her teeth, and returned to the table and poured more tea. Each sip brought more relief. She rose and peered in the mirror.

When she first returned from the tasting room, she'd simply flung herself on the bed and fallen asleep. Now her clothes were bunched and wrinkled and, except for her leather top, needed changing. Three wavy lines adorned her face, similar to the ornamental stitching of the bedspread. She massaged lotion into the lines until they faded. Her hair stuck out in all directions, but she tamed it with a vigorous brushing.

She swept off the leathers and hung them on the door of the closet. She hung her blouse and long pants in the personal, and turned on the hot water in the shower stall. She took a light wash, but continued to run the water at its hottest. A few minutes later, she shut off the water, exited the steamy room, and closed the door. By morning, she knew her clothing would be free of wrinkles. Slipping a night robe over her head, her stomach happy, she crawled into bed, and, as she faded into a dreamless sleep, the light globes dimmed automatically.

♋♋♋

Dawn, accompanied by bird song and the sounds of people at Godron House, woke Kat early. She wasted no time rising, performing her ablutions for the day, and set off for Mouse's room.

"Good morrow, Mouse."

He inclined his head. "Kat."

"Are you ready for your meal?"

"I am. I considered calling on you, but you arrived at my door before I had a chance to do so."

He closed and locked his door, and they set off again down the illustrated hallways, until they reached the dining lounge belonging to Godron House.

Although not as enormous as the hall at the inn, similar delicious smells of cooking food assailed Kat's nostrils. They chose a table for four when Mouse reminded her, that as Emrys's guests, they would be obliged to meet him and Tessia for the morning meal as well.

Mouse ordered tea for them both, which the assistant delivered within minutes.

"OK, Mouse, here is the note from Wynneth."

He took the parchment from her and read the lengthy note. "Wynneth says, she shared the latest dream with Deleth, but both of them are unclear as to the meaning. Wynneth asks permission to approach Eduardo and ask if he might possess any insight." He gave her a quick glance. "Do you wish to agree to this?"

She hesitated. "Uhm—I've told you about these dreams, Mouse. Do you think I should share them with Eduardo?"

"I believe you should. He may be privy to other information."

"I suspect you're correct. When we return to our rooms, I'll bring you parchment to write a note back to Wynneth."

"Fine. Now as to the antics of your pyrock, Wynneth says some of these creatures form such a close bond with the person who feeds them that they seem to wish to be even closer. Apparently from her behavior, Wink is very attached to you. Wynneth seemed surprised when you mentioned the flame which Wink expelled. She has no actual knowledge of this in any other pyrock, although rumors of such actions do exist."

Mouse signaled the server, and ordered meals for them along with refills of the tea.

"I believe Emrys and Tessia will be arranging a tour for us through their private winery," Kat said.

Mouse, about to reply, waved at their hosts to invite them to share the table.

The pen Godrons barely seated themselves when Tessia began her chattering. "Did you find our winery impressive?

The sound in the fermenting room is amazing. Right?" She resumed her incessant comments and questions, without waiting for answers.

Kat did her best to keep a bored expression from her face. *I'm so grateful we only need to spend one more night with this tedious girl.* At last, she interrupted to speak to Emrys. "You promised you would allow us to tour your private winery. May we do this before the noon-turn meal?"

He nodded. "I would be delighted to do so. As soon as we are finished this meal, I will personally take you on the tour."

"Must I come as well?" Tessia pouted at the suggestion.

He smiled at her. "No, Tessia, you and I need to prepare much for our eventual trip to Kaylin. I believe you would be best to apply yourself to those preparations."

"Oh yes. We are going to see Eduardo." She giggled at the thought.

Emrys changed his tack. "Kat, you travelled through much of our land. What interesting things have you discovered about Glowen?"

Dropping the veil over her mind so fast she thought it clunked, Kat swallowed. "Well, your people are enraptured by thoughts of pleasure. Much more than I initially thought. You possess an abundance of foods and flowers and the land is lush with greenery."

"Is that all? Are there no other secrets you discovered?"

"Secrets? I was not aware you possessed secrets, other than how well you manage your lands. Do you have others? What are they?" Kat determined that she would always use the veil on her thoughts when in the company of Emrys and Tessia.

He laughed. "If I told you, they would no longer be secrets. So, did you unearth some?"

"Hardly, since I didn't know you Glowen harbored any." *He's lying. He has no idea of any secrets about Glowen. But why is he interrogating me?*

Kat glanced at Mouse and saw him frowning at Emrys.

Tessia joined the conversation. "Kat, you do know a secret. I remember overhearing you mention one when we first met."

Mouse chuckled,.

However, Kat did not see amusement in his eyes.

"Tessia, Kat and I were only talking in generalities."

"Mouse is right, Tessia, I only recall discussing with him that I hide no secrets. As I told him, if I knew any, I wouldn't know if I should reveal them or not."

"Why did you talk about secrets if you were not hiding one?"

"Tessia, you interrupted a private conversation between Mouse and me. One which bore no topic about secrets. So drop the subject, because I do not possess any."

"You do not need to be so grumpy about this."

"I am not grumpy. I only wish to make sure the subject of secrets is sorted."

Tessia glared at her. "Hmph."

Kat shook her head in frustration. "Our meals are complete, Emrys. May we take the tour now?"

"Yes." He eyed her with suspicion in his expression. He then rose, followed by Kat and Mouse, but Tessia set off for her private rooms.

The three of them followed a different route through Godron House and arrived at yet another separate building, housing the pen Godron's personal winery. Emrys took them through the rooms, similar to those of the massive winery that was attached to the town of Dornish, but much smaller.

The biggest difference was in the fermenting room. While the barrels were the same size, the room contained only six fermenting barrels and was, therefore, much smaller. Four of them were labelled Blud wine, and the remaining two bore labels of Celebration and Orenberry wines.

It was Kat's turn to view Emrys with suspicion. *Interesting he keeps so much Blud wine. Every time I learn something about him, I trust him less.*

However, based on his annoying personality, she was unable to believe he knew of the Sha-hees. *I know he suspects I'm concealing some secret.*

On this tour, she and Mouse skipped the tasting, as neither particularly enjoyed drinking the wines.

After the tour, Kat excused herself to add information to her journal about the tour of both wineries, and to pack most of her possessions so they could leave early to travel to Deon House. She first obtained some parchment and went to Mouse's rooms to ask him to prepare her reply for Wynneth.

He answered the door. "I suspect you are here so I can write a note for you."

They ordered tea and cookies, and Mouse set pen and ink on the table.

A knock at the door, and the apprentice delivered the tea to them.

Kat, while drinking tea and munching cookies, dictated her reply to the healer. "Tell her … I think this would be …. an excellent idea to tell Eduardo … about my dreams."

Mouse looked at Kat, a worried expression on his face.

Kat frowned at him. "What?"

"Kat it is most important you avoid any discussions of secrets with Emrys."

"I did my best, but my morning was trying, Mouse."

He raised his eyebrows as if in question.

Kat sighed. "Tessia's chattering, the third degree by Emrys you're referring to."

Mouse interrupted. "Third degree?"

"An expression my people use when referring to an annoying interrogation."

Mouse nodded. "I think more than that upsets you. What else?"

"Another tour of a winery, which I didn't want." She frowned in puzzlement. "Don't you find it odd that Emrys keeps twice as much Blud Wine? I do not trust the man."

"I also find being in his company disquieting." Mouse handed her the note to send to Wynneth.

"Mouse, I'm going to consume my noon-turn meal in my room, as well as my evening one later. I will meet you for an early morning feed on the morrow. This way I can avoid any further contact with both the pen Godrons."

"I would find a free post noon-turn period relaxing. And I anticipate with pleasure our morning meal. Before I call to send my bags to the stable, I will check with you to make sure you are also ready."

"An excellent idea, Mouse. I shall see you on the morrow." Kat returned to her room. Once inside, she inserted the note for the Kaylin healer in a tube, which she attached to Wink's foreleg. Tossing the pyrock in the air, she directed the small creature to go to Wynneth.

She tugged at the tassel, and requested a light meal from the assistant. He returned after a short delay with a delicious musserel stew, and fara tea. Kat stopped him before he left. "When the evening meals begin, would you bring me a small serving of whatever the main meal is for this night, and a cup of karri-san tea, please?"

He bowed his head. "I will be delighted to serve you, my Lady."

After he left, Kat donned a casual robe, packed everything except for the clothes she would wear on the morrow, and extracted her writing gear from her diplo bag. She completed some rough illustrations of the vats in the winery, and of some of the others sights she had seen in the past two turns. She hoped that when she returned home, she would not only have notes, but illustrations as well for her planned games.

Leaving her parchment to dry throughly, she slipped under the comforter on her bed and settled for a nap.

The fluttering of wings and assorted squeaks and chirrups, roused her. She stretched luxuriously, and put out a hand for Wink. "You made a quick trip. Let's find out about Wynneth's reply." Kat removed the message tube, and tucked Wink back in her cage with a couple of treats. Kat laughed aloud when she read only one word on the parchment. "OK."

A knock sounded at the door, announcing her evening meal. When he left, he removed the noon-turn tray.

Kat ate her food slowly, but with relish, and then consumed her tea. Once completed, she finished her preparations for bed and slipped between the crisp sheets for a relaxing night.

Eyelids heavy, Kat drifted in a world of soft warmth.

I hope I won't need to encounter Emrys or Tessia again.

CHAPTER 40

Kat had left the curtains open so she would wake with the first light of dawn. She stretched, and a small furry object make a squeaky oof, when she put her hand on the pillow. She swiveled her head, and came nose to nose with Wink. "You should be more careful. I'm going to squash you one day."

A teeny pyrock tongue poked out and licked her nose, and Kat laughed aloud. She carried Wink to the desk. The creature opened a wide mouth lined with little teeth and chirruped for food and snuggled in her little bedding when placed back in her cage.

Once dressed and packed for the day, Kat answered the knock at the door and smiled. "Mouse."

"Good morrow, Kat. The apprentice is here to take my bags to the stable. Are yours ready?"

She waved her hand behind her, and the assistant entered and retrieved most of her luggage. The rest they hand carried.

The stable assistant left and as they walked the painted halls of Godron House, Mouse patted his map bag. "Over our meal, I will give you a quick glance at our route to Deon House."

"I hope Emrys and Tessia will be at the morning meal."

Mouse stared at her, an astonished expression on his face.

She grimaced. "Not because I miss them. But it will only be polite to thank them for their hospitality and to say farewell." Kat smirked. "Its the last part I'm particularly looking forward to."

He smiled. When they arrived at the entrance to the dining lounge, he pointed to the two Glowens, and he and Kat joined them at their table.

Kat smiled at both of them. "I'm pleased we joined you for the morning meal. We wanted to thank you for allowing us to stay in your beautiful home and for the extraordinary tours of the wineries."

Emrys stood until Kat seated herself. "You are more than welcome, Kat. It has been a pleasure being in your company." He reached for her hand, but Kat sidestepped, and avoided his touch. *I still don't trust him.* Even her stone felt cool.

Emrys continued. "Tessia and I prepared most things for our journey to Kaylin, and we will no doubt meet you again in Jasteen. In a few turns, we will travel to Tavollen to pre-book on a boat to Rifella. From Rifella we will travel up the Farralawn River, cross briefly into Morden, and take the tunnel to Shendea. The route is simple, along the foothills of the Clog Nordad, and we will use the Nordad Pass to cross into Kaylin. Although the route is lengthy, it is straight forward and free of unpleasant creatures."

Mouse nodded at Emrys. "It sounds as if you've planned everything well."

"I hope so, as Tessia is anxious to meet with Lord Eduardo."

The young woman nodded enthusiastically.

The meal passed swiftly, with much chatter from Tessia, and with more probing by Emrys about a potential secret known to Kat. Mouse remained silent, but when they completed the meal, he rose immediately, thanked Emrys again, and bid farewell to the two Glowens.

Mouse, map bag over his shoulder and Kat with her diplo bag, headed out to continue their journey. As they exited the lounge, Kat expelled a sigh of relief.

♋♋♋

The pair rode for Deon House, stopping only once for a mid-turn meal, which Godron House had prepared for them.

The first smudges of color in the sky indicated the descent of the Pridden star below the horizon, as they rode up to the stables of Deon House. The stable master greeted them. "Welcome. You must be Lady Kat and Sire Mouse. Kerryon pen Deon waits for you at the entrance to Deon House, and will answer any questions you may wish to put to him."

Mouse bowed to the master. "Our thanks. We will meet him at the entrance."

The man who introduced himself as second-in-command to Gaynore, the head of the pen Deon pod, and Chief Advisor to Brennan, stood waiting for them. Kerryon stood tall, a strong man, more bronzed by the star than the rest of the Glowens that Kat had encountered. His wolf eyes were most striking and added to his commanding aura. Kat was far more comfortable in his presence than in that of Emrys. Her stone was warm again.

Kerryon took and bowed over her hand, without adding romantic or sexual gestures. "Welcome to Deon House. Please attend your rooms, so you may refresh yourselves before joining us for our evening meal."

They both thanked him, and walked to their rooms to settle themselves.

Kat exited her room, met Mouse in the hallway, and they set off for the dining lounge together. An assistant escorted them to a table for six, at which Kerryon plus another male and two females sat. Kerryon and the other male stood.

"Sire Mouse, Lady Kat"—Kerryon gestured toward the male—"this is my lead berry grower, Tevalow, and his bond mate, Erathin." He took the hand of the other female, smiling at her as he did so. "And this is my bond mate, Afeena."

"We are well met." Kat bowed her head to each of the three. *The northern Glowens are overtly seeking other conquests even if they're bonded. These Glowens seem happy in their bonds without seeking additional couplings.*

The six sat and ordered meals and spent an enjoyable evening in conversation. Kerryon promised to provide Tevalow take them through a tour of the berry orchards, and Afeena and Erathin would escort them through the rooms where they bred and cared for the jeweled pollinators.

Kat enjoyed the suggestions of the others. "I will appreciate the tour." She hesitated. "I must confess to you, I would much rather view the berries on their vines than drink the wine, which is too strong for me."

Afeena laughed. "Do not be embarrassed. Our wines are strong. I water the Orenberry wine and never drink the Blud one." She shook her head. "Those who drink the Blud generally possess a darker side. They appear to lose their love of life."

Her mate added, "We are in the process of growing a berry which is milder and will produce a less strong wine. The Kaylins and the Shendeans, we believe, will be more likely to order the milder one. Rifella and Baklai are the lands that appreciate the stronger wine. Both lands possess less water, and we suspect wine is now part of their normal drinking habits. Both do, of course, dilute the Orenberry somewhat."

"What about the Mordens?" Kat thought they would not likely avoid wine.

"Interesting you should ask the question. We receive no requests for wine from Morden, and our travelers prefer not to enter their land." He seemed worried. "We heard rumors that northern Mordens consume Blud wine, but we cannot understand how this is possible. Glowens are forbidden to export Blud."

"I met southern Mordens in Shendea and Rifella who drink wine at the inns in other lands." Kat rubbed at her forehead. "Remember, Mouse? We saw southern Mordens bargaining for wine with Glowens in Shendea.".

"We did. But they appeared most discreet about their requests."

So Glowens avoid Morden, yet Emrys is passing through there. Strange, even if it is a shorter route.

The party completed their meals, and all sought their beds, promising to meet at the gates of Deon House to tour the vineyards on the morrow.

As they reached their rooms, Kat gazed speculatively at Mouse. "Did you remember when we toured Emrys's personal winery, he possessed four vats of Blud wine fermenting? I wonder if he is supplying Morden."

"An interesting observation, Kat. This is something to consider." He rubbed his chin, entered his room and closed the door.

I'll bet he is. I definitely do not trust Emrys.

♋♋♋

Kat woke refreshed, and, after feeding Wink, she dressed for the day in light comfortable clothing. She left her room and knocked at Mouse's quarters.

He opened the door. "I am considering consuming my morning meal in my quarters. Would you join me, and we can discuss our final journey before we leave for Baklai."

She nodded. “I agree. I particularly wish to discuss the pen Godrons. I am experiencing more discomfort around them.”

She sat at the table in the corner of the room, while Mouse tugged the tassel and, when the apprentice appeared, ordered meals and tea for both.

He pulled out his maps and showed Kat the route from Deon House and pointed at Tavollen. “Brennan mentioned he will meet us here to say farewell, so we can board a vessel at the jetty near Tavollen.”

“I hope the weather is better than when we arrived. I hate being seasick.”

A knock indicated the arrival of their food, and Mouse cleared the table to make room for the dishes.

While they ate, Kat continued to speculate about Emrys’s activities regarding Blud wine. “I’m convinced he’s not a man with integrity, Mouse. He acts more like the northern Glowens, and when he attempts to take my hands, my skin crawls.”

Mouse peered at her, curiosity in his expression. “Skin crawls. What a fascinating combination of words. I assume this means you experience—?”

“Revulsion. Did you ever undergo a sensation of insects crawling on you?” She shuddered. “That’s the sensation I mean. I do not trust the man.”

“Although we possess no proof that he is dealing with the Mordens, you might be wise to explain your feelings to Brennan when we meet with him in Tavollen. As to Emrys, we are unlikely to meet with him again, which should set your mind at rest.”

“How can I relax? He specifically told us he and Tessia intend to meet us in Jasteen.”

"I did not pay attention, and was not aware of his plan. If such a thing does occur, I suggest we remain alert."

"Oh I will." Kat rose from the table. "Shall we meet with Afeena and Kerryon for our tour?"

Mouse rose in assent, and they set off for the Gates of Deon House.

♋♋♋

Tevalow and Kerryon stood beside a cart drawn by a ponti, able to hold four people comfortably.

Kat smiled at the ungainly animal. "This is the first ponti I've seen outside Kaylin or Shendea."

Kerryon patted the animal. "This is Loftin, and she is invaluable in the vineyards. We possess six of these creatures to help our people move about the vines rapidly. When we pick and prune, we cannot take a long time to accomplish our tasks. At picking time, we must gather the berries hastily, so they do not rot on the vines."

"How did you manage to persuade Kaylin to part with them?"

"Although the Kaylins use them in abundance, pontis are Shendean creatures, and the Shendeans are not averse to trading with us. Thane Brennan and Lord Rhognor are men who respect each other."

Tevalow stepped forward. "Do climb aboard. We will inspect the vines, but only a small section, as they cover many areas of this part of Glowen."

Mouse stood aside for Kat to enter the cart, and climbed aboard and seated himself beside her.

The two male Glowens sat in front so they were able to use the reins, and they set off toward the masses of lines of berry vines Kat saw in the distance.

Kerryon kept them informed of what aspects of a vineyard they viewed. He stopped at long row of vines bearing fruit. "The Orenberry vines you see here will be picked within the next few turns, and will be sent to Godron house for juicing and fermenting. If you wish you may descend and view the berries closer up."

Kat jumped down and walked over to the berries. The sun shone on the almost transparent little globes, causing them to glow like iridescent pearls. "They're beautiful and would resemble fabulous jewels around the neck of any woman."

Tevalow laughed. "Spoken like a true female. If you think the berries are beautiful, wait until you view the jeweled pollinators. The myriad of colors are magnificent, and they shine as if lit from the inside."

"I'd love to see them."

"We will take you to view the Celebration and Blud berries, of which we also own vines waiting to be picked."

They all piled in the cart again, and Kerryon drove them to the Celebration vines. Once again he stopped so they might view the berries from a closer point.

Kat gazed at the pink pearl-like berries and marveled at their perfect color. These, though only slightly transparent, also glowed in the sun.

The last vines they visited were the Blud berries. Rather than being transparent, these berries were the color of venous blood, dark with an almost blue sheen.

Kat shivered when she saw the berries. They were not a pleasing sight but appeared to resemble the blood of dying life forms. Her visit with those vines was brief and she scrambled aboard the cart for the trip to view the jeweled pollinators.

When the cart stopped beside a large shed, Kat descended and she and Mouse met with Afeena and Erathin. Kerryon and his berry grower continued back to the vineyards, away from the shed, which was covered with a porous fabric that allowed the breezes to circulate. Kat entered and gasped at the mass of brilliant dots of color, moving slowly among delicate white flowers. She stepped closer and stopped, stunned. The dots of color were tiny spiders, spinning webs among the flowers. Kat shrieked and rushed outside the shed.

Afeena ran after her. "What is the matter, Kat?"

"They're spiders. I hate spiders." She shuddered.

"These are pollinators, not the word you called them."

"They're spiders. They've got eight legs, and there are lots of them, and they're spinning webs. They're spiders. I'm not afraid of much, but I'm terrified of spiders."

Afeena appeared perplexed. "You need to fear nothing about them. They are gentle creatures who pollinate our vines. Without them, we could produce no wine." She patted Kat on the shoulder. "I am so sorry you fear them. But since you do, you should avoid walking among the vines when they are flowering. You are safe now, since none are in flowering mode, and we do not not release them among the vines until all berries are picked."

Kat waited outside the hut until Mouse appeared, and the four went to consume their mid-turn meal. Kat still shivered occasionally when she thought about her narrow escape.

Afeena and Erathin eyed her worriedly. Kat was somewhat embarrassed at her extreme reaction to the spiders. *Indeed they're small.* She shivered. *But I saw thousands of them.*

She felt a need to express herself. "Afeena and Erathin, I do apologize for my fear toward your jeweled pollinators, and I know I exhibit a ridiculous terror of spiders. I cannot help my reaction, but I thank you for your tour."

After my meal,I should walk among the vines to feel comfortable near the berries. I'll avoid the spiders at all costs.

CHAPTER 41

Afeena and Kerryon ordered meals for the four of them, and kossil-kweth tea for Kat. "This will help calm you. We are sorry we cannot help you view the pollinators as the gentle and beneficial creatures they are. Changing the views we create over a life time is not simple. We do suggest you take some time after this meal to walk among the Orenberry vines, and enjoy their beauty. We can promise no pollinators are among them at this moment."

Kat agreed. "I do understand that I'm silly to be so afraid of something so small. There is no logic to my attitude, but I can't seem to help it."

♋♋♋

Kat wandered along the first row of Orenberry vines, enjoying the glorious warmth of Pridden's star, which was kept to a manageable level by the breeze blowing from seaward. Shading her eyes she gazed upwards at the puffballs of fluffy clouds scudding across the brilliant cobalt sky.

Bringing her gaze back to the ground, she saw spring green leaves fluttering in the wind, sheltering and exposing the pale gold translucent berries, bunched like grapes, and hanging heavily, laden with juice.

Her heart ached with the beauty of the scene, and she wandered in among the rows of vines, cradling the clusters in her hands. The berries glowed and, temptingly warmed by the star, she plucked and ate one. The berry burst in her mouth, releasing the sweet nectar.

She ate another, and another. Kat chuckled to herself. *They're like potato chips. One is never enough.* She continued her wandering among the vines, picking the occasional berry and crushing it in her mouth. After the substantial noon-turn meal, the berries felt heavy in her stomach. She'd probably eaten too many.

She rounded a line and almost collided with a vineyard worker carrying a basket over his arm. "I'm sorry, I didn't expect to run into anyone."

"No matter, my Lady. I am performing a sampling of the berries to determine which vines are ready for picking."

"There are already a lot of samples." She peered in his basket and noticed each cluster of berries had a written note tied on. "I guess those notes tell you where you picked them?"

"You are correct. I take these back to Kerryon or Tevalow to judge."

"Why are you wearing gloves?"

"Those of us who work daily in the vineyards all wear them to protect ourselves from the poison on the berries, which the juicing removes."

Kat's eyes opened wide. "Poison? I've touched them too."

"No need to worry my Lady. We touch them thousands of times each day, and the poison would build up on our skin. The few you touched may make you a bit unwell, but would not affect you for long."

"But I did more than touch. I ate them … and I also swallowed the skins."

The worker's face appeared worried. "How many did you eat, my Lady? We should take you to our healer at once."

"I'm not sure. Perhaps I consumed about two bunches."

"How are you feeling?"

"Only a little nauseous." At that moment, Kat doubled over in pain, and she cried out.

The worker gasped and grabbed at her as she sank to the ground, barely conscious. He whistled, and another worker in a ponti cart came riding up. They helped Kat into the cart and raced for the main house. Kat was breathing with difficulty, and the Deon house healer's face swam into view. Her vision was fading, and all sound seemed to come from a distance.

She heard someone say, "Quickly, take her to the healing room."

She was lifted onto a long flat surface, and someone appeared with a container filled with little jewels. "Spiders! No." She shriieked and thrashed about, doing her best to avoid the jeweled creatures and fight off those attempting stop her from moving.

Voices yelled back and forth.

"Hold her down. We must put the pollinators on her."

Kat flailed about even harder. "No. No." She screamed in panic. Memories flooded back of running through a web when she was a child, and screaming for help, a huge spider on her chest. Her parents pulled at strands of web all over her body. She could not stop screaming.

Someone called out. "Quickly, bring the skat-koska."

She hear frantic peeps. "Wink!"

Multiple hands held her in place and something stung in her upper arm. Vision and sound faded.

♋♋♋

Mouse heard the words "Kat" and "ill" and rushed for the healing room. "What is happening to Kat? Is she alive?" Her face had taken on a blue tinge.

The healer, with a harried expression on her face assured him that Kat would be fine. "For some reason she became terrified of the pollinators and exhibited extreme violence. We were required to sedate her with the skat-koska."

"Why did you use the pollinators?" Mouse stared, horrified he might need to explain Kat's demise to Eduardo.

The healer emptied a container of pollinators over Kat, and they scuttled all over her, stopping every now and then to sting her and draw blood, which they expelled into a dish on the table. "She poisoned herself with the Orenberries. The berries become benign after juicing. All our pickers are gloved to protect them because they touch so many berries during the picking season. If she had not eaten any berries, she would be fine, because she only touched a few and would not have absorbed enough poison to affect her."

The healer brought a fresh container of pollinators. She collected the rather pale ones from Kat's body and allowed them to enter another container, which she handed to one of her assistants. "Unfortunately, she also consumed a fair number of berries, along with the poisonous skins. This was too much for her body to handle on her own."

The healer walked over to a desk and sat. She invited Mouse to join her. He did so and breathed in relief to see Kat now turning pink again.

"She was so extreme in her reaction. At one point a pyrock appeared, but disappeared once we sedated her. We have no idea where it came from." The healer ran her hand through her hair. "We do not know why she showed such fear of the pollinators."

"Apparently similar creatures exist on her world which she calls er … spiders. From what I gather, they are not brilliantly colored, and they grow in all sizes from small to as large as one of our meal plates. Many are deadly poisonous, while others will merely make the person they bite quite sick."

"But our pollinators are so small."

"She mentioned that some of their smallest spiders are the most poisonous of all."

The healer rose and picked up an empty canister. She retrieved the rest of the now pale pollinators and handed them to another assistant. "I understand why she might be afraid of our pollinators, and I suspect the poison in her blood increased her fear. We will quarantine the pollinators who helped your friend and supply them with some clusters of berries. They will pierce the skins for the juice and thus recover their abilities."

"What about Kat? How long will she take to recover?"

"She is already recovered. We simply need to wait for the remnants of the skat-koska to disappear from her system.We will transport her to her rooms at Deon House. If you check with her just prior to the evening meal, she should be able to join you."

Mouse sighed. "My thanks to you, healer." He took her hand and bowed low over it.

The female smiled and patted his arm. "She is important to you? Yes?"

Mouse blushed. He suspected she meant something more intimate. "Yes. Er… but because Lord Eduardo made me responsible for her well-being."

Does Kat deliberately enter into challenging situations to cause me such worries?

CHAPTER 42

Ssestin paced the length of the small vineyard beside Godron House. Emrys delayed his arrival, and Ssestin was uncomfortable, although he dressed in typical Glowen clothing, with his hair concealed by a hat. Discomforted by the fact that others might be watching him, he kept nervously to the shadows as much as possible.

He jumped when a voice broke the silence. "Ah, you must be Ssestin." Emrys appeared in front of him, accompanied by a young woman. "This is Tessia, my sibling's offspring, and we are anxious to be advised what is expected of us and what our reward will be."

Ssestin nodded. "A rumor reached us that a valuable secret exists in your land. Your patron in Morden wishes to possess this secret, and, for bringing it to him, will be willing to supply you with gold." Ssestin named a princely sum for Emrys, whose eyes gleamed with greed.

Tessia scoffed. "The amount is quite adequate, but we are wealthy ourselves. What I desire is the opportunity to meet with Lord Eduardo and to be bonded with him. That is the only item of real value to me."

Ssestin regarded her with a frown. He glanced at Emrys for confirmation.

The Glowen nodded. "A bonding between Tessia and Eduardo is important to us, and all Glowen. We will search for this secret and, when we transfer it to you, will be willing to accept half the gold, but the union with the Lord of Kaylin is of primary value."

Interesting. Was Galdin aware of this? "I understand. I give you my word that Tessia will be introduced to Lord Eduardo as a potential mate. You must understand, however, that while we are able to bring her to Lord Eduardo's attention, we cannot guarantee he will wish to bond with her. We are unable to control his thoughts or actions."

Tessia piped up. "That is acceptable. I heard many rumors of this secret, although I am not able to confirm them." She eyed Emrys. "We must further pursue this with Kat. I am convinced she is aware of something."

Ssestin stared at her, startled by her words. "Lady Kat? Is she not the woman who is in Pridden from another world?"

"Yes, I believe she is." Tessia frowned.

"Do you truly think she is cognizant of the secret?"

Emrys stepped forward. "I doubt she is, but Tessia suspects she harbors designs upon Eduardo, and thus dislikes her and prefers to think of her as secretive."

Tessia frowned. "Emrys, the woman is sneaky. You are correct though, I do not like her. I am sure she does possess an agenda when it comes to Lord Eduardo."

Ssestin paced and rubbed at his chin. *If this woman is privy to the secret, will Galdin now wish me to capture her and bring her to Morden?* "I do believe, Emrys and Tessia, you will be in the best position to discover the secret if this is what this woman is concealing. She knows you both, and I am sure you can persuade her to release the secret to you."

Tessia jumped in again. "And you promise you will make sure I am presented to Lord Eduardo."

"Yes. I promise." *No wonder this woman called Kat conceals things from Tessia. She is tedious.*

Ssestin, anxious to free himself from Tessia's single-minded occupation with the subject of Eduardo, leaned toward Emrys. "When you next send a shipment of Blud wine to Morden, we would ask you to deliver a crate to us at the Assassins' Guild. Is this possible?"

Tessia stared at Emrys, aghast. "You ship Blud wine to Morden?"

"I ship but a small amount. Blud is the only wine Morden wishes to receive from Glowen."

Tessia appeared horrified. "But this is illegal. Thane Brennan forbids the shipping of Blud wine outside of Glowen."

"Tessia, my dear. I told you, Morden wishes only Blud wine. It behooves us to make some trade with Morden, and Blud wine is consumed by fewer and fewer Glowens. We do a lucrative trade with Morden in Blud, and there is no need for Thane Brennan to know of this. Soon he too will realize this is a worthwhile trade. We sell no other products to Morden."

"But Emrys, this might cause trouble for our entire family if Brennan discovers what you have done. You should tell him the truth and explain why this is necessary."

"I will be informing Brennan shortly of my plans. Remember, although our Blud wine vineyard is small compared to Orenberry wine, we would not enjoy the luxuries we do without the income from it." He took Tessia's hand in his. "My dear, please keep this information to yourself for the time being. I must wait until the time is ripe before informing Brennan of my plans."

Tessia turned a worried face to him. "Are you sure? Will I need to wait long?"

He smiled at her. "I will tell you when I inform him. Now return to your rooms. You still need to prepare much before we meet with Eduardo."

She released her hand from his. "I will do as you ask." She left for her rooms within Godron house.

Emrys faced Ssestin again. "My apologies. She can be very rigid in her beliefs at times." He pulled a piece of parchment from his pockets. "Come with me to my office. I will record exactly what you need."

Ssestin followed him. *Does Galdin trust this man? I do not.*

CHAPTER 43

Kat woke on her bed at Deon House. Her stomach growled as she rose, and drew back the curtains. Dusk, bringing with it deepening colors of reds and dark blues, sent a clear message that meal-time was imminent.

She walked over to Wink's cage, and regarded the creature curled up and snoring gently. She poked at Wink through the bars. "Hey, did you fly to my rescue?" The pyrock yawned and stuck her head under her wing and resumed sleeping. *My stone didn't get cold either. Perhaps the pollinators are not dangerous. But they're still spiders. Ugh.*

Passing the mirror, Kat noticed she still wore the same clothes as when she strolled through the vineyard. Then she thought again about her encounter with the pollinators, and, shaking, she shed her clothes as fast as possible. She rushed into the personal and washed herself thoroughly, including her hair. Ensuring nothing foreign was anywhere on her, she withdrew long pants and a shirt from her bag and donned them. Leaving the shed clothes in a pile on the floor, she strode to the tassel and tugged.

When the young assistant appeared, Kat apologized for the clothes lying on the floor, and asked if he could arrange to clean them overnight.

"Of course, my Lady. Why are they on the floor?"

"I think they covered me in pollinators because they were trying to do that when they sedated me, and I'm not sure if any are still among the clothes. I really hate spiders."

He regarded her with curiosity. “I will take care of them for you.”

He carefully picked up the clothing, but no pollinators revealed themselves. Kat sighed in relief as he left with the bundle of clothes.

Straightening her spine, she marched from her room to Mouse’s door, and asked if he wanted to join her for the evening meal.

He gazed at her, a slight crease between his eyes. “Are you now well?”

“I am.” She shut her eyes and shuddered. “They crawled all over me, didn’t they?”

Mouse sighed. “They did, but with the amount of poison from the Orenberries in your system, if they had not, you might be dead now. The pollinators removed all the poison from your bloodstream.”

“Mouse, my fear of spiders is so overwhelming, I might prefer to die than allow them to run over me.” She shuddered again.

“Which is why the healer for Deon House needed to sedate you. You became violent, and a number of the workers received injuries.”

“I’m so sorry about the workers.” Kat scrunched up her face. “I couldn’t help myself. I hate spiders so much, and while I can run away from one, there were thousands of them.” She closed her eyes again and trembled with the memory.

Mouse patted her arm.

She stared at him, still shaking. “So can we go to the evening meal?”

“Yes, and I believe kossil-kweth tea should be our immediate order.”

Mouse leaned back into his room, grabbed his map bag, and they headed for the dining lounge.

Once seated and tea ordered, they inquired of the server about the dishes available.

"You are in luck, Lady. Tonight we will serve a superb thick-cut slab of musserel, fire-grilled and seasoned with a unique Baklai sauce. You will be willing to swear you are consuming meat. We serve this with additional roasted vegetables, covered in an oil from Rifella. This is Thane Brennan's favorite meal when he visits Deon House."

So impressed with the description and the mouth-watering odor wafting from the kitchen doors, they ordered the meal. Kat said, "How can we go wrong eating Thane Brennan's favorite dish."

Drinking the kossil-kweth tea, Kat's fear dissipated and calm eased over her being.

Mouse pulled a map from his bag and pointed out their route to Jasteen. "Jasteen is populated by many sailors and dock workers. The shipyards are controlled by the pen Cadno pod, and the master is Gorhelion. However, his offices are located in Marnabee, which is the headquarters of the pen Cadno pod."

"Glowen has been fascinating, but I will glad to leave. The contrasts between the northern Glowens and the southern ones are extraordinary. But I hope we will no longer be in the company of Tessia and Emrys, despite what they indicated."

"I hope you are correct, although they do possess a habit of appearing from thin air."

At that moment, their server walked to their table carrying two sizzling dishes of musserel. All they saw was a seared steak, covered in sauce, with a small blue flame burning from it, adding to the heat in the room.

The server placed the dishes in front of them. "Please do not forget to extinguish the flame before you eat this dish."

Duh. Does he really think I'll put flames in my mouth?

As the flames diminished, Kat blew on the musserel to douse them completely.

She gazed at the browned slab, still hot and simmering, and almost drooled at the sight and smell. She cut a small piece and chewed it with relish. The flavor reminded her of rib-eye steak, covered in a pepper sauce. She moaned with pleasure. She often tended to eat to live, but this dish was a live to eat one. She did her best to consume it slowly, rolling her tongue around every delicious bit.

All too soon the meal was over, and the server came by to ask if they wished dessert.

"No, thank you." Kat smiled up at him. "I'm well satisfied. You were correct, that was delicious."

The assistant cleared the dishes but brought a fresh pot of kossil-kweth to the table.

As they drank their tea, Mouse suggested they complete packing their bags when they returned to their rooms. "On the morrow, I propose we head for a morning meal and send our bags to the stable, so that once we have completed eating, we can head directly for Jasteen."

"Perfect. Will you send someone to waken me?"

Mouse nodded. "I will. As I am ready for my bed, I recommend we make for our rooms."

Kat rose at the same time he did, and they left the dining lounge.

In her room, Kat readied herself for bed, and slid under the comforter.

♋♋♋

Squeaking and chirping, Wink woke Kat the next morning, from a dreamless sleep. She stretched and rose to check on the ball of fluff, who almost danced in her cage, mouth open, obviously indicating a desire for food.

"Ah, someone's hungry. Wait a minute." She withdrew three pieces of pyrock food from her backpack, then eased the furry creature from her cage, and fed her. After returning her to her little bed, Kat smiled. Feeding and petting Wink was one of her favorite parts of her day.

A knock at the door proved to be the assistant from the previous turn, returning her clean clothes.

"Thank you."

"Lady, Sire Mouse suggested I inform you he will be ready to go for his morning meal shortly."

"My thanks. I will join him."

She showered, dressed, and then attached Wink's cage to her back pack. Ensuring her dagger was properly concealed at her waist, the tiny knife neatly tucked inside her left boot, and baggage on its way to the stable, she was ready and waiting when Mouse knocked. Opening her door, she joined him to attend the dining lounge. He only carried his map bag and a small leather satchel.

When they arrived at the dining hall, he led her to a small table, and they ordered a morning meal.

"You appear to be extremely healthy today, Kat."

"I am so much better. I slept well last night. I was lucky enough to meet with the Deon healer on my way to bed and I expressed my thanks to her again. She mentioned that just before they sedated me, a pyrock appeared. I thought I heard Wink when I was losing consciousness.I wonder if she thought she was coming to my rescue?" Kat smiled at the thought. "Unfortunately, I did not get the opportunity to say farewell to Afeena and Kerryon for their hospitality."

Mouse grinned. "They mentioned to me they would join us for tea this morrow. You can express your thanks when they appear."

Kat glanced toward the entrance. "There they are now." She stood to greet them. "Afeena, Kerryon, I thank you for everything you did for us. Especially for me when I foolishly ate the orenberries."

Kerryon smiled at her. "You are more than welcome, Kat. We must admit that you are one of our most interesting guests."

Afeena smacked him on the hand. "Mate of mine, do not tease Kat. We should have thought to warn her not to eat the berries. It was natural she would consume some. We are much at fault ourselves."

"My mate is correct, Kat. In our defense, we are not used to travelers from elsewhere. It did not occur to us that you would not know about the orenberries."

The four chatted about the visit to the vineyards and, finally, Mouse rose. "Afeena. Kerryon. Once again our thanks, but Kat and I must depart so we may arrive in Jasteen well before dusk."

While the two Glowens headed to begin their working day, Kat followed her guide to the stables.

ꕥꕥꕥ

Once mounted and on their way, Mouse took the lead, attaching the pack animal to Kat's horse. "Our ride should be simple. We will arrive in Jasteen in time for a quick tour of the town if you wish. Although, being mostly inhabited by sailors and wharf men, the town has little in the way of interesting sites."

"I don't mind, Mouse. I am glad we don't need to listen to Tessia and her equally annoying relative, Emrys."

He laughed.

They rode until the Pridden star was directly overhead, and stopped briefly for a piece of journeyklim and water. Mouse told her, "We do not need to fill our canteens, because we will shortly view the buildings of our destination on the horizon."

As they set off again, a thudding of hooves from behind them caused both to turn and discover who followed them.

"Oh, no. Mouse, it's Tessia and Emrys. Can't they leave us in peace?"

"Remember Kat, they are important to Brennan. Please keep this in mind and treat them with respect, no matter what you wish to do." He grinned at her.

They paused to let the two Glowens catch up and greeted them.

As they rode on, Tessia blurted out, "We decided we would meet you at Jasteen for an evening meal. You will soon be leaving, and this will be our last chance to see you before you go. Although, Kat, I hope to meet with you in Kaylin."

"How kind of you to want to say farewell. However, Tessia, I doubt we will meet in Kaylin. Mouse and I still need to complete a lengthy journey, and it will be many turns before we arrive back at Lord Eduardo's Keep."

Emrys addressed Mouse. "Since we are both here and can join Lady Kat for the evening meal, why do you not, Sire

Mouse, head on to Marnabee to book your voyage to Baklai. In that way, you can be sure of a having a vessel when you are ready."

Mouse raised his eyebrows and pursed his mouth in speculation. "That is a fine suggestion, Emrys. I may do so."

Kat stared at him. She was sure horror was etched on her face. "But Mouse?"

"Do not worry Kat. I will return to Jasteen to join you for the morning meal on the morrow."

Kat was still horrified. *Good grief. Alone with these two for a whole evening.* She glanced upwards as if in prayer and wondered what she had done to deserve such a fate.

They soon spotted the buildings of Jasteen and headed for the stable. Mouse arranged for Kat's horse and the baggage animal to be settled for the night, and requested some hay and water for his horse. "Kat, I will head directly for Marnabee. The town is not far, and it is still light. I will meet with Gorhelion pen Cadno and arrange for a ship for us. I will stay the night but will leave early enough to join you for the morning meal. I hope you will agree to house my bags in your room."

"If you think this is best, Mouse, I'll see you on the morrow. Please do not be late."

An attendant carried their bags to her room and she stayed to say one last thing to Mouse. "I'm not happy about being left alone with these two. You owe me big time."

Emrys called back to her. "We will meet you at dusk for the evening meal, Kat."

She waved to indicate she'd heard him.

I hope I can escape for an early night.

CHAPTER 44

By the time Pridden's star began to sink below the horizon, Kat had fed Wink, made sure only her clothes for the morrow remained unpacked, and had her night clothing folded on her bed.

She sighed, because she would not be able to avoid joining Emrys and Tessia for her food for the evening. No doubt they would come looking for her if she failed to appear. She made sure the veil over her thoughts was firmly in place.

The hallways of the Jasteen inn, covered in nautical motif and pictures in bright primary colors, raised her spirits. Although she disliked sailing and the often subsequent throwing up involved, the pictures reminded her she would be leaving Glowen in a few turns.

This land, while fascinating because of the Sha-hees, contained much she found unappetizing. What with robbers, northern Glowens' overtly sexual desires, poisonous berries, spiders, winged biters, and Blud wine, it had its share of contrasts. However, she forced herself to admit, their Golden River and the lip glosses almost made up for the negatives. And musserel, which made the most delicious meals.

She arrived at the entrance, and saw Tessia waving her over to join her and Emrys. She sat at their table. "Have you ordered your meals?"

Emrys aimed a vulpine smile at her. "Not as yet. We were waiting for you."

Kat indulged in an internal shudder. “Let’s ask the server what is available this night.”

Tessia waved him over. “Tell us what is best on the this evening’s menu.”

The young man bowed his head. “My male parent, Farth pen Peskajorie, owns a large vessel with which he captures sea swimmers. This night, we have a delightful dish of them, which are roasted over glowing charcoal and dressed with the juice of the lymnava fruit and some spices from Baklai. I believe you will find this meal most pleasant.”

Emrys ordered a musserel dish, but both Tessia and Kat asked for the sea swimmers. Kat asked the server whether they might bring her cantobean tea, which came from Rifella. She needed a stimulating drink to keep her from zoning out while listening to Tessia.

The server smiled at Kat. “A number of Rifellan guards reside in Glowen, and they all favor cantobean, so we can supply you with it.”

Tessia, naturally, asked, “What is cantobean?”

Kat explained that the tea supplied energy, and was much loved in Rifella.

“Oh, well, I do not need any energy because after our meal we will no doubt go to our beds early.”

The server returned carrying the tea and their meals on a huge tray. He served the tea first, and Kat took a quick sip while the young man distributed their meals. The plate he placed in front of her resembled a painting, a thing of beauty. The swimmer, lightly browned, completely deboned and decorated with flakes of bright green, tempted Kat so much she felt herself salivating. The meal, accompanied by three types of vegetables, all carved and displayed like flowers in yellow, green, and purple, seemed far too pretty to eat.

Kat grinned at Tessia. "I'm so grateful they do not leave the head on."

"The head?"

"Yes, in my world, many dining places, leave on the heads of the swimmers when they serve them."

Tessia screwed up her face and wrinkled her nose. "Sounds revolting."

"I find the heads are a pretty nasty display. I hate having my meals looking at me. I don't wish to be introduced to anything I plan on eating."

Tessia appeared confused. "Food is for eating, not for socializing."

Kat took a hasty bite of swimmer to avoid answering and sighed with pleasure. The fish, light, flaky and delicate, fell apart in her mouth. The sauce poured over the swimmer tasted similar to a lemony butter. "Mmm. Delicious."

Emrys apparently spied someone he knew and excused himself from the table.

Tessia reached for her tea, and revealed a beautiful bracelet with pink stones. Kat grabbed the young woman's wrist. It was her stolen bracelet. "Where did you get this?"

"What do you mean?"

"This bracelet. Someone stole this from me at the Keep. Where did you find it?"

"Emrys gave this to me as a gift."

"Where did he obtain it?"

Tessia pushed her chair away from Kat. "He said he purchased the bracelet."

"Well, it's mine. I recognize it, because of the unusual cut of the stones."

Before Tessia could speak, Emrys returned to the table. "Kat, the time has come for you to reveal the identity of the secret."

She frowned at him. "Don't start that again. I keep telling you … I do not possess any secret. By the way, where did you get this bracelet you gave to Tessia?"

Emrys's eyes turned cold and flinty, and the outer ring of his iris changed from blue to black. "Do not attempt to change the subject. As to the bracelet, I bought it." He scowled. "I know you are hiding a secret. I can sense this."

"Sense what? How you can sense something I have no clue about?" She growled at him. "I'm tired of discussing this. Leave me alone." *He can't sense anything, 'cause the veil over my thoughts is strong.*

Tessia said. "Kat, I did overhear you discussing a secret."

Kat turned on the girl and almost spat her reply. "I told you before, we were not discussing a secret. You misinterpreted what you heard. And I've had enough of these discussions."

Emrys leaned toward her. "You do know something. My contact in Kadwee told me you were missing for a few turns. Perhaps you learned this information then."

"That's enough — I've had enough of the two of you." She jumped up and stalked from the hall. *I'd like to squash him like a bug.*

Kat left the inn and stomped down a path in the direction of Marnabee. She wished Mouse had not gone on ahead. He acted as a buffer between Tessia and her equally annoying relative. She strode aimlessly, grumbling to herself. Beginning to puff a little because she'd been walking so fast, she stopped to examine her surroundings. When she glanced back, she realized she'd come a long distance from Jasteen. Luckily, the night sported a full moon so visibility was excellent.

She shivered. The night had cooled, and it began to rain. *I'd better get back.* Something hard hit her head. Then another. *Ouch.* Before she could go any further, the rain turned to ice pellets. Although they were only the size of small marbles, they hurt when they hit. *The weather on this island is weird. First I sweat, and now I'm bombarded by hail.* She glanced around for shelter, but there were no trees big enough to hide under. *Ouch!*

As she scanned the area, she saw what resembled a tall mound off the path. She ran over to investigate, and found a substantial wooden door, set at an angle. It appeared to allow passage to a low-rock building. The hail was falling faster and thicker, and she needed shelter. This instsant. Kat hauled on the door with all her strength, and finally it swung open. Unfortunately, the door blocked the moonlight and hid the interior except for a single top step. Although she was reluctant to enter, another blast of hail drove her make her move.

She trod on the step and her feet slid from beneath her. The door slammed shut, and she rocketed down a slide. Landing on her bottom with a thump, she cried out. Nothing moved or spoke in the darkness. She remembered seeing others light the normal Pridden globes with a clap, so she tried. Globes, fastened to the wall in sconces, illuminated a tunnel leading downward. Further on, two doors beckoned, but they were locked from the other side. *What is this place?*

She followed the lights through the tunnel. Just past the two doors, she entered a massive room, lined with hundreds of carboys filled with Blud wine. All were stoppered with airlocks, which helped prevent air from entering the corboys and interfering with the fermentation process. Off to the one side, the same wine was bottled and stored in crates. Empty bottles, crates, and a tub of corks and stoppers lined the other side wall.

The smell in the room combined rich earth and the strong musk of wine, although, less heady than the pen Godron winery in Dornish. Although no wine expert, Kat was positive this was a final bottling and storage facility for Blud before being shipped to Morden.

She resolved to try to climb the slide and return to the inn before Emrys and Tessia discovered her. *I probably should have waited for Mouse before exploring this place.*

I wonder if this is the secret Emrys thinks I'm aware of?

CHAPTER 45

Kat began walking back to the slide entrance but voices from beyond one of the locked doors stopped her. Heart thumping, she frantically searched for a hiding place. As the door opened, she ran and tucked herself behind a stack of cases of wine.

Tessia's high-pitched voice came through clearly. "Emrys, this is a huge amount of wine. Is all this being sent to Morden?"

"Yes, over the next path. But wait before you approach Brennan. I did not get the opportunity to speak to him." His footsteps grew closer.

"Is all this wine why I am able to meet with Lord Eduardo? Is the wealth this wine will bring to our House the reason Brennan is so anxious for me to form a bond with the Kaylin Lord?"

How can I avoid them, there is no good place to hide? Her heart raced.

"Naturally, Tessia. Brennan and Eduardo want a compatible relationship between the two lands. Wealth and a bond between you and Eduardo will guarantee this."

His steps grew closer. And stopped. Her stone turned icy cold.

Oh, oh.

Kat looked up. Emrys stood before her.

He sneered at her. "Well, well, well. What do we have here?"

Tessia scurried over and peered around Emrys's waist. "Kat. How did you get here?"

Emrys's grin held part leer, part menace. "It appears, Kat, my dear, you are far too curious for your own well-being."

Kat couldn't think. Like her stone, her hands were freezing. "Coming here was an accident. I… I was seeking shelter because I got caught in the ice storm when I was trying to get away from you both. You kept asking me about a secret," She jumped to her feet and faced him, hands on her waist. *Sometimes the best defense is attack.* " I think the secret you are looking for is if I know of your illegal activities with Blud wine."

"You foolish woman. I doubt this is the secret spoken of in Glowen."

With her hands at her hips she inched her fingers toward her dagger. "You can't pretend any longer, Emrys. The secret is out. Brennan will learn about the Blud wine." Kat pointed at Tessia. "This child knows about this as well, and she will not be able to keep her mouth shut. Now I truly am also privy to a secret." Kat clamped the veil around her mind. *He must never learn of the Sha-hee.*

"Kat, my exporting of Blud wine is not that large a secret. You will tell me what the real one is, or you will suffer the consequences. Plus now, you are informed about my trade with Morden, I cannot risk you telling Brennan. I'm warning you. If you do not reveal the true secret, you will be of no value to me. I will ensure you and your guide, Mouse, disappear forever."

Tessia stared, her mouth hanging open.

Kat's heart skipped a beat. "You intend to kill us? Over wine?"

"Emrys? Kill someone? You cannot."

"Be quiet, Tessia. You must be aware that we cannot allow this woman to wander about our land with full know ledge of our Blud wine trade."

"But you suggested killing her."

"Tessia, listen to me. Not only is this woman conscious of our secret, but I am convinced she also knows of a secret hidden within Glowen. If we let her live, she might give the information to someone else."

Kat stepped toward him. "You forget one thing, Emrys. If you even attempt to kill me, Mouse will find out and will report this to Eduardo." She swung around to Tessia. "You can kiss your possible bond with Lord Eduardo goodbye. He would never bond with my killer, nor trust a criminal who deals with unsavory enemies in Morden."

Tessia rushed toward Emrys. "She is correct. You cannot destroy her. I do not wish to be part of any killing." She clutched at him. "Thane Brennan will never support you in this. Please, do not do this."

"Tessia, you are either with me or against me."

"Emrys, I am not against you, only against killing anyone. You must not do this." She cried out in horror, and ran toward the closest door.

Emrys called out. "Tessia, be careful where your loyalties lie. You, too, could be troubled by an accident." He headed after her.

But Tessia had fled, and Emrys turned back toward Kat, his face darker than before. Seeing his expression, she ran toward the slide.

He moved swiftly in her direction. "You. This is your fault." He pulled a dagger from his belt, grabbed Kat's left arm, and pulled her toward him. “You will tell me the secret or face death now.” He aimed the dagger at her throat.

Unseen by Emrys as he attempted to draw her even closer, Kat drew her own dagger, which she hid behind her back. She resisted him with all her strength. “Stop. You cannot get away with killing me.” Her heart was pounding in her body, and her stone sat like a shaft of ice on her chest.

He snarled at her. “I mean it, I want the secret.” His grip on her was painful.

Using a defensive move she learned during her martial arts training, Kat twisted her wrist from his grasp, and retreated. She brought her right hand in front of her, clutching her own dagger. “You are the one facing death, Emrys. I know how to use this.”

His eyes widened. He obviously did not expect retaliation. “We seem to be at an impasse.” He sneered. “However, I can cut your throat before you can kill me.”

“Can you? You’re not as close now. Are you willing to take such a chance?” Kat’s heart still hammered in her chest, and her pendant lay frozen upon her breast.

Time stopped. The two adversaries stared at each other, neither moving. Waiting. Watching.

The door creaked, and they both whirled toward the sound.

The Sha-hee appeared. “Kat. Sha-hee know of what this challenge is for you, but we wish to tell you, you face no danger from this one. I add my thanks that you are able to maintain the veil on your thoughts.”

Emrys eyes locked on the being in the room. He gasped. “This must be the secret. You creatures are the ones with the treasure. I know the secret. I am now wealthy and powerful beyond everything. Where do you keep the money? What do you know of power?"

Sha-hee regarded him. "This one has many confused thoughts, all of which protect me from assuming anything from his mind. However he does wish you harm, and that we cannot allow." Sha-hee walked toward Emrys.

The Glowen backed away. "Wait. What do you want?"

Sha-hee reached out, touching him on the forehead with three fingers. Emrys's eyes rolled up in his head, and he keeled over, unconscious.

Kat stared at the downed Glowen. "Did you kill him?"

"No. I told you before, we cannot kill. I removed most of his memories. You and your guide are safe from him."

My stone is warm. I am safe now. "Thank you." She blinked a couple of times and breathed deeply. Tension drained from her body.

"Lady Kat, the Sha-hee must thank you for so ably concealing our existence. You proved yourself a worthy ally of Glowen and of Sha-hee. We trust you, and allow you permission to share your knowledge of us with your guide. He is an honorable man, and, from our observations, we trust him, and so should you."

"I do, and I must admit I thought you had already suggested such a thing, but when I attempted to tell him of you, he objected."

"We are aware, and you are correct. As your trusted guide, we allow you to tell him. He may still refuse to hear, and he does so because of challenges that exist, of which you are unaware. He will request this knowledge when the time is appropriate."

"My thanks again. I am honored you trusted me enough to reveal yourselves to me. I will not betray your trust, ever, until my guide asks for your secret." Her heart no longer hammered.

"This too is part of our knowledge. We will always know of your place in Pridden. The one who we saw most clearly in your mind created a talisman for you. We believe this aids in our link to you." The Sha-hee bowed toward her. "Now, we will depart. When we leave, wake that one, and leave this place by the same door. He will remember nothing and will follow you back to the place where you arranged to meet your guide." With those words, Sha-hee left via one of the doors from the storage place,

Kat pulled Emrys to his feet as he regained consciousness.

He blinked at her several times. "What happened?"

Kat did her best to hide her smile. "You tripped and hit your head." She urged him to walk. "Let's return to the inn."

They exited through the second door, walked along a well-lit tunnel for what seemed like quite a distance, and emerged in a small building close to the inn. The moon illuminated the path back to the inn, and the first tendrils of light colored the horizon. *Is it dawn? Already?*

As they stepped stepped from the building, Emrys turned to Kat again. "Why did we come here?"

"You wanted to show me where you kept the excess Blud wine." This was the first thing that she could think of to say.

Emrys frowned and scratched his head. "You will not tell Brennan about this, will you?"

"But you said you wanted me to." Kat was running out of lies.

They reached the inn, and Emrys was shaking his head. "Something is not right. I cannot remember why I told you this. My mind is confused, and I am tired. I should sleep." Emrys nodded vaguely at her and plodded off toward his room.

Trudging along the halls of the inn toward her room, Kat thought about the night and yawned. Exhausted she entered, shed her clothes, and tumbled into bed. *I've got to get some sleep before I find Mouse.*

CHAPTER 46

Ssestin paced the rooms of the small house in which he stayed. *Why had Emrys not contacted him?"*

He thought about the promises he made to both Emrys and Tessia. The female, an annoying young woman, would only discuss Lord Eduardo and how wonderful and handsome all thought him to be. Would Galdin agree to the promise he made to her about meeting with Eduardo.

All of Morden thought the Thane unpredictable, and more than once, Ssestin suffered the consequences. He suspected, however, that Ssarff experienced most of the suffering.

He stopped his pacing at the window. No sign of Emrys. *Where was he?*

The Pridden star rose some time ago, and Ssestin needed to understand what Emrys discovered during his meeting in Jasteen with Kat. Ssarff would be anxious for a report, and Galdin, never one for patience, would be more than frustrated. While the Assassins' Guild possessed much power, they did not enjoy enough strength to openly defy the Thane. He was curious whether the secret, once he obtained it, would supply enough might for the Guild to break free of Galdin's rule. Ssarff was the only one who might possess some insight into any weakness on Galdin's part.

A knock at the rear door of the house alerted him to Emrys's arrival, and he rushed to admit the man. "What delayed you? Did you obtain the secret from the woman?"

Emrys appeared quite calm. “Secret? Ssestin, I bring you no secret. I interrogated Kat, and I threatened her, but she was unable to reveal anything.” He laughed. “She thought the secret was that I supplied Morden with Blud wine.”

“So this so-called secret is a false rumor?”

“Yes. However, despite the fact that we cannot supply you with any unknown and valuable information, I hope you will still allow Tessia to meet with Lord Eduardo.”

“The promise was predicated upon you obtaining the secret which would bring power and wealth to Thane Galdin. Now, I cannot guess.”

Emrys twisted his face in worried lines. “But—”

Ssestin held up his hand in a placating gesture. “But I will attempt to arrange the introduction for you. I will do this in return for your promise to deliver two crates of Blud wine to my Guild.”

“Yes, I will arrange for the wine.”

“I must return to Morden to take the news to my Guild Master. You should contact me when your arrival in Kaylin is arranged, and hopefully I will pass on word of your intent to visit Lord Eduardo.”

“I will, and I must tell Tessia about our plans.” He bowed his head to Ssestin and left.

The assassin paced the room. He needed to contact Ssarff and advise the rest of his men that their services were no longer necessary.

He went to the room where his bags were stored, and withdrew a messenger moth from a pouch inside the closet. He brought the moth to his mouth and dictated a message to Ssarff. “We discovered no secret about any power or wealth that exists. It appears the only secret in Glowen is about Emrys’s illegal exportation of Blud wine.”

Ssestin paused to gather his thoughts further and continued to whisper to the moth. "Emrys himself thought another secret might exist. He had forgotten how much effort he expended to keep his illegal activities unknown. Because of this, I can pass you no secret to give to Thane Galdin. I will dismiss my men and advise them to return to Morden via various circuitous routes, and I will depart for the Guild on the morrow."

He took the moth to the window and launched it from his hand and watched it flutter off on the journey back to Morden. He was glad he did not need to be the one to break the news to Galdin and was relieved he would avoid the Thane's temper.

Ssestin knew of a number of rumors about Galdin. People spoke in hushed voices about the cruelty of his male parent, Thane Gritch, and the suspicious disappearance of his female parent. He wondered if this was the reason rumors whirled around Galdin about his potential responsibility for the death of Gritch.

Ssestin called to his men and advised them that they were no longer needed in Glowen. "Each of you must make you way back to the Guild as carefully as you are able. Take extra care to remain out of sight. I will meet you at the Guild to pay your wages."

Most shrugged. It was not unusual for a mission to be cancelled. They headed to their rooms to pack and leave.

Did Galdin destroy Thane Gritch because he suspected he had killed his female parent?

CHAPTER 47

A knock woke Kat from her brief nap. She stumbled from her bed and asked who was there.

A young assistant called back, "Lady Kat, Sire Mouse requested I advise you he has returned, and awaits you in the dining hall."

"Thank you, please let him know I will join him shortly."

"Yes, Lady."

She checked the window, and dawn was painting the sky with a palette of reds, yellows, and blues. Her head felt filled with cotton, so she grabbed an icy cold shower and dressed. She fed Wink, and made sure all was packed.

She glanced at herself in the mirror. Her stone glowed brilliantly green. *What did Sha-hee mean by a link to my stone?* She frowned, and left her room, her mind filled with a jumble of thoughts about the pen Godrons, Sha-hee, and Blud wine. She arrived at the dining hall entrance, unaware of how she got there.

Mouse, seated at a table, waved her over. "I ordered groonnan for you and some stimulating cantobean tea."

"I'm glad you thought of it. I guess neither of us slept enough this night. I was not happy you left me to deal with Emrys and Tessia."

"I know you were not. Although we both need sleep, I suggest we leave immediately after our meal. We will arrive in Tavollen by the noon-turn. This will give us an opportunity to gain some sleep before we meet with Brennan. When we arrive, I will make sure he is advised of our plans, and hopefully he will invite us to join him for an evening meal. He will desire that we bring him up-to-date on our journey."

"Wonderful. I will need a decent nap when we arrive in Tavollen. And, to keep us awake in our saddles on the way, I will tell you what occurred after you left."

Mouse smiled. "I most likely managed more sleep than you, but passing on the information should keep you awake. I am more weary from being in the saddle for so long." He stretched. "I must say, I am looking forward to Baklai. From what I hear, they are straight forward people."

ꝏꝏꝏ

Mouse took the lead, and they passed through the village of Marnabee, where he had arranged for them to meet a boat to travel to Baklai two turns hence. "After we meet with Brennan, we will stay in Tavollen,because Marnabee and the jetty are so close. We will go to the boat from there and the dockhands will help to board our horses. They will secure them so that they will rest well in the makeshift stalls during the crossing."

"I'm pleased you told me. I am sure the poor animals encountered a rough time coming from Rifella."

"They survived, but as you may remember, we remained a few turns at Brennan's Keep, so we could allow them to gain enough rest to recover from the challenging voyage." Mouse gazed at Kat. "So, how much will you tell Brennan about Emrys?"

Kat made sure the veil covered her thoughts well. "Everything I've told you. The foolish man never realized the secret he kept attempting to discover was that he traded Blud wine illegally with the Mordens. It was a large secret, because he wanted to avoid his activities becoming public knowledge."

Mouse stopped his horse and gazed at Kat, his face expressionless. "Is this the secret you wished to tell me?"

She concentrated on keeping the veil strong, and faced him, keeping her own expression neutral. "Yes, that was it." *He did say if I ever mentioned it again, he would abandon me.*

He kept his gaze on her. "Good, then I did not need to be concerned."

She lifted her head. "It would seem so."

The air thickened with words unsaid. Kat's heart beat a little faster. *So he still isn't ready to ask what I know.*

Mouse clicked at his horse to move. "We should not tarry."

Kat followed him. "I notice more buildings ahead. Is Marnabee enormous?"

Mouse chuckled. "No, what you are seeing is Tavollen from the other side."

They rode up to the inn, and both dismounted, Kat doing her usual, hanging on the pommel and sliding down the horse. She knew she lacked grace, but this method guaranteed success without injury to herself. Mouse negotiated with the stable master for stalls, food and water for their animals. The assistants then led them to the inn to deliver their baggage.

Kat followed, with her back pack, and Mouse with his map satchel. Before either closed their doors, Marreth appeared.

"Welcome. I gather this last journey was no less challenging than your first."

Kat smiled tiredly at her. "We have much to tell you, Marreth. But I must sleep first. I suspect Brennan will want to meet with us as well."

"We have both come to join you here, and Brennan asks you meet with him for the evening meal." Marreth smiled at Kat. "Both of you appear tired. I suggest you take some rest, and I will come for you in time to join Brennan."

Kat thanked her, entered her room, and placed Wink's cage on the dresser. Too tired to do more, she shed her outer clothes, flopped on the bed, and slept.

♋♋♋

A light knock at her door woke Kat, and she called out. "Who is it?"

"Tessia. Can I come in?"

Tessia? Why was Tessia at the door?

"A moment." Kat rose, grabbed her robe from her duffel, put it on, and allowed Tessia entrance. *I do need to talk to her, though. She's subdued. Good.* "So why have you come here?"

"I grew afraid when Emrys said he would kill you. I wanted to make sure you were safe."

"If you were so worried, Tessia, why didn't you do something?"

"He terrified me. I never saw him act like that. My parents would not wish me to be in the company of a man like him." Her lower lip quivered. "I had no knowledge about his illegal exporting of Blud wine."

"Do you now understand that he is a criminal?" *The girl is beyond naïve.*

She shook with obvious fear. "Yes, but Lady Kat, what I should do?"

"Tessia, you are aware that I should report you to Thane Brennan, aren't you? You discovered Emrys was involved in exporting Blud wine to Morden, and you did not advise your Thane immediately." *Poor Tessia wasn't really responsible, but a good scare might help her to grow up.*

She lowered her head and nodded. She barely whispered. "Yes."

"Sit, Tessia. I'm going to tell you what I expect from you."

She sat.

"First, you will avoid Emrys's company at all costs. Your parents will soon be apprised of his crimes, so they will not question why you avoid him. Second, you will return my bracelet to me."

The girl took the bracelet from her wrist and handed it to Kat.

"Thank you. Third, you will forget about traveling to Kaylin to attempt to meet with Eduardo. You can understand that he cannot afford to bond with a woman who possesses a relative who is a known criminal."

Tessia nodded, a glum expression on her face.

Kat continued. "And fourth, I would suggest you meet with Marreth, the healer for Glowen and request that she allow you to become an apprentice to her."

"But I do not have any healing experience."

"No, but you will learn from Marreth." Kat sat at the table, opposite Tessia. "If you do these things, I will make sure Thane Brennan is advised that you took no part in any of Emrys's dealings." *I'm being hard on her, but ...*

Tessia gazed at Kat, hope in her eyes. "You will? You would do that for me?"

"I will. Now, return to your family, and advise them that you wish to seek apprenticeship with Marreth."

At last, tears escaped poor Tessia's eyes, and she rose and almost scuttled from Kat's room.

Kat returned to her bed and fell back to sleep.

♋♋♋

When she heard the knock on her door, she groaned. She guessed that Marreth had come for her to meet Brennan for an evening meal. She opened the door. "Marreth, can you give me enough time to stand under a brief but cold shower to wake me up fully and to allow me to throw on some clothes?"

Marreth blinked and grinned. "What an odd picture. I envision you throwing clothes in the air and them falling on you in a picture-perfect fit."

Kat laughed. "I must admit some of my world's expressions are odd. But can you allow me some time?"

"Of course. Come to Sire Mouse's room when you are ready."

When Marreth left, Kat hastened to unpack appropriate clothing. She fed Wink, took an icy shower, and dressed. She felt ready for anything—well, almost anything—and left her room and knocked at Mouse's quarters.

Marreth opened the door. "You certainly were brief. Are you awake now?"

"Mostly. While we head to Brennan's quarters, I will advise you about my discussion with Tessia. I assume Mouse has told you about Emrys's activities?"

"Yes he has."

During their walk, Kat told Marreth the four things she demanded of Tessia, particularly that she seek an apprenticeship with Marreth.

"Tessia? A healer apprenticeship with me? You are being demanding of her."

"Yes. I suspected you might think my request odd. But Marreth, she is most naïve and needs some sort of direction in her life. Even if she absorbs a little of what a healer apprentice must be conversant with, it will help her appreciate and listen to people, instead of acting like a spoiled child. Plus you can take this opportunity to tell her about the world. I doubt she will actually become a healer, but whatever she learns from you will be of benefit to the poor girl."

Mouse gazed at Kat. "You continually surprise me."

Kat frowned at him and resumed her chat with Marreth. "Think of this as healing Tessia's spirit."

"I surrender." She held her hands up. At last she shook her head. "You surprise me as well, but I will help the child."

"Marreth, she's not a child, but she does tend to act like one."

"You are correct in your assessment, Kat. Fine, I will accept her as an apprentice, and I will take on one other so they may help each other. After all, who can guess what Tessia will absorb—and, become."

Kat smiled. *Who can guess, indeed.*

CHAPTER 48

They arrived at Brennan's quarters. The guard opened the huge doors, advised Brennan they waited for him, and ushered them inside.

Brennan boomed a welcome at them. "Marreth, I would appreciate you joining us for the meal. You may possess additional knowledge that I will find helpful."

Marreth bowed her head. "I would be most willing, Thane."

He walked to a table set for four, which was less formal than the first dinner they enjoyed with him when they arrived in Glowen. He called for wine and asked them all to be seated. As they did so, the servers began pouring wine for each of them. Kat stopped him by placing her hand over her glass.

"You do not appreciate our wine, Kat?"

"Thane, on the contrary, I do appreciate your wine. However, I haven't enjoyed much sleep, and your wine might cause my head to end up in my dinner. Perhaps you would allow me to request cantobean tea." She grinned at him. "I do prefer to remain awake in your company."

Brennan roared with laughter. "Kat, if you fell asleep in my company, I would realize I am now old and boring."

Kat laughed with him. "Old and boring? Never. I can't imagine such a thing happening."

Brennan called for a toast for a successful visit by Kat and her guide. "So now I would ask about your journey after you left Tavollen the first time."

Mouse gave him a brief description of their visit to the Godron House winery in Dornish, and the astonishing sights and sounds. Brennan interspersed Mouse's report with additional questions. Mouse advised the Thane about the fright they all received when Kat was poisoned by orenberries, and her unsettling fear of the pollinators.

"I am astonished, Lady Kat, that you should be so afraid of those beautiful creatures. They are so tiny and valuable for our wine production. That a woman of your courage and resolve should be so fearful of them, I find quite odd."

Kat explained to him about spiders and how when she was a child, she accidentally walked through a series of massive webs, and they wrapped all over her, leaving at least two huge spiders on her body. She asked for some parchment and a pen, and shivering, drew a picture in actual size of a tarantula. *Brennan would't know that Tarantulas don't spin webs—but they're frightening.*

When she handed the parchment to him, his eyes widened. "Is this their actual size? I can understand why you may fear these creatures, but they are enormous compared to our pollinators."

"Some of the most poisonous ones are only the size of my fingernail."

"I see." He stroked his chin. "Do continue with your story."

Kat told Brennan about Emrys's illegal activities with Blud wine.

Brennan's eyes widened, his face twisted in an expression of horror. "He is sending Blud to Morden? How much? How often?"

Kat related what she learned but suggested Brennan investigate on his own. She also mentioned she suspected

Emrys operated a band of robbers, or at least dealt with them. She insisted she was not positive about this. However, her stolen bracelet ended up on Tessia's wrist, and Tessia insisted she received it from Emrys.

Brennan shook his head. "Since Emrys knows you discovered this, why has he not threatened you?"

As guilelessly as she could, Kat told him, "He did attempt to do so, but during our struggle, he fell and hit his head. This appears to have affected his memory in some way."

Brennan raised an eyebrow, but at this point, the server brought their meals and conversation ceased while he served.

Kat, ecstatic she could consume Brennan's favorite meal, musserel steaks with the spicy sauce, sniffed the air and smiled broadly. "This is delicious. Thane Brennan, you Glowens do possess wonderful taste in food."

Brennan insisted Kat continue with her narrative while he continued to ply her with questions. Between swallows, Kat covered what she assumed Brennan should know. When the meal was complete, the servers cleared the table and brought additional flagons of wine and cantobean tea for Kat.

Brennan raised his glass. "Lady Kat, this has been quite a tale you have told us. Our thanks for advising me of areas in Glowen which do indeed require changes. I thank you and acknowledge how astute Eduardo was in sending you here." He grinned at her. "You uncovered a major illegal export of our Blud wine. You also exposed the fact that our northern people are so steeped in sensual sensations that visitors need to be warned of the challenges they might face."

"Thank you, Thane."

"And, Mouse, I believe both of you discovered an area which might attract potential visitors to view our wine making. Your description of the fermenting rooms was vivid. This might persuade those from Shendea and Rifella to visit us and, thus, import more wine. From what you tell me, we could even attract those from southern Morden."

Kat asked, "Brennan, what do you suspect will happen when the Mordens from the north discover they can no longer import Blud wine?"

"An excellent question. I believe that rather than create a potential war, we may have to allow a limited amount to be exported. And, we will destroy much of the blud berries that Emrys is cultivating. If we produce only a small amount and export but half, Morden cannot complain that we are limiting them. I plan to destroy the storage facility you discovered. This will immediately reduce the amount of Blud wine currently available."

Mouse was looking at Brennan with an expression of admiration. "A unique but effective solution. I am sure Lord Eduardo will support such a decision."

"I admit I hope he will. I admire Eduardo's leadership skills."

The four sat in silence.

Brennan rose from his chair. "Mouse, once again, I thank both of you for your help in uncovering some of Glowen's challenges. I suspect you will want to be leaving for Baklai. I will make arrangements for a boat for you."

Kat smiled up at him. "Our thanks, Thane Brennan, but my ever-efficient guide has made the arrangements for us to board within two turns."

"You are an efficient guide, Mouse. I am sure both of you are ready for sleep. I do not need to keep you from your bed any longer, Lady Kat. However, perhaps you will both join me for a farewell meal in the evening of the morrow."

Kat desperately attempted to hide a yawn. "My thanks, and I would be most honored to meet with you on the morrow."

"Excellent. Marreth, would you please remain with me for a brief conversation."

Kat was unable to hide her yawn any longer, and she and Mouse departed Brennan's dining room and headed for their own quarters.

Kat's only thought as she prepared for bed was about the Sha-hee. *They are strong, but convey no fear, and I managed, despite severe temptations, to keep their secret during this whole trial.*

♋♋♋

She woke the following turn refreshed, with Wink demanding food as soon as Kat moved in the bed. After preparing for the day, she tugged on the tassel and ordered a light morning meal.

She ate and sat to write in her journal and covered the happenings with Sha-hee. The only person who would ever be able to read her journal would be Mouse, so she was safe recording their existence. She trusted Mouse, and he was right, she also trusted other men: Liandock, Eduardo, Bardu, Arrogol, Rhognor, Bannigus, Nick, Garren, Brennan, Godrith, Walden, Jagloran, Kerryon, Penrow, and Thontook.

Reluctantly, she also trusted Haydar, despite the fact that he annoyed her. As she thought about these men, she realized that there were many other men she had encountered on her journey that she also trusted, such as Ariang the Master Miner, and Ballinor the Rifellan guard leader in Roothlan.

Mouse was right. My old way of thinking no longer applies. I have trusted many men during my journey. She laughed to herself. *I do trust men.* She smiled, surprised she had changed her attitude so much. She also trusted the Sha-hee although whether to classify them as male or female, she had no idea. *I guess they aren't either. They're simply Sha-hee.*

Leaving the parchment on her desk to dry, she checked on Wink, who was sleeping soundly, and left to find Mouse. She knocked and asked if he was ready for a noon-turn meal.

"Your timing, Kat, is impeccable."

They headed to the dining lounge, and when seated, with meal ordered, Kat said,"You are correct, Mouse. I do trust many men. You, obviously."

"Thank you. How do you now feel about the males in Glowen?"

"I'm happy to realize how many excellent men do exist in my life, both in Pridden and my world. So many helped me in various ways, and even some whose names escape me, were of aid. It's freeing to meet a man and not automatically dislike him. I'm not talking about those to whom I'm attracted. Trust and physical attraction are two very different things. My life seems more positive now." She clasped her hands and leaned on the table. "But you asked about the men in Glowen. I believe I must deal with each of them on their own merits."

"I am pleased you understand this and hope you will continue to do so."

Kat frowned. "Just because I trust you Mouse, does not mean you can lecture me." She chuckled.

Mouse shook his head.

Kat smiled behind her hand. "I realize we leave tomorrow to board the ship to Baklai. Are there supplies we might need? I was thinking a short trip to the shops might be fun, and we will still enjoy time to pack and meet with Brennan for our meal this evening. I need to ask him something."

"Shopping is not an entertainment for me, Kat. However, if you wish me to accompany you, I will."

"I would like that, if only to ensure I don't forget anything."

They rose, and Mouse led her toward the market.

♋♋♋

Kat, following the apprentice to Brennan's quarters, shrugged at Mouse. "You were right. I found nothing I considered unique at the market."

"At least you were brief. I anticipated with horror a lengthy shopping trip."

Kat snorted at him.

When they arrived at Brennan's door, one of his guards admitted them.

Brennan greeted them with wine and seated them at his table. "I planned a simple meal. Since you will be traveling by boat on the morrow, you will find it best to keep only simple foods in your stomach."

The evening consisted of laughter and conversation. Kat delighted in the jovial side of Brennan. The conversation flowed along with the wine until Mouse suggested it was best if they departed for their beds.

Before they left, Kat asked Brennan for a quiet word. He agreed with a puzzled expression and stepped aside to hear what she wished to say. She explained about the deal with Eduardo. "I must find people with energy of power in each land to help me return to my own world. Will you be one of those from Glowen to aid me, Brennan?"

"Kat, I will gladly help you in any way I can. But I must tell you. I am not a Wielder. I am not sure what energy I can supply."

"Brennan, you are blessed with power. Power in leadership and power in your unique way of thinking. No doubt that will be of value. My thanks for agreeing to this."

ᘓᘓᘓ

Wink's squeaks woke Kat. The first streaks of dawn colors splashed across the sky. Another beautiful day in paradise dawned, or so she felt. She got ready and bounced her way to Mouse's door and knocked. "Rise up, sleepyhead."

The door opened and he stood there, appearing well rested. "I awakened before the dawn, and my bags are on their way."

"Terrific. Let's eat."

After eating, Kat asked the server if she might obtain a canteen filled with red-leaf tea. Despite the calm weather, she would appreciate having the tea on hand, just in case of seasickness.

They walked to the stable and mounted their previously saddled horses.

Mouse led, with the baggage animal attached. "The jetty is not far, and once we arrive at the docks, they will give us a stateroom to hold us and our baggage. The horses will be tied into individual stalls."

"It sounds efficient."

Mouse was correct. They arrived soon at the Marnabee jetty, and the crew directed them to the ship that was to sail that day for Baklai. Two dockhands removed the baggage, plus bridles and saddles, and placed all on a cart, which they wheeled up a gangplank to the vessel, and in through an opening halfway up the ship.

Mouse followed and beckoned to Kat to join him. The cart paused outside a cabin, and the dockhands removed everything and stowed their belongings inside. Kat ran to the place through which they'd entered to catch what happened next. Three grooms led their horses into the bowels of the ship.

She turned to Mouse, excited. "I never watched any of this before. It was night, and the weather was awful."

"We can go and watch the people boarding. The best view is from the upper deck, where the crew have already laid out food for a noon-turn meal."

Once all passengers had boarded, and the gangplank stowed, the crew raised the sails. The ship had a weird mast and sail configuration. To Kat, it almost resembled a barkentine. The foremost mast had square sails, which were perfect for running with the wind. The second mast had a huge jib, while the third mast sported a large mainsail. As they prepared to leave the harbor, with the wind from behind, the crew rigged the second and third masts as "wing-on-wing," with the mainsail to one side and the jib to the other. They sailed from the harbor, catching the ebb tide.

The sea was calm despite an excellent breeze that blew from the land, and Kat made her way to the bow area. Holding tightly to the rail, old tunes her parents had collected during their travels, ran through her head. She began to sing softly. "What will you do with a drunken sailor… early in the morning." She breathed in the sea air and recalled the next verse. "Shave him with a blade of a rusty razor, early in the morning." She had forgotten most of the words, but continued to hum the lively tune.

Mouse beside her, asked a question. "An odd song, but the words are interesting. Where did you learn it?"

She turned and smiled at him. "From my parents. Many, many, many years… uhm paths ago." She gazed up at the few fluffy clouds. "I have a fine feeling about this voyage to Baklai."

Plus I'm getting much closer to going home.

DRAMATIS PERSONAE

NAME	DESCRIPTION	FROM
Aenid	A hunter from Tirenna	Rifella
Afeena	Of the pen Deon pod and bond mate to Kerryon	Glowen Shendea
Anwen	Apprentice Healer & Guide for Mouse & Kat in Shendea	Shendea
Ariang	Master Miner at Haligon	Rifella
Argelwyd	Original Lord of all Pridden	Morden
Arrogol	Praetor of Murwenna's guards, bond mate of Olwyn	Rifella
Bardu	Praetor of Eduardo's guards bond mate of Irina	Rifella
Ballinor	Leader of Guards in Roothlan	Rifella
Banhadron	Refugee from Morden	Morden
Bannigus	Horse-master in Rifella	Baklai
Bannon	Caretaker of Pontis in Kaylin	Kaylin
Benden	Stable master at Geronna	Rifella
Brennan	Thane of Glowen - of the pen Taddyn pod	Glowen
Brigden	Leader of Morden travelers in Shendea	Morden
Brith	Seamstress for Eduardo's keep	Kaylin
Bodeth	Assistant to Tythan, with the guard unit in Geronna	Rifella
Bronwyth	Head of functions for Eduardo	Shendea

NAME	DESCRIPTION	FROM
Caleesh	Goddess for Pridden	Pridden
	Spirit only (except in Morden)	
Carlo	Designer/coder for Nick	Our world
Carrog	Busta bonded to Brynn	Rifella
Casseg	Busta bonded to Kat	Rifella
Clune	Financial clerk for Eduardo	Kaylin
Colwin	Apprentice serving Kat in	Shendea
	Shendea	
Cranna	Busta bonded to Arrogol	Rifella
Dafid	Door guard for Eduardo	Kaylin
Dayleeya	Bond mate to Rifellan guard	Rifella
	leader Jagloran, in Glowen	
Deleth	Healer to Lord Rhognor,	Shendea
	womb mate to Wynneth	
Derwynn	Head of Thieves Guild	Shendea
Drainin	Counselor to Eduardo	Morden
Ebron	Of the pen Darryn pod, a	Glowen
	well respected artist	
Eduardo	Lord of Kaylin, related to Mouse	Morden
Emrys	Of the pen Godron pod &	Glowen
	uncle to Tessia brother to	
	Gwindon, and is in charge of	
	the Orenberry winery in Pridden	Glowen
Erathin	Of the pen Deon pod and	
	bond mate to Tevalow	
Fardith	Assistant to Halfin	Shendea
Farnon	Headmaster for Dizerth	Shendea
Farth	Of the pen Peskajorie pod G	lowen

NAME	DESCRIPTION	FROM
Fenneth	Healer to Murwenna	Shendea
Ferren	Apprentice to Marreth	Shendea
Flank	Burgomaster of Magwin S	hendea
Galdin	Thane of Morden	Morden
Garren	Of the pen Darryn pod, and talented Glass blower	Glowen
Gaviska	Of the pen Yuwen pod, manages the pathways around Kadwee	Glowen
Gaynore	Of the pen Deon pod, chief advisor to Brennan	Glowen
Godrith	Tapestry Master in Shendea	Shendea
Gorhelion	Of the pen Cadno pod, and Master of the shipyards.	Glowen
Grendel	One of Murwenna's honor guards	Rifella
Gritch	Male parent to Galdin and previous Thane of Morden	Morden
Gwinrick	Leader of Murwenna's guards	Rifella
Gwindon	Of the pen Godron pod, brother to Emrys and father to Tessia. He is head of the wine-makers	Glowen
Halfin	Lady of Shendea, Lord Rhognor's bond mate	Shendea
Hamrid	A servant to a Morden, rescued by Kat	Baklai
Haydar	Horse-Master for Eduardo, Mayda's father	Baklai
Hesginn	Grey Magician, Head of Magician's Guild and advisor	Shendea

NAME	DESCRIPTION	FROM
Hesgian	coinued -- to Lord Rhognor and Brother to Walden	
Illian	Apprentice builder, Penrow's daughter	Kaylin
Irina	Member of Keep guards, Bardu's bond mate and sister to Liandock	Rifella
Istra	Serving woman at Vendi's Inn	Shendea
Janella	Murwenna's Bond Mate, sister to Tiwellan	Rifella
Jagloran	Praetor of Guards to Thane Brennana	Rifella
Kadnu	Bardu's second in command	Rifella
Kaleen	Met Kat at Ponti Inn, member of Rifellan guards	Rifella
Karen	Friend to Kat, Nick's wife	Our world
Kanorang	Of the pen Darry pod, and is a master musician	Glowen
Kat Karim	Katherine Karim - Mother a Scot and Father Arabic	Our World
Kaydith	Serving woman for Kat in Shendea	Shendea
Keedin	Rifellan warrior stationed at Roothlan in Shendea	Rifella
Kerryon	Of the pen Deon pod. Second in command to Gaynore who is head of the Wine growers and bond mate to Afeena	Glowen

NAME	DESCRIPTION	FROM
Koosela	Of the pen Yuwen pod, manages pathways around Kadwee	Glowen
Kraklin	Grey Magician, second in command to Hesginn	Shendea
Krogen	Leader of the pen Yuwen pod	Glowen
Kurdin	Rifellan guard in Brevista	Rifella
Laylin	Serving woman for Kat in Kaylin	Kaylin
Liandock	Master Metal-Smith of Kaylin, brother to Irina, lover to Kat	Rifella
Lanerch	Lord of Kaylin prior to Eduardo, and adoptive father to Eduardo	Kaylin
Lilliwon	Of the pen Iselon pod, now of the pen Taddyn pod, bond mate to Thane Brennan	Glowen
Makinti	Praetor for Thane Cathked, Bardu's friend	Rifella
Manga	Of the pen Yuwen pod and Manager of the camp	Glowen
Marreth	Healer to Thane Brennan	Shendea
Master Keeper	Keeper of the village of furred stingers	Glowen
Maxwell	Cousin to Kat's ex-husband world	Our World
Mayrin	Bond mate to Horse-Master Haydar, female paretn to Mayda	Baklai
Mayda	Serving woman and apprentice Wynneth daughter to Haydar	Baklai

NAME	DESCRIPTION	FROM
Mazon	Head of the Mazon Family who welcome guests in Dizerth	Shendea
Melindar	Chief Advisor to Murwenna, sister to Murwenna	Rifella
Merrindock	Prefect of Pakanna	Rifella
Milva	Of the pen Darryn pod, bond mate to Ebron	Glowen
Morshag	Legendary horse thief of Baklai now a curse word	Baklai
Mouse	Serves Galdin, Guide for Kat in Pridden related to Eduardo	Morden
Murwenna	Lord of Rifella, bond mate to Janella	Rifella
Neerin	Assistant to Walden	Shendea
Nick	Kat's supervisor, husband to Karen	Our World
Nooville	Guard leader in Brevista	Rifella
Penrow	Master Builder of Kaylin, Illian's father	Kaylin
Pentramore	Prefect of Tirenna	Rifella
Pilar	A Tirennian hunter	Rifella
Ponsin	Leader of Glazenwyth	Shendea
Rantor	Store Owner in Blain	Rifella
Rhognor	Lord of Shendea, Titular head of all Guilds and Bond mate to Halfin	Shendea
Saglin	Ssarff's second-in command	Morden
Salssin	Agent of Assassin's Guild	Morden

NAME	DESCRIPTION	FROM
Sherwyn	Head of Housekeeping for Eduardo's Keep	Kaylin
Skonya	Of the pen Yuwen pod, manages the flower reserve	Glowen
Souris	Waiter at hotel in Tortola	Our world
Ssarff	Leader of Assassin's Guild	Morden
Ssayleese	Snake Goddess in Morden (Spirit only)	Morden
Ssestin	New assistant to Ssarff	Morden
Ssorin	Assassin in Brevista	Morden
Taddyn	Last Lord in Glowen	Glowen
Tammyn	Servant to pen Godrons	Glowen
Tannis	Brings Gornog Meat to Rifella	Kaylin
Tessia	Of the pen Godron pod and niece to Emrys	Glowen
Tevalow	Of the pen Deon pod, lead berry growe and bond mate to Erathin	Glowen
Thontook	Master Weaver of Kaylin	Kaylin
Tiwellan	Economic advisor to Murwenna adopted brother to Janella	Morden
Trevalynn	Of the pen Godron pod. 2nd-in-command to Emrys pen Godron	Glowen
Troyon	Heir to the Rifellan Throne, son of Murwenna	Rifella
Tythan	Head of the Rifellan guards in Geronna	Rifella
Walden	White Magician, brother to Hesginn	Shendea

NAME	DESCRIPTION	FROM
Wealin	Taylor in Murwenna's keep.	Rifella
Wolfdrang	Second in command to Arrogol	Rifella
Wynneth	Healer to Lord Eduardo, womb mate to Deleth	Shendea

THE GLOWEN PODS

pen Taddyn	Royalty and royal relations
pen Deon	Vineyard growers and cultivators
pen Godron	Wine makers
pen Darryn	Artists of all kinds, including musicians
pen Cadno	Shipbuilders and keepers of wharves
pen Yuwen	Growers of foodstuffs
pen Iselon	Responsible for relationships with other lands
pen Peskajorie	In charge of fishing

FLORA AND FAUNA OF PRIDDEN

NAME	DESCRIPTION	FROM
Blicks	Small rabbit like creature delicious in a stew	Rifella
Blud	The rare strong red Glowen wine	Glowen
Bonbrie	Delicious fruit similar to peach	Shendea
Boradai	Furred creature size of a kitten who can read minds	Shendea
Brantor	Small, short-legged, carnivores who hunt in packs, with massive claws, two small horns and black teeth.	Rifella
Brynosh	Tall plants which are used for tapestries and by Rifellans for their leather armor.	Shendea
Busta	Intelligent creatures who bond with Rifellans to fight the Crosa (see specific busta in Personae)	Rifella
Cantobean	A chocolate-like bean for a stimulating tea	Rifella
Cathnog	Large ferocious cat-like creature with four huge canines resembling a saber-toothed tiger.	Shendea
Drag	Largest snake in Morden, similar to a python in that is crushes it's prey	Morden
Difoona	Flower whose scent helps waken	Glowen

NAME	DESCRIPTION	FROM
Eedhenna	Vicious bird resembling buzzards	Glowen
Eethnaire	A root vegetable which when combined with dried brantor produces a delicious and nutritious stew	Rifella
Fara tea	A tasty balancing tea made from fara root and leaves	Glowen
Fire Mouth	A hot spice that is similar to Peri Peri sauce	Baklai
Furred Stingers	similar to our bees and they produce Golden River, which is similar to our honey	Glowen
Flying Nips	similar to mosquitos, they draw blood and leave behind a a dreadful itch	Glowen
Gondal	Two-foot long lizards with black tongues, and which are excellent for eating.	Baklai
Gornog	Pig-like animal, size of a jaguar, grey & black, covered in stiff bristles two sets of tufted ears, six clawed feet, 12 inch tusks in a warted mouth. Meat is tender, sweet and delicious, although causes gas in those who consume it.	Kaylin
Groonnan	A dish made from grains from Kadwee, used for morning meals	Glowen
Gwindle	A health tea for mind & body focus	Shendea

NAME	DESCRIPTION	FROM
Haggapoe	Large carrion bird which is attracted to shiny objects.	Rifella
Hissar	Rodent-like creature 1.5 feet, with the temper of a Tasmanian devil, three rows of barbed teeth, and the strength of a creature 10 times its size.	Baklai
Horse	Almost the same as in our world, except much larger in size.	Baklai
Hydodd	Large elk-like animal with huge horns, cantankerous and a match for the ferocity of the Cathnogs.	Shendea
Kamelona	small scaled creature which almost resembles a chameleon. About 6 inches in length, with a tail 3 times as long can spit toxic saliva which can swiftly cause death in its prey. One bonds with Kat and she calls it Brade	Rifella
Karri-san	Tea which blocks out Rifellan hormones Kaylin	Kaylin
Kithra	Dog-sized rodent with black eyes, needle sharp teeth and brown hair. Travel and attack in packs.	Kaylin
Klim	Plant which produces nut-like and is cooked into journeyklim, a porridge-like meal, or dried in pieces to be used for eating while traveling.	Shendea
Koska	Flowers whose scent helps sleep	Glowen

NAME	DESCRIPTION	FROM
Kossil-Kweth	Tea with calming qualities	Glowen
Liquid Sha-hee	Huge creatures which live in the sea have enormous teeth and resemble whale sharks, are parrot Sha-hee	Glowen
Loftin	Ponti which escorted people among the vineyards of Glowen	Shendea
Lowen	Flowers whose scent conveys happiness	Glowen
Lymnava	A fruit which tastes much like a lemon but which resembles an avocado	Glowen
Musserel	A large vegetable which mimics the flavor of steak.	Glowen
Nerthon	Flowers who convey energy	Glowen
Orenberry	The berries from which the white wine is pressed	Glowen
Panwon	Thick glue-like substance produced from the horns, claws & hooves of brantors.	Rifella
Ponti	Resembles a horse, but with very large head for it's body size, large splayed feet, short legs, wide girth very sure footed in mountainous regions. Pontis grow to about ten or eleven hands high.	Shendea
Prickle-fur	Blue plant with red berries and soft barbs on the leaves, is toxic to human skin and leaves	Rifella

NAME	DESCRIPTION	FROM
Prickle-fur cont.	a red itching rash when touched.	Rifella
Pyrock	Tiny, furry animal, with long tail and leathery wings can transport instantly, and locate any person anywhere on Pridden. Answers only to one person during lifetime. When rolled in a ball, fits in one hand.	Kaylin
Red-Leaf Tea	A tea which helps nausea	Baklai
Red-line berries	Sweet berries which taste similar to strawberries	Glowen
Red Rash	A dangerous virus, which emerges every seven years, and unless treated may cause excruciating pain and death	Pridden
Repella	keeps winged biters away	Glowen
Sea Swimmers	Fish from the Bay at the Mora, usually either roasted over coals or presented in a stew called cassolet	Shendea/
Shade	A huge black panther-like animal with brilliant emerald eyes that became Kat's protector in Shendea	Shendea
Skat-koska	A strong sedative used as a bring about unconsciousness	Glowen
Syeth	Small but deadly poisonous snake, venom causes almost instant death but is used by Shendean	Morden

NAME	DESCRIPTION	FROM
Syeth	continued	
.	...Healers to produce potion to combat Red Rash	Morden
Wullawerth	Sheep-like animal with masses of fine soft hair, excellent for clothing. Prized for eating.	Kaylin

ABOUT THE AUTHOR

J. M. Tibbott is a prize winning author, a writing instructor and editor. She has been writing since grade school, and has continued to study literature and the English Language ever since. She believes there is always something new to learn.

Her works include magazine and newspaper articles, newsletters, online blogs, and story collections. This most recently book, "The Pleasure Seekers", Book 4 of The Pridden Saga, a myth/fantasy series, was published in March of 2021. Book 5 of the series is currently in the works.

J. M. feels strongly that the well-being of any author is maintained by belonging to a number of writer's groups. Since early 2020, her groups have morphed into virtual ones.

A HINT OF BOOK 5

THE HORSE MASTERS

Keeping the veil on her mind firmly in place, Kat's voyage continues as she and her guide, Mouse, sail for Baklai. On the otherwise pleasant trip, she meets an odd Rifellan, named Ssestin, who broadcasts no Rifellan pheromones. Although she does not completely trust the man, she finds him interesting.

Mouse seems to have become smaller around Ssestin, and advises Kat that he too is uncomfortable around the man.

As a survivor of the last Red Rash outbreak, Ssestin explains he lost the hair on his head, and thus is forced to wears a strange type of turban to protect his bare head from the burning rays of Pridden's star. When they reach the harbor at Baklai, he departs hastily for the Rifellan guard's keep at the border of Morden.

For Kat, her challenge in this land is only beginning when she discovers her faithful horse has died. Accident or deliberate? She know not which. Her most arduous journey begins this day, because the Baklai hold her responsible, and refuse to grant her another animal.

Can Kat survive in this extreme patriarchal society? But when she meets the women of Baklai, she discovers she may actually be in a strong matriarchal culture. How can these two extremes exist in one land?

In Baklai, where horses are glorified, and whose enemies include the challenges of blick burrows and attacks on their foals by packs of haygas-kaths, vicious animals who resemble cheetahs. Kat must find a way to convince the horse masters she can be responsible for a valuable new animal.

Sent to Baklai by Lord Eduardo of Kaylin, will she uncover hidden problems for Thane Cathked, the ruler of Baklai, in this new and challenging voyage?

BE SURE TO ENJOY OTHER BOOKS IN THE SERIES OF THE PRIDDEN SAGA BY J.M. TIBBOTT

The Arrival: Book One:.......Amazon.com

A computer whiz trapped in a tech-free world. Can she save an enchanting new world from a savage civil war?

Video game designer Kat Karim has never been much of a team player. So when her attitude causes friction at the office, her boss sends her on a forced vacation with instructions to think hard about her future. But while exploring ancient ruins in the Virgin Islands, she is thrust into a vortex which transports her to a spellbinding realm.

Desperate to return home, Kat strikes a bargain with the lord of Kaylin to help uncover troublemakers in exchange for a way back to her world. But with enemies lurking around every corner, she must defend against a villain with sinister plans for the power she doesn't know she possesses…

Can Kat survive in a land hurtling towards destruction?

The Healers: Book Two:..........Amazon.com

Plunge into the next tale of Kat's journey as she wends her way among the spiritual healers of Shendea, but encounters heart-stopping challenges from a ferocious cathnog. Attacked by unknown and violent strangers, our video game designer must fulfill her promise to Eduardo of Kaylin to help Pridden avoid a devastating war, but unfortunately without clear or specific instructions.

CONTINUED

In this second fantasy edition of the enthralling Pridden Saga, she is escorted by her mysterious guide, Mouse, and the glorious big cat, Shade. Without real knowledge of these people, and hindered by her tendency to blunder when faced by peculiar customs, she is astonished by a Thieves' Guild who do not steal, a Magicians' Guild who demonstrate no magic, and the wiles of the alluring Rifellans. Will she survive these wily assassins? How will she keep her word to help Lord Rhognor of Shendea, and still return safely to her own world?

The Warriors: Book Three: Amazon.com

The exciting fantasy continues as Kat, with only her guide Mouse and her pyrock, Wink, enters Rifella. In this land, she is often mistaken for a red-headed, royal-born Rifellan, with all the abilities of these powerful warriors. She encounters strange new creatures, some violent, and some delightful. The inhabitants she encounters are strong, fine-looking men and women, and who are surprisingly welcoming. Rifella is a harsh land, filled with dangerous creatures, and often grim terrain, but, she is nevertheless, entranced by the beauty she encounters.

She is drawn to Liandock, the intensely attractive Metal-Master when he walks into her life again. Can Kat help Lord Murwenna, Rifella's ruler, to discover the challenges to her land, and gain additional ways to return to her own world?

If you like unstoppable female protagonists, seductive companions, and action-packed quests, then you'll love volume 3 of this epic fantasy.

www.ingramcontent.com/pod-product-compliance
Lightning Source LLC
Chambersburg PA
CBHW07204219072[illegible]6
48294CB00005B/1368
9781738974283